WORLD W~~AR II LI~~ ◁ P9-CJH-064

For the hundreds of thousands of readers fascinated by
World War II history, Dell has created the World War II
Library—outstanding nonfiction narratives that convey
the total experience of war with historical accuracy and
detailed immediacy that until now could be understood
only by those who had fought it.

THE RUSSIAN FRONT

All around us were the crack of rifles, the boom of mortars, and
the hollow chatter of machine guns. We overran their first line.
While we were attacking the Russian second line, we became
suddenly aware that we were taking fire from behind. The Russian
soldiers in the first line of trenches, who should have surrendered,
had turned and were shooting us in the back.

Our soldiers went berserk. From that point on during the
assault they took no prisoners and left no one alive in a trench or
foxhole.

I did not try to stop them. Nor did any other officer, because
they would have killed us too if we had. They were out of their
minds with fury. The Russians were all killed, without mercy or
remorse.

C.A. Ball
April 2000

THE DELL WAR SERIES

The Dell War Series takes you onto the battlefield, into the jungles and beneath the oceans with unforgettable stories that offer a new look at the terrors and triumphs of America's war experience. Many of these books are eyewitness accounts of the duty-bound fighting man. From the intrepid foot soldiers, sailors, pilots, and commanders, to the elite warriors of the Special Forces, here are stories of men who fight because their lives depend on it.

☆ ☆ ☆ ☆ ☆ ☆ ☆

QUANTITY SALES

Most Dell books are available at special quantity discounts when purchased in bulk by corporations, organizations, or groups. Special imprints, messages, and excerpts can be produced to meet your needs. For more information, write to: Dell Publishing, 1540 Broadway, New York, NY 10036. Special Markets.

INDIVIDUAL SALES

Are there any Dell books you want but cannot find in your local stores? If so, you can order them directly from us. You can get any Dell book currently in print. For a complete up-to-date listing of our books and information on how to order, write to: Dell Readers Service, Box DR, 1540 Broadway, New York, NY 10036.

SOLDAT

Reflections of
a German Soldier,
1936–1949

—

by
SIEGFRIED KNAPPE
with
TED BRUSAW

—

A DELL BOOK

Published by
Dell Publishing
a division of
Random House, Inc.
1540 Broadway
New York, New York 10036

If you purchased this book without a cover you should be aware that this book
is stolen property. It was reported as "unsold and destroyed" to the publisher
and neither the author nor the publisher has received any payment for this
"stripped book."

Copyright © 1992 by Siegfried Knappe and Charles T. Brusaw

All rights reserved. No part of this book may be reproduced or transmitted in
any form or by any means, electronic or mechanical, including photocopying,
recording, or by any information storage and retrieval system, without the
written permission of the Publisher, except where permitted by law. For information address: Orion Books, a division of Crown Publishers, Inc., New York,
New York.

Dell books may be purchased for business or promotional use or for special
sales. For information please write to: Special Markets Department, Random
House, Inc., 1540 Broadway, New York, N.Y. 10036.

Dell® is a registered trademark of Random House, Inc., and the colophon is a
trademark of Random House, Inc.

ISBN: 0-440-21526-9

Reprinted by arrangement with Orion Books

Interior design by Jeremiah B. Lighter

Printed in the United States of America

Published simultaneously in Canada

September 1993

10 9 8

OPM

*This book is dedicated
to the endless columns of German soldiers
who disappeared into the Soviet Union
at the end of the Second World War,
never to return.*

CONTENTS

PREFACE

THOSE OF US who were soldiers in the German Army during World War II were young men fighting for their country. We were not "Nazi" soldiers; we were just German soldiers. This is the story of one of them.

SIEGFRIED KNAPPE
Xenia, Ohio
September 1991

The amount of detail in this narrative is possible because Siegfried Knappe kept a diary from his midteens until he went into Russian captivity on May 2, 1945. Additionally, he smuggled many photographs of his war years from his mother's home in East Germany when he tricked the East Germans into allowing him to go to West Germany upon his release from Russian captivity in December 1949. During approximately 450 hours of interviews, we used these photographs to help trigger his memory as we covered every episode of his war years many times.

Siegfried also had General Weidling's account of the 56th Panzer Korps' part in the fighting from the Oder River to Berlin and the defense of Berlin, which Weidling wrote for the Russians immediately after surrendering. And when Siegfried was released from Russian captivity in December 1949, one of his first acts was to write his own account of the same period and of his Russian captivity as well. Finally, Siegfried had a day-by-day report of his artillery battery's participation in the invasion of France in May 1940, written by his battery commander.

A writer could hardly ask for a more thoroughly documented subject.

TED BRUSAW
Dayton, Ohio
September 1991

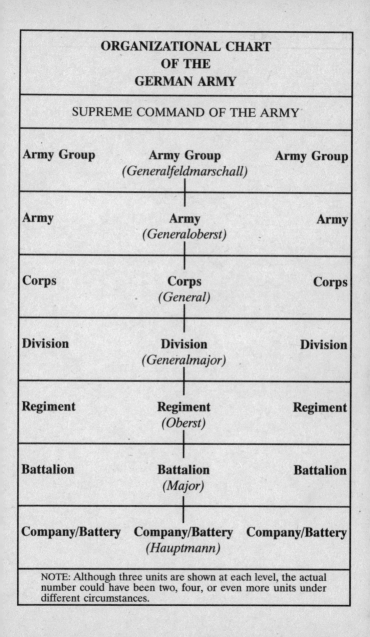

ORGANIZATIONAL CHART
OF THE
GERMAN ARMY

SUPREME COMMAND OF THE ARMY

Army Group	Army Group *(Generalfeldmarschall)*	Army Group
Army	Army *(Generaloberst)*	Army
Corps	Corps *(General)*	Corps
Division	Division *(Generalmajor)*	Division
Regiment	Regiment *(Oberst)*	Regiment
Battalion	Battalion *(Major)*	Battalion
Company/Battery	Company/Battery *(Hauptmann)*	Company/Battery

NOTE: Although three units are shown at each level, the actual number could have been two, four, or even more units under different circumstances.

GLOSSARY

abiturient. gymnasium graduate

abteilung. Labor Service unit (equivalent to Army battalion)

abteilungsführer. Labor Service unit leader

achtung. attention

Braunhemden (Brownshirts). members of the SA

Dolchstosslegende. a theory that the German Army was never defeated on the battlefield in the First World War, but that Germany was instead fatally weakened by an attitude of defeatism in a significant portion of the civilian population. Many politicians in the 1920s and 1930s, including Hitler, exploited this "stab-in-the-back" theory to make themselves popular with the army and with First World War veterans.

fahnenjunker-gefreiter. cadet lance corporal

fahnenjunker-unteroffizier. cadet lance sergeant

fähnrich. ensign

fahrer. "driver"; horse handler in artillery unit

feldwebel. senior sergeant (infantry)

Führer. leader; Hitler

gauleiter. equivalent to a state governor in the United States

gefreiter. lance corporal

general. lieutenant general

generalfeldmarschall. general of the army

generalleutnant. major general

generalmajor. brigadier general

generaloberst. general

gruppenführer. Labor Service group leader

gymnasium. roughly equivalent to American high school and community college

hauptmann. captain

hauptwachtmeister. battery sergeant major (artillery)

hausfrau. housewife

Hitler Youth. organization composed of young people in their early and middle teens

Jawohl. Yes, sir

kanonier. gunner in artillery unit; artillery private

kriegsschule. military academy

kübelwagen. equivalent to an American jeep

leutnant. second lieutenant

Luftwaffe. German Air Force

*major.** major

NKVD. predecessor of the KGB, the Soviet Union's intelligence agency

oberfähnrich. senior ensign

obergefreiter. corporal

oberkanonier. private first class (artillery)

oberleutnant. first lieutenant

obersoldat. private first class (infantry)

*oberst.** colonel

oberstleutnant.* lieutenant colonel

panzer. tank

panzerfaust. shoulder-fired rocket weapon, similar to a bazooka

pferdehalter. horse orderly

SA. *Sturm-Abteilung,* or "attack unit." This was the official name of the Braunhemden.

soldat. private (infantry)

SS. *Schutzstaffel* or *Schwarzhemden* (Blackshirts). Originally an elite group of Hitler's bodyguards, they became Himmler's private army, and still later they were divided into the Allgemeine SS (black uniforms) and the Waffen SS (gray uniforms). The Waffen SS fought alongside regular Army units as combat soldiers, but they remained part of the SS under Himmler. The Allgemeine SS supplied concentration camp guards rather than combat soldiers.

stabsgefreiter. a career corporal. Someone who could not accept responsibility and would never achieve a higher rank.

unterfeldwebel. sergeant (infantry)

unteroffizier. lance sergeant

unterwachtmeister. sergeant (artillery)

Volkssturm. "people's attack force," composed of overage men and used principally for defense

wachtmeister. senior sergeant (artillery)

Wehrmacht. armed forces

* The designation "i.G." after these three ranks indicated general staff officers.

PART ONE

The Witch's Caldron

1945

1

HAUPTMANN KAFURKE, MY AIDE, woke me by knocking on the window of my automobile.

"Herr Major, the stationmaster has a message for you," he said.

I willed my sleepy body and mind awake and looked about. My car was secured on a railroad flatcar that was part of a train on which we had traveled through the night on our way to join General Wenck's Twelfth Army, which was just being formed in the Harz Mountains. I had slept in my car because it was more comfortable than anything else available. Thinking we would be near Leipzig by morning, I had left instructions for my orderly to wake me at Eilenburg so I could take a motorcycle and visit my wife, Lilo, and our infant son, Klaus, in Leipzig and then catch up with the slow train in another city. We were not in Eilenburg, however, but in Bautzen. I stretched, got out of the automobile, climbed down from the railroad car, and went into the station.

"You have a message?" I asked the stationmaster.

"*Jawohl,* Herr Major," he said. "I have received an order that your train is to be diverted north, toward Berlin."

His comment startled me. "Has the railroad to the west been cut?" I asked, searching for a reason we were being diverted north.

"No. Travel has been moving slowly but freely."

I thanked him and returned to the train. They were probably just going to take us to Berlin and put us on a

different route to the Harz Mountains, but it killed my
hopes of being able to visit Lilo and Klaus. It was against
all regulations for me to visit them anyway, but I had decided not to pass up a chance to see them if it was possible.
Well, now it was no longer possible.

At about 11:00 A.M., we reached the south ring of the
railroad circle around Berlin. We had just rolled into the
subway station at Neukölln when the air raid sirens began
to wail loudly. On checking with the stationmaster I
learned that we would not be able to continue until the air
raid alert had ended. I posted sentries on the train and
sent the rest of our men into air raid shelters in the vicinity.

As operations officer of the 56th Panzer Korps, I was
overseeing the transfer of the corps' staff from Silesia,
where we had just been in combat against the Russians, to
the Harz Mountains. Oberstleutnant i.G. von Dufving,
chief of staff of the 56th Panzer Korps and my immediate
superior, had gone to the Harz Mountains ahead of us with
an advance party.

Hauptmann Kafurke, Major Wolff (personnel officer
of the 56th Panzer Korps), and I went into an air raid
shelter that was occupied mostly by civilians. The mood of
the civilians was sober, yet composed. There was no joking,
but they showed no resentment toward us for continuing to
fight, as some civilians were beginning to do.

As the alert continued and we heard no explosions, I
decided to go out and have a look. The streets were empty,
of course, and high overhead I could see Allied bombers
passing over. No German defenses against them were in
evidence. I looked at the wave of bombers and wondered,
as always, if Michaelis—a Jewish friend with whom I had
gone through Petri Gymnasium, whose family had moved
to England in 1938—might be in one of them. Finally, at
4:00 P.M., the all clear sounded, and everyone returned to
the train. We pulled out slowly—but, to my alarm, toward
the east! When I received orders that we were to unload at

Müncheberg, about fifty kilometers from the Russian front, it was obvious that we were going back into combat against the Russians—*and my heart sank.* We unloaded the train at Müncheberg, and I drove to Waldsieversdorf, where, I was told, our headquarters were to be. Oberstleutnant i.G. von Dufving was already there with the advance party. He was a rather small man with a wiry build and dark eyes.

"I think somebody has pulled rank on us," he said, with just a trace of anger and bitterness in his voice. "Apparently we are trading places with another corps staff—one that has a commanding general." Our old commanding general had been reassigned, and our new one had not yet arrived.

At Waldsieversdorf, we learned that we were to relieve a panzer corps staff that commanded two divisions of Army Reserve here—in the expected *center* of the coming Russian offensive! We assumed that the commanding general of the corps that was being relieved had political pull at the Supreme Command of the Army and had managed to have his corps staff take our place in the Harz Mountains and have us assigned to the Ninth Army in his place. The corps staff we were replacing knew the area, they knew the divisions, they knew the combat situation, and they had the necessary communications equipment. We, on the other hand, had arrived in a completely strange area, did not know anyone in the divisions assigned to us or any of the corps or division staffs on either side of us, and had only about 50 percent of our telephone and 35 percent of our radio equipment because we had just been taken out of combat in Silesia. And with these handicaps, we were supposed to take over the very difficult task of leading a mobile defense against an enemy who had overwhelming superiority in both numbers and equipment! Our new commanding general, General of Artillery Helmut Weidling, was on his way, but he had not yet arrived. Well, there was nothing we could do about it. Von Dufving and I took

command of the corps section of the front from our predecessors, who quickly disappeared.

General Weidling arrived the next morning, April 13,
1945. Von Dufving, who knew Weidling, coached me on
Weidling's likes and dislikes, and I acted on von Dufving's
advice when I reported to Weidling, giving him a very brief
and concise rundown on the situation. He was very nice,
and I felt I had made a good impression on him. Since he
relied on first impressions to form his permanent opinion
of subordinates, it was very important for our future work
together that I, as his operations officer, make a good first
impression.

In the afternoon, Weidling took Wolff and me to look
over the area and make contact with our own divisions and
our neighbors'. Weidling grilled us during the trip to find
out how much combat experience we had and how much
help we were really going to be to him. He seemed content
with what he heard. The situation at the front showed continuing Russian preparation for an offensive across the entire front. The Russians had established three bridgeheads
west of the Oder River, and we still held footholds on the
east bank of the river at both Küstrin and Frankfurt. Aerial
photographs showed one Russian artillery piece for every
ten meters of front! Large batteries of artillery, with twelve
artillery pieces each, were posted in straight lines, along
roads or railroads, without even any camouflage. The Russian guns would have provided a virtual "turkey shoot" for
the Luftwaffe of previous years, but by now the Luftwaffe
no longer existed as a fighting force, so the Russian artillery was in no danger. The Russians also had an endless
supply of tanks and everything else. It was obvious that we
had no hope of stopping them. At best, we would only be
able to delay them. We estimated that the Russians outnumbered us six to one in infantry, ten to one in artillery,
twenty to one in tanks, and thirty to one in combat aircraft.

General Weidling, Major Wolff, and I then drove to
the hills north of Seelow, which offered an overall view of

the front at the Oder River, on both sides of Küstrin. This ridge of hills about seventeen kilometers from the Oder, known as Seelow Heights, was considered our second line of defense—except that no troops were available to occupy it. It was only a defensive line we would be able to fall back to. We also visited Generalmajor Mummert, who commanded the newly formed Panzer Division Müncheberg, which was under our command for the coming operation. We found that the division's equipment was good but incomplete, and that the troops were trained and experienced but had been together only a few days. Panzer Division Müncheberg really was a makeshift force. The Supreme Command of the Army had known for some time that the final attack would come here, on the road to Berlin, and every available soldier was sent to the town of Müncheberg. Panzer Division Müncheberg was hastily organized from these troops. That was the way divisions were often being formed at this late stage of the war.

After dinner at the officers' mess at Panzer Division Müncheberg, we drove to the 20th SS Panzer Division, our other division for the coming fight. It was also not quite fully equipped and ready for combat, because it had recently been in fierce fighting with us in Silesia. (All the combat SS units were Waffen SS, which means they were combat soldiers as opposed to the political SS units that ran the concentration camps.)

When we returned, I tried to call Lilo but could not get a connection. I then called my mother and learned that the American Army was on the outskirts of Leipzig!

"Siegfried, what shall I do?" she asked plaintively.

"Stay at home and do nothing," I told her. "If shooting starts, go to the basement and wait it out. If you try to leave, you will become just another refugee. Don't risk that, Mother. What happens to refugees is cruel."

The conversation was under surveillance (the lines were not supposed to be used for personal calls), and a woman's voice interrupted and asked the purpose of the call, so I had to cut the conversation short. I could only hope that my mother would be safe and that Lilo and Klaus were still all right. I shook off the sense of impending doom and helplessness and forced myself to concentrate on business.

Our 56th Panzer Korps was now the reserve corps for the Ninth Army, which was commanded by General Busse. The Ninth Army's two other corps were in position at the Oder River and around the Russian bridgeheads. We were behind those two corps, kept in reserve for whenever there was a breakthrough or a situation that called for reinforcements.

Russian Marshal Zhukov's offensive started at 5:00 A.M. on April 14, when the greatest massing of artillery in military history—over forty thousand guns—opened up on our front. As reserve, we were behind the front line. We had a good view of the entire area, although we could see little more than where the action was taking place. General Busse had correctly guessed the timing of the Russian offensive and at the last minute pulled our infantry out of the positions being shelled by the Russian artillery. We could see airplanes dropping bombs and artillery shells exploding, but very little more. Because of our combat experience, however, we could make an educated guess about what was happening. We could hear the roar of the battle (artillery, rockets, bombs), and we could see the depth of the battlefield and judge how well it could be defended. The massed artillery was awesome, and it was accompanied by increased air activity as well.

Seelow Heights was about ten kilometers from the front, and the area between Seelow and the Oder River was flat, open terrain, with no woods. Although the area was flat and unwooded, much of it was swampy and not a good area for tanks, so the Russians were somewhat restricted in what they could do. We spent the early hours of the battle preparing to conduct mobile combat when we were committed to the battle. The reports from the divisions fighting at the front indicated that the Russian offensive was being conducted with unimaginable force. The first day, our divisions in the front were able to stop them, even though there were some deep pockets in our line. As the reserve corps, we were on constant alert, awaiting orders to join the fight, but General Busse was hesitant to commit us to the battle because we were his only reserve. The Russians continued attacking through the night and even intensified the attack at dawn. Their incessant artillery and aircraft bombardment was now beginning to devastate our positions. We knew we could not stop them in front of Seelow, but we could see that Seelow Heights presented us with a good fallback line of defense.

Although we knew this was the decisive battle before Berlin, we also knew, with a terrible sinking feeling, that we could not hold them, although we wanted desperately to hold until the Western Allies reached Berlin, so that the city would be spared occupation by Soviet forces. Once we had been committed, there would be no further reserves, and without reserves the situation was hopeless. The countryside in the seventy or so kilometers between Berlin and the Oder River was fairly flat, with a few chains of hills. The area west of Seelow Heights had many lakes and woods, but the woods contained service roads for foresters that could accommodate Russian tanks and motorized equipment. The only serious natural obstacles to the Russian tanks between us and Berlin were the lakes.

When we worked on our plans for combat and looked over the maps and sketches left by our predecessors, we found that we had no information about defensive positions in the area closer to Berlin. Since we were supposed to fight in this area, we asked the Ninth Army for the necessary information. In reply, we received some very sketchy position maps that showed nothing of the defense ring around Berlin. When I asked for more detailed information, the Ninth Army operations officer became angry and told me he did not have more detailed information and that it was *none of our business*! Perhaps they really did not know any more than they gave us, or perhaps they did not want us to know until the last moment for fear we might pull back too soon. A lot of people were secretly questioning why the government did not negotiate an end to such a hopelessly lost war—even if it meant unconditional surrender—and the Ninth Army staff may not have trusted us.

The Russians took three days to reach Seelow, even with their vast superiority in men and artillery. They also had reconnaissance planes, which gave them an advantage that was not available to us. The hilly terrain on both sides of Seelow, however, made the Russian advance more difficult. On the evening of the second day our front line was still intact, but we could not tolerate their deep incursions without the breakdown of our defenses.

Our corps headquarters was in the basement of a villa in Waldsieversdorf. Motorcycle runners were always ready to be dispatched at a moment's notice. They always knew where the divisions were, and when Weidling went somewhere he always took one or two runners with him. He could not always be certain that the Russians were not listening in on the telephone, so he would send a runner with a message instead.

Finally, at 6:00 A.M. on April 16, we became actively involved in the battle for Seelow Heights by taking command of the divisions already fighting there in addition to our own two divisions. From then on, we worked around the clock, catching an hour or two of sleep whenever conditions permitted. Our headquarters stayed where it had been, but Weidling went to the divisions to have a look at the situation and conduct the battle from there, taking me with him. We drove to the headquarters of our two new divisions to discuss the situation with the division commanders. The headquarters of the 9th Parachute Division was under both artillery and mortar fire. At their division headquarters I ran into my good friend and former General Staff College classmate Major Engel, but unfortunately there was no time for small talk. The 9th Parachute Division commander was an Air Force generalleutnant who was much too old and had apparently been assigned to this position after a falling-out with Göring. Weidling immediately asked for his relief, and the next day a young paratrooper, Oberst Hermann, took over the division. The Ninth Army's 101st Korps was to our right, and a Third Army panzer corps was to our left.

The next day, April 17, brought new enemy attacks, and the Russians threw more and more tanks into the battle. The 9th Parachute Division destroyed forty Russian tanks in one battle, and still the Russians kept coming, making constantly deeper incursions in our front. In some places, the Russians had already reached Seelow Heights. Panzer Division Müncheberg, however, was not yet released for combat. It was on alert in the area west of Seelow, ready to be dispatched immediately if a breakthrough should occur. The situation was most threatening at the outermost flanks of our corps sector, where we kept losing contact with our neighbors, but we succeeded again and again in patching up the front. During the night, Weidling decided to pull back to the hills on both sides of Seelow to prevent our combat units from being decimated individually if the Russian incursions in our front got any deeper. Thus we again formed a continuous front in a prepared position.

Seelow changed hands several times during the battle. A few Russian tanks broke through the defense line first, and then Russian infantry followed. A little gap had been opened, but the line was still holding to the right and to the left, so the Russians had to wait for reinforcements. During the wait, the defending German commander threw his reserve battalion into Seelow and drove the Russians out again. Then the Russian reinforcements arrived, and they took the town again. Then our defending division threw in extra reserves and took it back. This seesawing back and forth continued for some time. The cold words on paper look clinical and antiseptic, but with each change of hands Russian and German soldiers were dying in agony and terror.

The fierce German defense persisted, even though we were outnumbered ten to one and our divisions were quickly becoming decimated. Every day, we suffered more and more losses—losses we could not make good—and finally the Russians began to break through. We were holding in the middle, but the Russians were streaming through on both sides and trying to get north and south of Berlin. They could have surrounded us, but for some reason they did not. They probably thought we had strong defense lines east of Berlin, and they wanted to avoid them by going north and south of the city. If they had known that Berlin was defended only by Hitler Youth and Volkssturm, they could have cut us off and Berlin would have been theirs. When they reached our deep flanks, we had to fall back. Behind Seelow Heights were some hills and behind the hills were many lakes, so we decided to use the hills as our next line of defense.

2

AT 7:00 A.M. on April 18, 1945, heavy bombs fell close to our headquarters in the villa at Waldsieversdorf, and we began preparing a command post in a wood somewhat distant from there. On the same day, the Russians broke through to the north and south of us again. Weidling now committed Panzer Division Müncheberg on the right flank of the corps because Russian tanks had broken through in the Müncheberg area. On the other side of our front, the situation on the left flank of the 9th Parachute Division became more and more precarious. A breakthrough to the left became probable, and there was a danger that our corps would be encircled in the area around the lakes. The situation seemed to become more desperate almost hourly, and it was becoming increasingly more difficult to keep our spirits up. The Ninth Army promised to transfer the 18th Panzer Division to our corps the next day, April 19.

Early on April 19, I moved into the woods with the most essential staff personnel. Only a few bunkers were ready, but we wanted to be ready to work from there when it became impossible to remain at the villa. At first it was still very cold, but soon the sun came up and I could take off my fur-lined overcoat. At about 9:00 A.M., von Dufving arrived.

Then General Heinrici, commander of Army Group Weichsel, of which we were part, arrived. He approved Weidling's combat decisions and warned about the danger of the front breaking apart between the Ninth Army and the Third Army. We expected the 18th Panzer Division to arrive during the day from the Stettin area and to be placed under our command.

A short time after Heinrici departed, General Busse arrived. He, too, approved our conduct of the fighting and told us that we might also get the SS Panzer Division Nordland under our command. The SS Division Nordland was a division of Norwegian, Swedish, and Danish volunteers, except for a few German officers. (In many of the occupied countries, volunteers were recruited for special divisions from among young men who agreed with Hitler's political philosophy. This was especially successful in the Scandinavian countries because Hitler's philosophy of the superiority of the Nordic race appealed to them.)

During a short pause in combat on April 19, Reich Hitler Youth Leader Artur Axmann arrived at our corps headquarters. Axmann, who was in his early thirties, had lost an arm fighting the Russians in 1941. At his request, we briefed him on the situation, and then he offered us a battalion of Hitler Youth for combat. Weidling did not want to accept at first because he did not want to put children into the fighting, but then he reluctantly, almost grimly, agreed to put the boys in a blocking position behind the front to protect the corps' northern flank against enemy forces breaking through there. Goebbels had also sent some Volkssturm civil defense battalions to us here, which he should not have done (he should have contacted us to find out where we wanted them sent).

Then we received another high-ranking civilian visitor. Reich Foreign Minister von Ribbentrop appeared at our basement headquarters at Waldsieversdorf. After being briefed on the situation, von Ribbentrop asked permission to drive to one of our divisions, and Weidling directed him to Panzer Division Müncheberg. Von Ribbentrop appeared depressed, even somewhat confused. He wore an officer's leather overcoat without insignia, and a uniform hat with the big eagle of the diplomatic corps.

It was out of line for him to be at the front. It would not even have been appropriate for him to come to us just to learn the situation. This was not his job, and it had nothing to do with his job. If he had wanted to learn the situation at the front, he had only to ask the Chief of the General Staff of the Army at Führer Headquarters what was happening, what he could expect, how long we expected to hold, and so on. But he had no business at the headquarters of a corps that was actively engaged in combat. Some time after his departure, I received a call from Panzer Division Müncheberg informing us that von Ribbentrop had requested that he be allowed to accompany a combat reconnaissance patrol. I relayed that information to Weidling, who refused the request, pointing out quite logically that at Ribbentrop's age and without infantry training or experience—and wearing a uniform that would have made him stand out as a very inviting target—he would certainly be killed on an infantry patrol. With that, von Ribbentrop departed from the division without returning to us.

In the meantime, the Russian attacks continued undiminished, and we began to have difficulty maintaining contact between the Third and Ninth armies, as Heinrici had predicted. Our 9th Parachute Division reported the final disruption of their contact with the Third Army's 101st Korps to the north. Then, after five days of massive attacks, the Second Russian Armored Army succeeded in breaking through our front, threatening our left flank. Parts of the 18th Panzer Division began arriving, and, in desperation, we threw them into the battle piecemeal as they arrived. With that, we managed to stop the Russians on our left. On our right, Panzer Division Müncheberg was engaged in fierce fighting with Russian tank forces, and here we lost contact with our neighboring corps on the right during the evening. To prevent our being outflanked on both sides and giving the Russians unimpeded access to Berlin, Weidling decided to fall back to the Müncheberg-

Waldsieversdorf line, which we had determined would be our next main defense line.

In places, however, the Russians had already breached the Müncheberg-Waldsieversdorf line. By 6:00 P.M. we could hear machine-gun fire, and mortar shells were exploding nearby. Therefore, we moved our corps headquarters to Kolonie-Herrenhorst, a small community on a pine hill south of Strausberg. By 8:00 P.M., we were again ready to conduct combat. The SS Division Nordland arrived during the night. In addition, the heavy antiaircraft units in the Strausberg area were put under our command. Unfortunately, they had only immobile, pivoted 88mm guns, but they could at least prevent a surprise tank attack into our deep flank. I drew up their orders for Weidling's signature and advised the antiaircraft units of the combat situation.

Our single corps was now facing an entire Russian army group, which they called a "front." If not an army group, we should have been at least an army instead of a corps. Obviously, we were not going to be able to hold out here any better than anywhere else and would have to fall back to Berlin proper. Already, the Russians were shelling the city.

Finally, in the early hours of April 20, I could close my eyes for a few hours. While drifting off to sleep, I thought of the stirring speech I had heard Goebbels make on the radio recently about new wonder weapons that would yet enable us to win the war. The endless slogans and propaganda coming from the government in Berlin sounded to us at the front like sheer childishness. Our headquarters then was in the home of a railroad employee, who had been utterly believing as he listened to Goebbels. Although I could not tell him and his wife that the Russians would probably overrun their home within thirty-six hours, I advised them to send their sixteen-year-old daughter away.

I was awakened by detonations of light shells all around. I decided that it was probably fire from tanks that were still a mile or so north of us. Our new main defense line was already in Russian hands in some places. Russian tanks and infantry had broken through to the right of us and were already southwest of our corps headquarters. We threw the SS Panzer Division Nordland against this enemy force with orders to secure the corps' southern flank.

We explored a new line of resistance toward the south, in the lake area of Strausberg. If we could secure all the land between the lakes in this area before the Russians arrived, we could hope to make another stand there. If only Goebbels had sent his civil defense battalions here instead of where he had sent them! On the trip to Kolonie-Herrenhorst, I learned that most of Goebbels's civil defense battalions had already been dispersed by air attacks. Only the remaining parts of the two battalions could be sent to the Strausberg lake area to help man the new defense line there.

The frontal attacks against us decreased during the day as the Russians now put everything available into exploiting the gaps on either side of our corps. The Hitler Youth battalion that Weidling had been so reluctant to use had had its baptism of fire the night before in its position north of Waldsieversdorf. Attacked by Russian tanks, the leader of the battalion, a nineteen-year-old senior Hitler Youth leader, had completely lost control at the very outset of combat. The crying of his wounded boys had deprived him of his nerve. Crying himself, he had ordered the position to be abandoned—without making a report to the corps or to anyone else! The boys were dispersed in all directions. Because of this, a very serious situation had arisen on our left flank. However, by dispatching antitank gunners of the 18th Armored Infantry Division, we were able to close the gap that had resulted.

In the afternoon, severe fighting developed about three kilometers north of our corps headquarters, between Russian tanks proceeding toward Strausberg and our antiaircraft emplacements. In spite of their courageous resistance and the destruction of many Russian tanks, the antiaircraft crews could not stop the enemy in the long run, especially when infantry was dispatched against them. With that, facing the danger of being surrounded again, we ordered the front moved back to the lake line in the Strausberg area. At 8:00 P.M., we moved our headquarters to Elisenhof, about three kilometers south of Altlandsberg.

On the way there, we observed intense enemy aircraft activity everywhere. Along the road from Altlandsberg, I could see burning houses as well as burning Russian tanks that had been stopped by antiaircraft guns when they approached our positions from Altlandsberg. That village itself was in Russian hands—and Elisenhof was only three kilometers from there, without any troops in between! Major Wolff immediately organized the local defense with the clerks and drivers as they arrived. I lay down for a while to get some rest, since communication lines had not yet been established and there was nothing I could do. Besides, it was clear that the corps headquarters could not remain here because with the loss of Altlandsberg, the position of the corps in the narrows between the lakes was already outflanked again.

By midnight on April 20, Weidling and von Dufving arrived from Kolonie-Herrenhorst. They decided to move the headquarters again, to a location where we would have the protection of the divisions; the new headquarters was supposed to be in the southeastern part of Petershagen. Over country roads, dodging to the south since new enemy movements had been reported, I reached Petershagen. The inhabitants had mostly left; only a few elderly people were in some of the basements. I found some individual houses that were suitable for our headquarters, and our communications people quickly established communications lines to our divisions. The lines were disrupted constantly by Russian artillery fire, however, and we had not had wire connection with the Ninth Army command for several hours.

At 7:00 A.M. on April 21, as I was eating some scrambled eggs, a radio message arrived from Ninth Army headquarters reading, "I expect resolute fighting from now on. Corps headquarters is to be moved immediately to the east edge of Berlin. Busse." Apparently, Ninth Army thought we were inside Berlin! I gave the message to Weidling, who became angry and had the following radio message sent to the Ninth Army: "Corps headquarters is engaged in infantry fighting five kilometers east of the edge of Berlin. Weidling."

From the divisions came reports that the frontal attacks of the Russians were becoming stronger again, and we had to dispatch our last reserves. In some places, the enemy already had broken through the narrows between the lakes or had unexpectedly crossed the lakes in boats. That meant that now we had no other choice than to put all troops able to fight into the direct defense of Berlin, although there, too, break-ins had already occurred in the north, near Altlandsberg.

In Köpenick on that day, I witnessed a truck, loaded with bread and stopped because of traffic, being looted by passing women, children, and old men. The driver stood there, unable to do anything about it except make parrying gestures. His truck was emptied within a few minutes.

The eastern Berlin suburbs of Friedrichsfelde, Kaulsdorf Süd, and Karlshorst were already under constant fire from light artillery, probably from the direction of Altlandsberg. Our corps headquarters had been established in the meantime in some villas at the south edge of Kaulsdorf Süd. With our right flank at Müggel Lake, we intended to try to hold a line connecting Hoppegarten, Kaulsdorf, and Marzahn. There we should be connected with the Berlin defense line. To the left, however, we would not have any connection with the 11th SS Panzer Korps. From the Ninth Army we asked permission to close this gap. In response, we got orders to leave the north bank of the Spree River, connect at our left to the Berlin defense line at the Treptow Park, and prolong the right flank along the Spree

River to the southeast to gain contact with the Ninth Army again.

For this night, it was too late to make these movements. The orders were issued to the divisions for execution during the next night. For the remainder of the night, I could sleep on a bed for about three hours. I was awakened in the small hours of April 22, 1945, by the fire of light artillery and mortars in the surrounding area. I went to the air raid shelter of the Children's and Senior Citizens' Institution next door, where our headquarters had been prepared in the meantime. Three or four rooms had been emptied for us there. The other, larger rooms were occupied by forty or fifty children and fifteen to twenty nurses.

Outside, it was becoming more and more dangerous because Russian tanks that had broken through at Köpenick were driving around nearby. German tank-hunter groups with bazooka-like panzerfausts were chasing them, and the tanks were shooting wildly in all directions. All divisions reported new Russian attacks with tank support. The Russian pressure was especially strong on the right flank, where the advance had been stopped successfully before the Spree River. In the north, the Russians marched into a wide gap that occurred at Werneuchen, toward the west.

On the morning of April 22, we moved our headquarters to Rudow, seven kilometers southwest of Köpenick. I was to stay at the old headquarters until 9:00 P.M. and then follow after all our divisions had reported. During the day, I could hear the sounds of infantry fighting coming closer and closer. It appeared as if the children's home would be in Russian hands by the time I was to leave at 9:00 P.M. I posted guards so I would at least get a warning in time to escape capture.

One after another, the divisions reported abandoning their present headquarters. At about 8:00 P.M., the operations officer of the 9th Parachute Division and my General

Staff College classmate, Major Engel, appeared. He had been my closest friend at the General Staff College. We talked about the situation that he was reporting to me and I was reporting to the Ninth Army. The fight was obviously hopeless, and we could not understand why the government did not sue for peace and stop the senseless slaughter. Slogans and propaganda were not going to throw the Soviets out of Germany! At the most optimistic, we could continue to resist a couple more weeks. We had not during the entire war had the kind of firepower the Russians were now unleashing against us on one small front, and what was happening to our troops was inhuman. They were now fighting with little more than determination, desperation, and raw courage. I recalled the name many were now sarcastically using for Hitler: Gröfaz (*Grösster Feldherr aller Zeiten,* "the greatest general of all time").

Engel and I discussed the situation as personal friends rather than as corps and division operations officers. I gave him the picture of the overall situation as it looked according to our information. In the west, the Western Allies were at the Elbe River, with a few small bridgeheads on the east side of the river, but they had stopped there without carrying out an attack farther to the east. This had stunned us, because we had fought so fiercely against the Russians in the hope that we could hold them off until the Western forces arrived to take Berlin. Now it seemed obvious that they had no interest in taking Berlin to keep the Russians out.

The Russians had torn open the front of the Fourth Panzer Army of Army Group Schörner near Guben and Forst and were marching behind us. We had to deal with a breakthrough between the Ninth and Third armies through which motorized Russian infantry were streaming toward the west without resistance, passing by Berlin. Unimpeded traffic out of Berlin would probably be possible for only a short time.

For a brief moment, Engels and I discussed getting

into my car and leaving this witch's caldron. The end had to come with the encirclement of Berlin by the Russians. To stay meant Russian captivity or death. If we escaped to the west, it would mean freedom, or in the worst case British or American captivity, which was not too disturbing. But it also meant abandoning those men who were still fighting so desperately, and neither of us could bear the thought of deserting such brave men. We decided to stay and do our duty to the end. There was no question that, with the red stripes on our trousers and the corps flag on my car, we would have made it through all the road blocks and controls. No one in our respective staffs would have questioned our disappearance; they would have assumed that we had not been able to get away from our old headquarters and had been killed or captured. But our pride and sense of duty would not let us do it.

3

AT 9:00 P.M., after the last division had reported, I got into my kübelwagen. Combat activity had quieted down somewhat. The nurses wanted desperately to go with me (many others and some of the children had left earlier, with our other cars). The poor, hapless women, having heard many stories of rape and wanton killing when the Russians took a place, were terrified of the Russian soldiers. I could take only one of them, however, because several members of my staff had to go and there was room for no more in the car. With an aching heart, I could only leave all of them but one to their fate. I left it to them to decide which one would leave with me. I have no idea how they decided, but at the appointed time one of them appeared.

In Ober-Schöneweide, we had to drive through continuous artillery fire, now including heavy artillery. It was a feeling akin to terror, with heavy artillery shells exploding all around us, and roof tiles, window frames, and chunks of street pavement flying through the air. It seemed as if the whole world were exploding around us. Artillery fire in a city is much more frightening than it is in the open. Whenever a shell hit something above us and exploded there, it sprayed shrapnel and fragments of whatever it hit all over. I was glad when we had the bridge over the Spree River behind us, because it was probably the target of all the Russian artillery fire. And beginning in one hour, two of our divisions had to cross this bridge.

When I arrived in Rudow, there was great excitement

in the basement of the large school building where our headquarters was located. South and west of Rudow, Russian tanks and armored vehicles with motorized infantry had appeared in several villages. Major Wolff again had to organize sentinels in the immediate vicinity of the corps headquarters. Although these enemy troops were clearly reconnaissance forces that would have retreated at the slightest resistance, it could have become very unpleasant if suddenly three armored cars had appeared in the courtyard of our school.

The withdrawal movements of our divisions from their positions had already started. Because of the exact timing of the marching orders and well-prepared traffic control, the movement of our four divisions away from the enemy, over two bridges, began rather well during the night of April 22. The SS Division Nordland, which now stood at the left flank and would be free first, was to form a reduced bridgehead around Ober-Schöneweide to protect the retreating parts of the other divisions. The division commander, SS Generalmajor Ziegler, objected when he got this order because he thought Weidling intended to sacrifice his division to save the other divisions. Only an outburst by Weidling made him accept his task. This incident indicated that discipline was beginning to break down. Earlier, Ziegler would not have questioned such an order.

After a short rest, I began to receive the first reports. Without heavy losses, the disengagement from the front had been successful. It was now April 23, 1945, and the bridgehead to Ober-Schöneweide was still in our hands.

In Köpenick, however, something had gone terribly wrong. Our 20th Division was supposed to hold Köpenick so we would have a stable front from there on south of the Spree River, but the division could not hold and Köpenick was overrun. Of course, the division was to blow up the bridge across the Spree if it had to retreat, but the Russians struck with such overpowering force that the Spree bridge was not completely blown up and was still usable.

This gave the Russians a bridge over which they could bring tanks, so Weidling issued orders to the division commander to retake that bridge and finish blowing it up. The division commander, Oberst Scholze, to everyone's shock, replied that his division was exhausted and decimated and unable to mount the ordered attack.

Weidling was naturally infuriated that a division commander would refuse his order, and he exploded. Since I was at hand and he knew I had been trained at the General Staff College to lead a division in combat—and that I would carry out the order—he ordered me to go to Köpenick, take command of that division, lead the attack, and blow up the bridge. The idea of a major leading a division was preposterous, but he had no one else to send. He could not spare von Dufving, who substituted for him at corps headquarters in his absence, and he knew I could and would do the job. That would have probably made me, at twenty-eight, the youngest and lowest-ranking division commander in the history of the Germany Army!

Köpenick was about six kilometers away in a straight line, but I had to take a circuitous route to avoid the fighting. My mind was in a turmoil during the trip because I knew that the division commander I was to relieve was a good man with an excellent combat record, which would now be ruined by a court-martial. But I knew Weidling, and I knew he could blow up like that. Of course, he could not tolerate a division commander's refusing an order, and it was in fact an order that simply had to be carried out. It would have been very bad for the Ninth Army if the Russians held that bridge and got their tanks across the Spree River.

When I arrived, I talked first to the division's operations officer, an oberstleutnant i.G. I learned from him that just before Oberst Scholze had received Weidling's order, he had learned that his wife and children at home had been killed in a bombing raid. He had just lost control of himself for a while, which was understandable to me. But

Weidling had no tolerance for such weakness. I am sure that if it had happened to him, it would have hit him as hard personally, but he would not have let it interfere with his duties. The operations officer told me now that Scholze had regained control of himself and ordered the attack on the bridge. Under those circumstances, I discreetly withdrew and returned to corps headquarters, where I informed General Weidling of the changed circumstances. I took a chance by returning, because that meant that I was not carrying out his orders either. Since the attack was being made, however, Weidling was content. The bridge was recaptured and blown up, but with heavy losses.

In the meantime, alarming news came from the 18th Panzer Division regarding enemy pressure across the Spree River. Weidling and I drove to Alt-Glienicke, to the headquarters of the 18th Panzer Division. Weidling wanted to see the situation personally. The community was under uninterrupted artillery fire. Enemy infantry attacks came out of the southern part of Köpenick and from the east, where the Russians, who were already crossing the river with ferries, had been stopped until now. Antiaircraft guns—unfortunately immobile—were there and could be used against Russian tanks. The division commander, Generalmajor Rauch, believed he could hold until evening. To the south, he had only weak defensive positions along the Spree River, where the Russians had not yet attacked.

We had to move our corps headquarters into the outskirts of Berlin regardless of anything else, so I set out in search of a location. In spite of our efforts, we still knew nothing about the position of the Berlin defense line. I had to make contact, therefore, as quickly as possible with some local command post. But first we had to have new headquarters, because infantry fire was becoming heavier and heavier. At about 9:00 A.M., riding in a kübelwagen and under mortar fire, I managed to get into Berlin on an autobahn. When I arrived at Schöneiche, a suburb of Berlin that we had tentatively selected as our next headquarters, it was apparent that here too it would be impossible for our staff to work because Russian infantry was already moving along the subway tracks from Erkner and Köpenick.

Deciding that the subway station at Rahnsdorf would be the best location for our new headquarters, I telephoned von Dufving to come there. When he arrived, he approved my decision and began to supervise the installation of the corps headquarters. Now I finally could go try to make contact with those in charge of the defense of Berlin. We had to find these people and try to coordinate their defense with ours. We knew only that something had been prepared, although we guessed that whatever had been prepared would be manned by Hitler Youth and by Volkssturm rather than by soldiers.

I was shocked when I found the prepared defense ring around Berlin. It was empty foxholes and trenches and roadblocks—*completely unmanned*! Disgustedly, I realized that it was no more than a line on a map. It had been Goebbels's responsibility, as defense commissar for Berlin, to prepare these defenses, but it was painfully obvious that he had no idea how to do it. So much for Goebbels's ability to assume military responsibility. I managed to get maps of what were supposed to be the defense lines around Berlin so we could plan where to put our divisions when it came to that. All I found was a command post and a headquarters with several officers who were amputees. They commanded no troops, and some of them did not even know where the prepared defenses were. Incompetence seemed to be the order of the day in Berlin.

So Berlin was without defenses, and light, fast Russian units were floating in between our corps (as the northernmost corps of the Ninth Army) and the southernmost corps of the Third Army. If either of the two corps had had reserves, either could have repaired the situation—but neither of us had reserves, and the best we could hope for was to slow the Russians down a day or two.

When I returned to our headquarters, a radio message from General Busse had arrived (we did not have wire connections) that we were to protect the left flank of the Ninth Army, at a line from Königswusterhausen to Rangsdorf, about twenty kilometers south of Berlin, with our front facing north. That meant giving up Berlin! So we would leave the city to its own fate, which, with the inadequate forces available for its defense, would mean the end for Berlin within a few days. This order indicated that General Busse was now thinking only of the Ninth Army and that he probably intended to break through to the west to surrender there. His decision was a logical one, because trying to defend the city with over a million civilians still in it would result in senseless casualties. For us as well, this was a much more comfortable prospect than going into Berlin, which was little more than a heap of rubble, to conduct a hopeless fight there.

We had been thrown into Berlin without anticipating it or having a chance to prepare for it, having been pushed back from the Oder River in less than a week by the most prodigious offensive of the war. During their massive attack, the Russians kept breaking through on each side of us, and we kept falling back to keep from being encircled. Their continued attempts to encircle us eventually cut our corps off from General Busse and the Ninth Army to our south. We finally lost all contact with them and did not know what the situation was. We could see Russian light tanks and trucks to our south, between us and the Ninth Army. General Weidling initiated the actions necessary to comply with General Busse's order to form an east-west front that faced north. Then he turned to me.

"Knappe, you know Berlin from your time at Kriegsschule Potsdam," he said. "Let's go see General Krebs [Chief of the General Staff of the Army] at Führer Headquarters and see whether we can establish communication with the Ninth Army from there and find out what the overall situation is."

Von Dufving stayed at corps headquarters to run things in Weidling's absence, which is the primary function of a chief of staff, and Weidling and I left for the Reich Chancellery. We took one car and driver and two motorcycle runners. The city was under fire from heavy artillery, which was probably mounted on a railroad car somewhere thirty or more kilometers away, and there was also some bombing by Russian aircraft. Fortunately, the artillery was not concentrated; it was scattered all over the city, with a heavy artillery shell landing somewhere in the city every few minutes.

Smoke and dust covered the city. Streetcars were standing disabled in the streets, their electric wires dangling. In the eastern suburbs, many buildings were burning and the civilian population was queueing up in bread lines and in line to get water from any source that was still working. Civilians were everywhere, scurrying from cover to cover because of the artillery shells and bombs. To avoid creating a possible panic, Goebbels had refused to issue orders for civilians to leave the city, even women and children, and now thousands more were fleeing into Berlin from the east. Defending Berlin was obviously going to be very ugly business, and many civilians were going to die in the fighting.

Arriving at the Reich Chancellery at about 6:00 P.M., we left our car and driver to proceed on foot, taking the motorcycle runners with us. The area around the Reich Chancellery was pitted with deep craters. Fallen trees were scattered about like matchsticks, and the sidewalks were blocked by piles of rubble. The Reich Chancellery was badly damaged, with only shells of walls remaining in some places. The entrance hall on the Wilhelmstrasse had been completely destroyed. The only part of the Reich Chancellery that was still usable was the underground bunker system. In the underground garage, we saw several Mercedes-Benzes we had seen Hitler use in parades and political rallies. There was an entrance to the passage to Führer

Headquarters in the underground bunker from the garage. SS guards at the entrance saluted Weidling, with his Knight's Cross and Swords. These first guards were SS unteroffiziers, but the deeper we went toward the bunker, the higher the rank of the guards became.

The bunker system under the Reich Chancellery had become a virtual underground city, housing hundreds of people, including civilians. Many of the civilians probably were employees who worked there and now no longer tried to go home at night. Others probably worked in the surrounding government buildings and found this the safest place to be now. The population of the bunker was controlled, of course, but it was shelter for many people. It was badly overcrowded, because it had been built as an air raid shelter, not as a place for hundreds of people to live. There were also many wounded soldiers, apparently from General Mohnke's SS unit assigned to defend the bunker. Some were on mattresses on the floor and others just sat around.

Führer Headquarters was about three levels down from the garage. We were stopped at many guard posts, even though Weidling was a general with many impressive military decorations, and we were searched by the guards before being admitted to the actual Führer bunker. The SS guards were respectful, but here we were carefully investigated as to who we were, where we came from, and what our business was. We had to show proper identification and surrender our pistols.

Then we finally entered the antechamber to the offices of the Chief of the General Staff of the Army, General Krebs, and the chief of the Personnel Department of the Army, General Burgdorf. We were announced, and Burgdorf's adjutant, Oberstleutnant Weiss, came to welcome us. He led us to the next room, where both Krebs and Burgdorf awaited us.

The reception General Weidling received from Krebs and Burgdorf seemed reserved and strange, considering that he had known them both for years and had attended the General Staff College with Krebs. They invited us to be seated and had ham sandwiches and a bottle of Hennessy cognac brought in for us (at higher staffs, this kind of hospitality was standard procedure for visitors from the front). They had talked to us only briefly when Krebs said he would announce Weidling's presence to Hitler and see if Hitler wanted to talk to him. That was surprising, since Weidling had not come to see Hitler and knew of no reason Hitler would want to talk to him.

When Krebs and Burgdorf were out of the room, Weidling said quietly, "Something is wrong. They are behaving strangely." After about ten minutes, Burgdorf returned and told Weidling that Hitler wanted to see him. I stayed behind, of course, and talked to Weiss, Freytag-Loeringhof, and Boldt (Burgdorf's and Krebs's aides). They wanted to know what was happening where we were. (Weidling had filled Krebs in on that briefly, and also had told him about the order we had received from Busse to form an east-west line twenty kilometers south of Berlin.) I got information from them about the big picture, which was what we had come for. They told me that the Western Allies had stopped at the Elbe River and that General Wenck's Twelfth Army was getting ready to relieve Berlin. They were optimistic, and I did not attempt to discourage their optimism even though I was certain that Wenck could not relieve Berlin.

After Weidling, Krebs, and Burgdorf had been gone about twenty minutes, Krebs and Burgdorf returned. They offered me cognac, and Krebs began to question me about our situation at the front.

After about twenty more minutes, Weidling returned and told me that Hitler had ordered us to come into Berlin and take over the eastern and southern fronts of the city and that we had to get in touch with von Dufving and stop him from carrying out Busse's order. Using Krebs's telephone, I talked to a civilian telephone operator who got me through to our corps headquarters. I told von Dufving briefly what was going on, and then Weidling gave him orders to stop the north-south movement and prepare for our divisions to come into Berlin instead. We planned to establish our headquarters at Tempelhof Airport.

When Weidling and I were alone again, Weidling exploded. "What bastards Krebs and Burgdorf are!" he said. "They did not warn me that Hitler was threatening to have me shot because of a report that we were abandoning Berlin and escaping to the west. Hitler greeted me with the words 'Weidling, I will have you shot!' "

And on top of that false report, Hitler had also learned that we were swinging around to form an east-west line and leave Berlin open to the Russians—but he did not know that Weidling was acting on General Busse's orders. When Hitler had shouted himself out and Weidling could finally get a word in, he corrected Hitler's inaccurate information. After Weidling's complete report, Hitler calmed down and became friendly and finally ordered us into Berlin to defend the east and south fronts. What a difference between the haphazard way things were being done now and the professional way things had been done in 1940 and 1941!

While I talked to von Dufving on the telephone about the details of the move into Berlin, Weidling flushed down his anger against Krebs and Burgdorf with cognac. I had two more to try to help empty the bottle, since Weidling seemed determined to finish it off by himself. He was furious that Krebs and Burgdorf had not warned him of the situation. They parted in anger, and the cognac did not help the situation. In addition to everything else, Weidling was also angry because we were now trapped in Berlin, which guaranteed that we would eventually be captured by the Russians instead of being able to escape to the west with the Ninth Army.

Finally, at 9:00 P.M., I got Weidling to leave Führer Headquarters. We had a lot to do this night! Weidling wanted to inform the defense sector commanders on the east and south sides of Berlin that our divisions would be taking over from them and that they should pass on to the division commanders their knowledge of the area. Weidling could hide the fact that he was drunk only with a great effort as we set out to visit the defense sector commanders. Our first stop was at Tempelhof (Sector D). An old "exhumed" Air Force generalmajor named Schröder was in charge here. He had no concept of infantry fighting, which resulted in his being chewed out by the inebriated Weidling. To appease Weidling, he offered us the use of the basement of his building as our headquarters. I got on his telephone and ordered our advance group to this location to set up new corps staff headquarters. Then Weidling and I went to Hasenheide. There an infantry oberst who had lost an arm was in charge. The man was asleep when we arrived, and we had to wait for him to get dressed. Weidling, impatient from too much cognac and still angry about his experience at Führer Headquarters, began to berate the unfortunate man because he did not get dressed quickly enough and kept Weidling waiting. He was completely unreasonable with this poor man, who also began to get angry because he had done nothing wrong and had only one hand with which to dress—and it was obvious to him that Weidling was drunk.

I intervened in the argument and eventually succeeded in getting them both quieted down. I then suggested to Weidling that he stay at our new headquarters at Tempelhof and turn in. I could visit the other sector commanders. He agreed, and I went on alone. Even though the sectors were not far apart, the trip was a harrowing one in the dark, with all the obstacles in the streets (we had only little slits for headlights). At all the sectors I visited, I found un-front-like conditions. Much had to be done here if we really wanted to put up a fight against the Russians! We had five experienced division staffs, however, and we had to make them the skeleton of a fighting force that we would flesh out with the inexperienced personnel.

The date was April 24, and it was on this night that the apocalyptic battle for the city of Berlin began in earnest. The next day, Russian assault troops fought their way into the suburbs of the city. For the next eight days, Berlin was to be one huge urban killing ground.

4

WHEN I RETURNED to our new headquarters at Tempelhof Airport, the drive through Berlin at night revealed spectacular and gruesome images of the burning city. The glare from flaming buildings silhouetted the gutted hulls of other buildings. In a basement passage of our new headquarters, I found a spot amid civilians who were sleeping there and lay down to close my eyes for a few hours.

In the morning, our staff arrived and the work began, producing orders to the divisions and to the sector commanders. We set up our headquarters and established communication with the divisions through the civilian telephone network. Our headquarters was a beautifully furnished former command post for an air raid protection unit. There was no shortage of good office furniture, radios, and other luxury items. When I saw all the luxuries that the Army had squirreled away, I grimly remembered watching the civilians looting a bread truck for food.

The divisions went into their assigned positions. Then at 11:00 A.M. we received a call from Führer Headquarters that Hitler wanted to see Weidling again. He wanted to know whether our move had been executed successfully. I did not accompany Weidling this time, because I was busy with the divisions. Hitler ordered Weidling to assume command of the defense of the entire city, instead of just the east and south, by taking over the Berlin Military Command in addition to our divisions. In this position, Weidling was replacing Oberst Kather, who had just been

promoted the day before to generalleutnant for the dura-
tion of his position. Weidling was the fifth commander to
occupy this position in the last few months because of
clashes the other commanders had had with Goebbels.
Weidling, therefore, had made one very astute condition—
that he must be in *sole* command of the defense of Berlin,
without any interference from Goebbels, who was gauleiter
and defense commissar for Berlin but who knew nothing
about defending a city in a combat situation. It was a courageous thing for Weidling to do, because generals simply
did not impose conditions on the acceptance of an order
from Hitler. But Hitler probably realized that Goebbels
would otherwise be a problem for Weidling, and he accepted the condition. Weidling also decided to establish
our new headquarters at the headquarters of the Berlin
Military Command.

During a trip to one of the sectors in the southeast of
the city, I witnessed an event that said everything about the
state to which Germany had been reduced. Water pipes in
the city had been ruptured by the bombing and the shelling, and people had to stand in lines for hours for water at
the few sources still available. The food problem was even
worse; some storage houses had been destroyed by bombing and shelling, and the others had been plundered by
civilians. I was in a kübelwagen, and the part of the city I
was driving through was under continuous artillery fire. In
spite of the artillery bombardment, civilians—mostly
women—were queueing in front of the food stores and
water spigots. Just as we were about to drive past such a
line, an artillery shell exploded beside the line of women.
As the smoke began to clear, I could see that many of the
women had been hit. Those women who were unhurt carried the dead, the dying, and the wounded into the entrances of nearby buildings and cared for them—and then
again formed their queues so they would not lose their
places in line!

The sector commander I was visiting during this trip

had his headquarters in the basement of a brewery. The entire sector staff consisted of amputees, but that at least meant they had combat experience. They all were very confident, still believing in Goebbels's speeches, which was amazing under the circumstances. They even interpreted our taking over of their command as a positive sign! I had the adjutant of the sector brief me on the situation in his sector and learned that they did not see even the most obvious things, in spite of their front experience. They should have known that the few civil defense units (old men and young boys) could not stop the Russian tanks, and if those tanks turned around at the first indication of resistance, it was by no means a sign of "victory" by the civil defense or of the Hitler Youth—it only meant that it was a reconnaissance unit that was not supposed to fight but to find out what was opposing them. We received news that SS Group Steiner, which was supposed to break through to Berlin from Oranienburg, had been repulsed and driven back to its initial positions. The offensive of Wenck's Twelfth Army was supposed to have begun from the area of Wittenberg, but it had not begun to have any impact yet.

Early in the morning on April 25, Weidling and I drove to the Berlin Military Command at Hohenzollerndamm, in Wilmersdorf, a southwestern suburb of Berlin about five kilometers from the Reich Chancellery. The Berlin Military Command was just like a corps staff. It was a big operation, with a peacetime staff of about three hundred, including many telephone operators (now mostly women). When we took over, therefore, all our positions existed in duplicate. The Berlin Military Command's chief of staff was Oberstleutnant i.G. Refior, an old acquaintance of General Weidling's. Weidling decided to keep both chiefs of staff, von Dufving for fighting and tactical matters and Refior (who knew everyone in both the political and military command structures in Berlin and knew how to get things done) for political matters.

The Berlin Military Command's operations officer, Major i.G. Sprotte, made a bad first impression on Weidling, who dispatched him to Potsdam. Sprotte, not in the least disappointed, was in a big hurry to get out of Berlin anyway. To turn everything over to me in an orderly manner would have taken several days, so he showed me his maps and drawings with a sweep of his hand and promptly disappeared. With that, I was sitting alone in a room with three telephones that rang constantly. When I realized after three phone calls that they were all from offices of city, party, or ministry authorities who were calling to get information about the military situation, I took all three phones off the hook so I could get my work done.

We had to act quickly now to distribute our five division staffs in such a way that each of them got two to four defense sectors, so we would have all around the city a firm skeleton of experienced combat officers whom we knew and who knew us. Then, as quickly as possible, we had to establish a secure military communications network—it was impossible to continue to lead our troops via the public telephone network!

Life here now became like a typical day in combat: constant crises. When I could sleep two hours in a row, I was lucky. In addition to all the crises, I had to coordinate all the reports from the field. They would come to me by telephone, and I had to prepare a daily report at night that summarized all the telephone reports I had received during the day. Since the artillery shelling and the bombing strikes were becoming more and more frequent, we moved into the basement shortly after we moved into this building. Again, we found some of the rooms to be filled with food, coffee, liquor—even wristwatches.

All military personnel in Berlin, except the SS troops that guarded Führer Headquarters under SS General Mohnke, were now under Weidling's command—the Army, the Hitler Youth, the Volkssturm, the antiaircraft crews, the convalescent battalions from hospitals, and so forth. We had our own four divisions (the fifth one, the 20th SS Panzer Grenadier Division, had disappeared to the west, apparently to surrender there). In its sector, each division took command of whatever Hitler Youth and Volkssturm happened to be there. After a day or so, we had a defense that could hope to resist the Russians at least for a little while. We did not have long to wait. The disappearance of the 20th SS Panzer Grenadier Division left a gap, and the Russians soon drove a wedge through it.

By now, we could see the infantry fighting from our building. During the evening, I entered a room where Weidling was meeting with both von Dufving and Refior. They were discussing whether to defend Berlin dutifully or whether it would be appropriate to stay here and let the Russians pass by on both sides of us and then break through the Grunewald (woods to the west of the city), escape to the west, and surrender to the Western Allies. If we stayed to defend Berlin it would be necessary to move our headquarters to the center of the city, because within two days at the latest the Russians would be occupying this building. Weidling then made his decision to stay and defend Berlin.

The night was extremely turbulent. Outside we could hear the sounds of combat nearby. Major Wolff and his counterpart on the Berlin Military Command staff, Hauptmann Bärenbeck, had organized the immediate defense of the building. I returned early in the morning of April 26 to the second-floor office I had occupied before we moved into the basement. There were continuous artillery bursts all around, and I could see hand-to-hand fighting in the garden parcels to the south. We were obviously in a very dangerous position.

Weidling decided to move corps headquarters to a big antiaircraft bunker near the Berlin zoo. I was quite glad to be ordered to go to the air raid shelter bunker at the zoo, with Major Wolff, as an advance party to establish our new headquarters. Major Wolff and I made our way to the zoo bunker separately, to try to ensure that one of us would get there. The zoo bunker, a heavily fortified place with heavy antiaircraft guns on the roof, would be safe against bombing and artillery.

I was accompanied by a driver and a motorcycle runner. When we left our headquarters, we had to be careful, because the railroad embankment behind our building was under fire and we had to cross it to get to our kübelwagen and motorcycle. We crossed it by dashing from cover to cover, finally arriving safely at our vehicles. As we drove through the city, the earth trembled with each exploding artillery shell, and a huge geyser of earth and debris erupted from the ground with each explosion. The noise was deafening, and the heaving of the earth was unsettling. A sliver of shrapnel from an exploding artillery shell finally punctured one of the tires on my kübelwagen.

While my driver was changing the tire, a woman watching from a house nearby offered me a cup of tea. She was about forty-five years old and matronly, with worn clothes, bedraggled hair, and a kind face. She was the wife of a feldwebel and the mother of a gefreiter, and she had no idea what had happened to either of them. Apparently my lack of personal care showed, and she asked if I would like to wash up as well, so after several days I was able to experience the luxury of washing. I greatly appreciated her generosity, especially since many civilians were understandably beginning to turn against the Army for defending the city instead of surrendering it. Her apartment was in shambles from the artillery blasts. Small knickknacks, little pieces of her life, lay shattered on the floor about her.

"When will the Russians arrive, Herr Major?" she asked.

"In a matter of hours," I told her honestly. "A day at most. You will be safest if you stay in your basement."

Parts of Berlin were a virtual junkyard of disabled military equipment, and the smell of death now permeated everything. In addition to human corpses, many of the animals from the zoo had escaped and been killed. I arrived at the zoo bunker at about noon and found that Wolff had already arrived. There was a big flak bunker at the zoo, seven or eight stories high, with six big 128mm and six 20mm antiaircraft guns on its roof. The bunker could house six hundred people. Every room was occupied, so we selected those we would need and told their occupants they would have to leave because the rooms were needed by the commanding general of the Berlin Military Command. Several of the rooms had been reserved as a private refuge for Goebbels, because the place was so safe from attack. I did not attempt to dispossess Goebbels, of course, but I took over the offices of other superfluous staffs.

I sent Major Wolff back with the information that rooms had been assigned and that the communications officer should come to see to the appropriate telephone connections. After Wolff had gone, I put up signs directing the various units of our corps staff to their assigned rooms. When I had done everything I could do, it was late at night, and I lay down to rest, having had very little rest or sleep in a long time. Every half hour or so a bomb would hit the building. The building would sway visibly, the lights would flicker out momentarily, and a fine spray of plaster would descend from the ceiling. But the building was completely safe because the walls were several meters thick and bombs could not penetrate them. In my state of exhaustion, the motion of the giant bunker swaying on the marshy soil of the Tiergarten Park only helped put me to sleep.

When I woke after a few hours and the staff had still not arrived, I began to wonder if perhaps they had decided to leave through the Grunewald after all. Since I could not reach anyone by telephone, I decided to take advantage of the situation and get a full night's sleep for a change; there was nothing I could do anyway. Finally, the next morning, Wolff returned with the news that Weidling had decided to move instead to the old headquarters of the Supreme Command of the Armed Forces. It was closer to Führer

Headquarters and it had direct telephone lines to it. Because it was located on Bendlerstrasse, everyone in the Army referred to it as "Bendlerstrasse." It had been a full city block of buildings, but everything except the basements had by now been pretty much destroyed. In the center of the huge courtyard was a large bunker, three or four stories high, which was safe against the most formidable bombs—just like the zoo bunker. It was used as the communications center not only for the Army in Berlin but also for Führer Headquarters.

When I arrived there, our staff had been established in the basement. The actual working headquarters of the Supreme Command of the Armed Forces was no longer in Berlin; it had moved out of Berlin when the Allies began to bomb the city on a regular basis. By the time we moved in, the place had been almost abandoned except for civilians living in the basements.

Our staff had already been at work there since midnight. I found Refior at his desk—with coffee, cognac, asparagus tips, and ham! Von Dufving was working on a plan to break out of Berlin to the northwest, across the Pichelsdorf Bridge. I joined him and helped put together the time calculations and the distribution of our forces. I also drew the necessary maps for the operation.

General Weidling was in a room in which we were told Count von Stauffenberg and some other officers had been shot following the July 20, 1944, attempt to assassinate Hitler. It was chilling to see the bullet holes in the wall. It occurred to me that Germany would probably not be enduring this terrible final battle if von Stauffenberg had succeeded.

At noon, I had to leave to take the city map with the current military situation to Führer Headquarters. It had become very dangerous outside, with shell bursts everywhere. The acrid smell of smoke mingled with the stench of decomposing corpses. Dust from pulverized bricks and plaster rose over the city like a heavy fog. The streets, littered with rubble and pockmarked with huge craters, were deserted. I had to be careful not to get entangled in the streetcar wires dangling everywhere. At the Reich Chancellery, my identification card (signed by Goebbels personally so I could get quick access to the bunker) secured entrance for me. To get to the actual Führer Headquarters, I had to show another identification card signed by Johannmeyer, Army adjutant to Hitler. Then I had to surrender my pistol, and finally I was admitted to the antechamber, which was furnished with green leather chairs along the walls. Such fine furniture seemed out of place in a concrete bunker deep under the ground. I thought I remembered the green chairs from my visit at the Chancellery six years earlier.

Martin Bormann, who was sitting in the antechamber, immediately jumped at me and asked what I wanted. I told him I was bringing the latest situation map. I wanted to go to Krebs immediately, but Bormann insisted that I have soda and cookies while he pumped me with a lot of questions concerning the situation outside and what I thought about it. Bormann was about fifty years old, short and heavy, with a broad nose punctuating a round face that sat atop a bull neck. As political chief of staff to the Führer, he determined who was and was not admitted to see Hitler.

In Krebs's antechamber, I met Weiss and Freytag-Loeringhof, aides to General Burgdorf, and gave them the situation map. In turn, I copied the overall situation from their map. According to it, Wenck's Twelfth Army had begun its attack on April 25 and had progressed well in the beginning. Today, however, Wenck had been able to proceed no farther than the Beelitz State Hospital and was engaged in heavy fighting with Soviet troops who had attacked it from the east. Nobody here in the map room of the Chief of Staff of the Army really believed any longer that Berlin would be relieved.

I learned when I returned to our bunker that Göring had been arrested for attempting to replace Hitler as Führer and that Hitler had ordered Himmler's arrest for attempting to negotiate with the Allies. The government was disintegrating as rapidly as the military situation. But Hitler was apparently determined to fight to the last possible moment, no matter how many lives it cost or how much destruction to the city.

Interestingly, the Reich Chancellery did not have a large radio transmitter. All messages had to go through our communications center in the bunker of the old headquarters of the Supreme Command of the Armed Forces, so we knew what was happening everywhere. From Führer Headquarters, only a telephone connection of the public telephone network existed, and it was now being interrupted constantly by the fighting. We had laid four military cables to Voss-Strasse, where the Reich Chancellery was located, of which only one was still occasionally operational, even though we had men working constantly to keep the lines in service. For that reason, I always had to make the trip myself whenever something important came up.

The trip was becoming increasingly dangerous, because at some places Russian shock troops had already crossed the Landwehr Canal and were located in some of the houses at Matthäus Churchyard and in the vicinity of the Hotel Esplanade. All the buildings in this area had basements, and people were living in them. There was food in the buildings; many things had been stored in these buildings, because this had been the headquarters of the Supreme Command of the Armed Forces. There was even cognac, and other things that were very scarce for civilians. The Army had obviously prepared to take care of itself.

During the day, either von Dufving or I stayed in close contact with our divisions by telephone or radio, and of course each night I prepared a consolidated report from the divisions' reports. In addition, I made at least one daily trip to Führer Headquarters to report—not only because our lines were constantly being destroyed by artillery fire but because we could never be sure that the Russians were not listening in.

One of the worst things about the defense of Berlin was that the Russians always had fresh reserves to put into the fighting, so they could rest their troops, but our people had to just keep fighting, hour after hour and day after day, until they were killed or seriously wounded.

5

THERE WAS NO such thing as a typical day. Sometimes the Russians would hit us at three in the morning, sometimes at six, and the day just unfolded from there. Our time was spent responding to crises that incessantly occurred. I would get reports from the divisions. I would get cries for help. I was constantly involved, solving logistical problems, receiving and compiling reports, and informing the divisions of new developments. General Weidling was always out visiting the divisions, going where things were worst to get his own view of each situation in person, and von Dufving was directing the fighting from corps headquarters.

We all caught a few moments' rest whenever work permitted. I learned that I had to stand up whenever I was wakened to take a telephone call. Several times I took a call that woke me, listened to the problem of the caller, gave instructions to handle the situation, and then went back to sleep. Then when I woke I had no recollection of the conversation and did not know I had given such orders, although eventually I would remember it. After that, I put the telephone far enough away that I would have to stand up to answer it. I had to report the decisions I made to the chief of staff and to the commanding general, so it was essential that I remember what I had done.

I spent a lot of my time now going back and forth between Führer Headquarters and our corps headquarters on Bendlerstrasse. There were hardly any buildings remaining in the neighborhood, and even those that still stood were badly damaged and nearly unrecognizable, although most of the basements were still usable. The whole area was in ruins, having been bombed earlier in British and American air raids and now shelled by Russian artillery. Artillery shells exploded continuously, with thundering detonations. When I went outside now, the smoke from the burning city sliced through my nostrils and lungs like a jagged blade edge. The streets were full of both debris and bodies, although the bodies were hardly recognizable as such. The corpses of both soldiers and civilians who had been killed in the shelling and bombing were under debris, and everything was covered with a gray-and-red powder from the destruction of the buildings. The stink of death was suffocating. We had no way to dispose of the bodies, or even to collect them, because we were under constant air and artillery bombardment and infantry fighting was now everywhere. The city smelled like a battlefield, which in fact it was, with the smell of the plaster and brick dust from disintegrating buildings, of burning wood, of burned gunpowder, of gasoline, and of decomposing corpses. Fortunately, the nights were still cool, so the smell of death was still just bearable.

When I made the trip to Führer Headquarters now (approximately one kilometer), I had to dart from cover to cover, watching not only for incoming artillery rounds but for rifle and machine-gun fire as well. From our command bunker, I went straight up Bendlerstrasse to the Tiergarten, then along the south side of the park or through it. (The Russians were already in parts of the park, and they fired at all movement.) Then on to the southwest corner of the Reich Chancellery across from the park (I would enter the bunker from the basement of the Chancellery). Some of the SS troops defending the Chancellery were dug in before the building. At night, both sides would shoot at any movement.

To the people at Führer Headquarters, we represented the outside world. Nobody there had left the bunker for several days. They were safe in the bunker, with its many feet of concrete under many feet of earth, but they did not know what was going on outside—that the fighting was only a kilometer away or that the "rescuing" armies had been halted. Hitler and the high command were juggling divisions that no longer existed or were just skeletons of themselves.

Every time I came into the bunker, Martin Bormann especially was eager to know what was happening. He was *always* there, in the big antechamber in front of Hitler's office and living quarters. Every time I came in he would insist that I sit down on one of the green leather chairs and have some of his goodies and tell him about the situation on the outside. It was very important to him to know the situation on the outside before anyone else did. As a civilian chief of staff to Hitler, he had a reputation for being a ruthless intriguer. Everyone knew his power, and everyone had a certain fear of him because he had constant access to Hitler, but he was not held in high esteem by military leaders.

The effort to supply us by air had practically ceased, since the East-West Axis (the parade avenue through the Tiergarten) was now under constant mortar fire. The last plane that had landed did not make it off the ground again and was still sitting there, crippled by enemy fire. It was impossible to land ammunition for fifty thousand men, let alone to parachute it in. The airdrops had produced only six tons of supplies. Above all, there was no way to distribute them to the troops.

The situation was such that we still had control of an area shaped like a dumbbell. In the east, we had an area about three kilometers in diameter, with the Reich Chancellery in the center. The shaft of the dumbbell was the Heerstrasse, about eight kilometers long, which was being crossed from time to time by Russian tanks. In spite of that, the subway tunnel under it was still a safe connection to the west, where we still controlled an area about three kilometers in diameter surrounding the Olympic Stadium. The fighting out there was being done by the Hitler Youth, who, with exceptional courage, were keeping open the Pichelsdorf Bridge for a possible breakout to the west. The main push of the Russians was directed toward the center of Berlin, which they had attacked from the south, east, and north. For some reason, they had not hit upon the simple idea of attacking along the Heerstrasse, which they could reach without much effort, moving east, and just driving through the Brandenburg Gate into the center of the city.

The city's defenders—the remnants of our 56th Panzer Korps and General Mohnke's one thousand SS troops defending Führer Headquarters—were red-eyed and sleepless, living in a world of fire, smoke, death, and horror. Much of Berlin was burning like a bonfire. The fighting was being shared by soldiers and civilians alike. When the shelling got bad, the women queueing up for water would press closer to the building walls to hold their places in line. Since such a front could not possibly be held for more than a few days, Weidling decided to make a determined plea to Hitler to break out as long as the route to and across the Pichelsdorf Bridge remained open.

Once again, von Dufving and I went over the plan to break out of Berlin to the west and northwest, across the Pichelsdorf Bridge. We worked through the night, preparing the necessary orders and issuing them to the divisions. Only the code name "Spring Storm" was necessary to set everything in motion.

Our plan to break out in three groups promised real safety for Hitler and the other occupants of Führer Headquarters. A group of SS shock troops with about a dozen self-propelled guns would open the way, the twenty-five or so tanks that were still operational would surround the armored personnel carriers containing Hitler and his entourage to provide flank protection, and the infantry now fighting the Russians in the eastern sectors of Berlin would provide the rear guard. The plan was to start at midnight and be out of the city by morning. We had broken out of encirclement before, in Silesia, and we knew that those riding in armored personnel carriers in the center of such a fighting force would get through safely. Once out of Berlin, we would have to march for a few days to the northwest, toward Lübeck. The Russian Air Force was not a big threat because it was not very efficient, although it would certainly lob some bombs at us.

At about noon, General Weidling and I took the maps and departed for Führer Headquarters. Outside, conditions were more dangerous than ever. Since morning the Russians had held the Lichtenstein Bridge, and before the day was over the entire Tiergarten would be in Russian hands. Russian artillery shells were exploding everywhere, causing the earth to tremble and sending dirt, pavement, bricks, and other debris high into the air to fall back to earth and injure anyone below. The roar of flames from burning buildings and the crunching sound of falling walls were terrifying. We dashed from doorway to doorway in short bursts to avoid not only shrapnel and other debris from the artillery shells but also rifle and machine-gun fire. At twenty-eight, I did not find the running especially strenuous; at fifty-seven, General Weidling had a more difficult time.

We no longer had to surrender our pistols at Führer Headquarters, because we were so well known. When we arrived at Hitler's headquarters several flights of stairs below ground level, the situation briefing had just begun. General Weidling was announced to Hitler and immediately admitted to the briefing room. I waited in the large outer chamber with detailed maps that Weidling might need. The bunker smelled damp, and the sound of the small engine that ran the exhaust system provided a constant background noise. The ever-present Martin Bormann accosted me again. I had one of Bormann's sandwiches and filled him in on the battle that was being waged above ground.

After about forty-five minutes, the meeting in the briefing room ended. Hitler emerged, followed by Dr. Goebbels, General Krebs, General Weidling, and some other people. I saluted, and Hitler walked toward me. As he neared, I was shocked by his appearance. He was stooped, and his left arm was bent and shaking. Half of his face drooped, as if he'd had a stroke, and his facial muscles on that side no longer worked. Both of his hands shook, and one eye was swollen. He looked like a very old man, at least twenty years older than his fifty-six years.

Weidling presented me to Hitler: "Major Knappe, my operations officer."

Hitler shook my hand and said, "Weidling has told me what you are going through. You have been having a bad time of it."

Being accustomed to saying *"Jawohl,* Herr General," I automatically said *"Jawohl,* Herr . . ." and then, realizing that this was wrong, I quickly corrected to *"Jawohl, mein Führer."* Hitler smiled faintly, and Goebbels smiled broadly—but Weidling frowned because his subordinate had made a social error.

Hitler said goodbye, shook my hand again, and disappeared in the general direction of Goebbels's quarters. Although his behavior had not been lethargic, his appearance had been pitiful. Hitler was now hardly more than a physical caricature of what he had been. I wondered how it was possible that in only six years, this idol of my whole generation of young people could have become such a human wreck. It occurred to me then that Hitler was *still* the living symbol of Germany—but Germany as it was now. In the same six years, the flourishing, aspiring country had become a flaming pile of debris and ruin.

Weidling and I left the bunker through the basement hallways of the Reich Chancellery. We had found a safe passage through the basement all the way to a window facing Hermann-Göring-Strasse.

"Did he approve the plan?" I asked with trepidation.

"No," Weidling said angrily. "But it was the way he did it!" This man whom I had seen remain calm under even the most adverse circumstances was so furious that his voice quivered. "He listened to my proposal, and then he said, 'No, Weidling, I do not want to risk dying in the streets like a dog.' Our soldiers have been dying in the streets of Europe for the past six years—*at his command*! For him to imply now that such a death is somehow dishonorable is *loathsome.*" Weidling was so angry that he was throwing caution to the wind. If someone had overheard and reported what he had just said to me, his life would have been in very great danger.

But our men had been dying in the streets of Berlin every day and every night since we had arrived in the city, and they had died in the streets of other cities before Berlin. For Hitler to be so disrespectful toward the men who were sacrificing their own lives every day just to keep him alive one more day filled me with anger also. Many men who had served under my command had died since the beginning of the war. My own brother had died "for Führer and Fatherland." No wonder Weidling was angry. We had both been in the war from the beginning, and we had both seen countless deaths in our almost six years of war. As soldiers, we had accepted death—even our own if it came—as a natural part of our lives. We accepted it as a price we had to pay for a cause we had thought just, at least in the beginning. We were perhaps only now, at the last possible moment, beginning to see clearly what kind of man we had been following.

When I reported to the Führer bunker the next day with the daily situation map and saw Hitler going from one room to another in the bunker, my hand moved involuntarily toward my pistol. I had a terribly strong urge to kill him and stop all the suffering. It would have been easy to do, since he had no personal bodyguards inside the bunker. I would not have got out alive, since SS guards were at all the entrances and exits, but I could easily have killed him. Certainly it was not fear of death that stopped the movement of my hand to my pistol. With the escape plan out of the question, my fate was sealed and unavoidable. The Russians had been shooting captured German officers following every battle in their march across Germany. My life would undoubtedly be over in a few days in any case. In the instant I had to make a decision, I must have instinctively concluded that I should not risk making a martyr of Hitler and possibly creating another *dolchstosslegende*.

By late April, we no longer had any chance of defending Berlin. The horrible, hopeless battles in the streets continued, but our divisions were little more than battalions, our morale was poor, and our ammunition was almost gone. Theoretically, we had four divisions with which to defend the city, but in fact the divisions were at less than half strength, and that included many wounded. By including Hitler Youth and Volkssturm we may have had enough bodies to man four full divisions, but the Volkssturm was staffed by old men and the Hitler Youth was composed of children (although some Hitler Youth were somewhat effective in defensive positions). Even if we'd had four fully staffed, experienced, and rested divisions, we were still a corps fighting *two army groups*! And on top of everything else, we knew we would receive no more ammunition.

Being outdoors in the city was becoming more dangerous, because Russian tanks were now driving around the city, German tank-hunter groups were chasing them with panzerfausts, and both were shooting wildly in all directions. To go anyplace in the city now meant darting from cover to cover, from doorway to doorway, climbing over and around the piles of debris and the decomposing bodies that littered the streets. When a soldier walks over and around and sometimes inadvertently on human corpses daily, his sensibilities start to numb. I was beginning to wonder if we could still be called "human."

The loud roar of combat filled our days and our nights. We could usually detect from the sound what kinds of weapons were being fired. Mortars sounded slow, artillery shells were a little faster, and heavy artillery was much faster. Of course, the detonation of heavy artillery was much louder than that of light artillery and mortars. We could also tell the direction a shell was coming from by its sound, and we could tell by the sound whether it would pass over our heads or hit in our vicinity. After a while, our senses were automatically tuned to these sounds, and our reactions became instinctive.

We still had not given up on the idea of breaking out of Berlin. It was obvious that a breakout could succeed only as long as we could get to the Pichelsdorf Bridge without heavy fighting. The divisions urged us to begin the breakout soon. The morale of the men leaped when they learned about the possibility of a breakout. Weidling kept urging Krebs to press Hitler on the subject, but Krebs said that Hitler could not be made to change his mind. Hitler's refusal frittered away precious hours and days while the Russians constantly reinforced the ring around Berlin—especially to the west of the city.

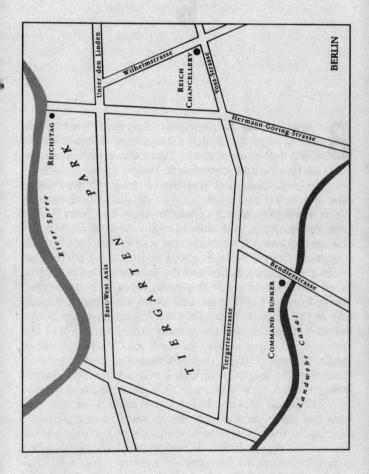

BERLIN

REICHSTAG

River Spree

P A R K

T I E R G A R T E N

East-West Axis

Unter den Linden

Wilhelmstrasse

REICH CHANCELLERY

Voss-Strasse

Hermann-Göring-Strasse

Tiergartenstrasse

Bendlerstrasse

COMMAND BUNKER

Landwehr Canal

6

BY APRIL 29, the Russians were less than five hundred
meters from the Reich Chancellery. I could hardly
steal a full hour of sleep. There was always work: reports to receive and consolidate, orders to write, instructions to give, maps and sketches to draw, phone calls to
take and make, and endless other details to take care of.
We learned that Wenck's Twelfth Army had been beaten
back conclusively, and with that any hope for a military
change was gone. Everybody now wanted to place hope in
a political change brought about by increasing friction between the Western Allies and the Russians. But could that
be of any help to us at this point, even if it happened?
Weiss, Freytag-Loeringhof, and Boldt answered this question in the negative when they left the sinking ship during
the afternoon, through the subway tunnel and across Lake
Wannsee, to carry Hitler's last will and testament out of
Berlin. However, they did not mention anything about
their plans to me, even though I talked with them daily; I
learned about their departure only after they had gone.

At Bendlerstrasse, individual members of the staff
who had no immediate job to do were having parties—
dancing on the volcano, so to speak—with the women auxiliaries for signal duties. It was a relief to me to again
submerge myself in my work. In another area, a feverish
activity developed: everybody wanted to take advantage of
being so close to the Personnel Department of the Supreme Command of the Army to get bigger decorations
and even a promotion. Von Dufving was promoted to

oberst at this time, and he surely had earned it. But other promotions were given very generously now at the last moment. Decorations too were processed rather quickly if they were related to bravery in the fight for Berlin. Several times I saw fourteen- and fifteen-year-old Hitler Youth members pick up their Iron Crosses for destroying Russian tanks.

Weidling was considering trying the breakout on his own if Führer Headquarters did not want to come along. It was a difficult decision for him to make, however, and he could not quite come to grips with it. We had almost given up any hope of getting out of the rubble and debris that was now Berlin when suddenly on the morning of April 30 a call came from Führer Headquarters—one of the cables actually was functioning for a change—requesting that I come over immediately and report again about the time calculations of the breakout plan. I left immediately.

Through the springtime foliage of the Tiergarten the shells burst without interruption, destroying everything in their immediate vicinity, and small-arms fire was everywhere. Blinding sunshine lay over a gruesome scene. On the lawns of the Tiergarten under mutilated age-old trees, I could recognize artillery pieces, all put out of action by direct hits. The gunners who had not made it were lying around, so mutilated they were hardly recognizable as human remains. Everywhere in the streets, the dead were visible among the piles of dust-covered debris. Empty shoes lay here and there. I remembered the first combat dead I had seen in France so long ago, and how shocked I had been at the sight. Now my sensibilities were so numb that a corpse was little more than an obstacle to step over. In those moments when I paused to catch my breath or to let a salvo of artillery shells get over with, I could see in gruesome detail the outlines of a human torso, or part of one, between fragments of bricks, rocks, and concrete. However, I could not let such observations distract me. I had to try to get in one piece across Hermann-Göring-

Strasse with my papers. Maybe Hitler had decided after all to make the breakout!

This time I did not have to endure Bormann's courtesies. General Krebs was waiting for me in the Führer's conference room. I laid out my maps and made another presentation on our intended breakout. Krebs then asked a lot of questions about the details of our time calculations. He was especially interested in the amount of advance notice that had to be given to the divisions before the beginning of the operation. I told him that we had everything prepared so that we could start tonight if the order went out this very moment, but that fourteen hours of startup time was required. A quick decision was necessary if the breakout was to be successful—tomorrow night could be too late. Krebs indicated that Hitler was still opposed to a breakout, but Krebs wanted to try again to change his mind. We would hear from him about the results. So all our hope had been for nothing. He had not even approached Hitler about it!

With a very heavy heart, I returned to Bendlerstrasse. The hours went by without anything happening, without word from Führer Headquarters to dispatch the code name to put the divisions in motion. Then it was noon—for tonight, it was now too late. And tomorrow, perhaps, it would be too late altogether.

Still, the front was holding firmly—almost inexplicably. Why did the Russians insist on attacking at all the most difficult places? Across the Spree River at the Charité Hospital and across the Landwehr Canal at the Lützowufer? At Potsdam Square and in Leipziger Strasse, where General Mohnke's SS units defended the immediate surroundings of the Reich Chancellery? The Russians apparently wanted to conquer the Reichstag and the Reich Chancellery as quickly as possible. It was lucky they did not know that the easiest way would have led them very quickly and directly to their goal! Each time I drew a new situation map, it was a puzzle to me why the Russian general staff could not recognize that.

During April 30, the Russians captured the Reichstag and then concentrated on the few hundred meters to Führer Headquarters against fierce resistance. General Mohnke's SS troops and the remnants of our 56th Panzer Korps were defending the bunker valiantly; even though their own deaths could be the only possible result of their continuing to fight, still they fought on.

At about 7:00 P.M., an aide of General Krebs arrived with an order for Weidling to come with a small working staff to Führer Headquarters. Whatever that might mean, it was a change. And there was hardly anything now that could make things worse. Weidling decided to take von Dufving, a clerk, and a liaison officer along. I was to stand by and follow, the next morning at the latest, with the latest situation map.

At around 6:00 A.M. on May 1, Major Kirsch, our liaison officer with General Mohnke, arrived from Führer Headquarters. He reported very strange things. Incredibly, Weidling was apparently being held there against his will, under something like house arrest! I took my maps and set out again on the horrible trip to Voss-Strasse, as Weidling had instructed me before he left.

In the conference room of the Chief of the General Staff of the Army, I met Weidling, von Dufving, and the others from our staff. Weidling somehow looked completely different. Something had happened that had thrown this man, who could not be discouraged even in the most hopeless situation in battle, completely out of kilter. Weidling informed me quietly that Goebbels had told him last night that Hitler, after first marrying Eva Braun, had taken poison, together with his wife, and shot himself. (None of us had known about Eva Braun before, but now it occurred to me that she must have been among the women in the bunker whom I took to be secretaries.) The corpses were rolled in carpets, drenched with gasoline, and burned in the courtyard of the Reich Chancellery so that they would not fall into the hands of the Russians. Goebbels had Weidling come to the bunker so he could continue leading his troops from there.

I was stunned. For some reason, it had never occurred to me that Hitler would commit suicide. If he planned to commit suicide, why had he not done it long ago, when it was obvious that the war was lost? Why had so many people had to die so senselessly, right up to the moment the Russians were knocking on the bunker door? Such selfishness was unbelievable to me.

Goebbels, as the highest Reich minister in Berlin, had taken command and apparently was afraid that Weidling might take action on his own. Weidling told me that he was not free to leave the bunker and advised me to try to maintain my base at Bendlerstrasse so I would not be restricted to the bunker as well. I had to be his connection with the divisions. He said he would try to get the agreement for the breakout tonight. He told me that the night before, von Dufving and Krebs had gone to the Russians to explore the conditions for a surrender (both spoke Russian), but the Russians had insisted on unconditional surrender.

Von Dufving then told me the details about his trip across the front lines. After Hitler's death, Krebs had immediately got in touch with the Russian command by radio and asked whether a German delegation could cross at Wilhelmstrasse to talk to them. Krebs, who was a former military attaché in Moscow, walked with von Dufving along Wilhelmstrasse, partly through the subway tunnel. They were received by Russian officers and driven to General Chuikov's staff headquarters. Although their conduct was correct, the Russians were adamant in their demand for unconditional surrender and for extradition of Hitler (whose death was not yet known to them), Goebbels, and all other nonsoldiers responsible for the war.

The next morning, Krebs gave his consent to begin the breakout during the night of May 1. Weidling gave Refior the order to issue the code name to our divisions. It was now too late for a massed, centrally led breakout in one direction, so breakouts were to be made individually by each division, beginning at 9:30 P.M. Weidling also gave each division commander and each soldier the choice to either join the breakout action or to go into Russian captivity.

In talking with Generalmajor Mohnke, Weidling and I learned that SS Brigade Mohnke intended to leave at about 9:30 P.M., gather at the subway station at Friedrichstrasse, and break out in a northerly direction. Weidling decided that our corps staff would join this group, and he instructed me to have our corps staff personnel ready to leave Bendlerstrasse at 8:00 P.M. We would, of course, have to fight our way through to the Reich Chancellery in order to join Mohnke's group.

The Reich Chancellery personnel, or those who were left, also intended to join this group. Krebs and Burgdorf decided to stay and take their own lives. During my walks through the Reich Chancellery this day, I saw wounded people everywhere who were being cared for by Army medical corpsmen and by Red Cross nurses. SS men were helping themselves to such delicacies as canned sausages and soda or beer.

It was obvious that the end had finally arrived. Plans were being made now by individuals rather than by commanders. At 7:30 P.M., I sat down to a "last supper" with all those from Hitler's immediate entourage who were still present in the Führer bunker. I was probably the only outsider in the group. Sitting around a large table with me were Martin Bormann, Admiral Voss (a liaison officer representing Admiral Dönitz), Ambassador Hewel (a liaison officer representing Foreign Minister von Ribbentrop), and four or five women whose identities I do not recall but who must have been secretaries. There were also two or three other people. We had tea, Army bread, corned beef, and canned liverwurst. The conversation, of course, was about the forthcoming breakout through the Russian lines. Since I was an experienced combat officer and therefore an "expert" in this group, I was bombarded with all kinds of questions. The appearance of the group was unusual, because all were dressed for the breakout. Fat Bormann could hardly have been comfortable in the regulation enlisted man's uniform he wore. The admiral and the ambassador also wore enlisted men's uniforms. Even the women were dressed in Army uniforms. The attitude of the women was fatalistic. Whatever happened could not be helped. Hitler was dead, and that was almost more of a shock than they could handle. They had all been with him for many years, and their minds were probably now blank with the inability to cope with what was happening.

During this meal, at about 8:00 P.M., Dr. Goebbels came in with Frau Goebbels to say goodbye to the Reich Chancellery staff. One of the secretaries whispered to me that Goebbels's children, who had still been running around in the bunker in the afternoon, had already been put to death. The attitude of Frau Goebbels was very composed, under the circumstances, and Dr. Goebbels also showed an amazing composure. It seemed astonishing to me that they could come around and calmly say goodbye to everyone, knowing what they had just done and what was to come next. They were in control of their emotions, however, and their voices sounded firm. With solemn expressions, they wished everyone luck for the future. They shook hands with everyone and then without apparent emotion they turned around and walked back through the hallway toward the Reich Propaganda Ministry to take their own lives there.

Although Weidling had made arrangements to break out with Brigade Mohnke, he wanted to go back again to Bendlerstrasse to address the staff and give everybody the choice of breaking out or surrendering. It was still daylight. The Russians had already taken the Reichstag and were throwing everything they had against the Reich Chancellery. The Tiergarten was now the center of the battle, and we were subjected to targeted artillery fire, machine-gun fire, and small-arms fire. I did not wait for Weidling, because two men would just present a bigger target than one. We had no protection, and it would have been pointless to fire back with our puny little pistols. The best thing to do was to concentrate on being a small, quick target and reaching the next cover alive. I jumped from cover to cover swiftly. Weidling, who was twice my age, could not move as quickly.

This extremely dangerous and physically exhausting trip, together with the events of the past twenty-four hours, must have finished off Weidling's nerves. He might also have been influenced by von Dufving's report about being treated correctly by the Russians. In any case, in the bunker at Bendlerstrasse, Weidling declared that he did not want to break out but to surrender to the Russians instead.

I told him I would like to take my leave, since I did not want to surrender but, according to the arrangements we had made earlier, would rather take part in the breakout with Brigade Mohnke. Weidling turned on me in a terrible outburst of fury. This was the only time he ever became angry at me, apparently because he felt that I had deserted him on the return from Führer Headquarters, although he did not say that directly. But he certainly had no right to accuse a soldier who had survived as much combat and been wounded as many times as I had of cowardice, and I told him so in rather explicit terms. We were probably both on the verge of nervous collapse. The human system can only take so much, and certainly we had put our systems to the test.

Perhaps he took my desire to break out as a reproach, since he had told Mohnke an hour earlier that he would join him with his entire staff. Of course, we would have suffered losses getting to the Reich Chancellery, but most of us would have made it. In any case, he forbade me to leave the bunker before 10:00 P.M. (until then, according to him, he still needed me), but of course it would be too late for me to join the Mohnke group then. So with his order, Weidling sealed my fate and prevented me from trying to escape Russian captivity. I was still soldier enough to follow orders instead of deserting to try to break out on my own, although anger raged inside me.

There was still work to do: preparation for the surrender, burning of all our papers and files (the official diary of the 56th Panzer Korps and Major Wolff's personnel files), orders to surrender to all units that could still be reached. After von Dufving gave a brief speech about his "decent treatment" by the Russians the night before, almost all the members of the staff were in agreement to surrender without further fighting and to become prisoners of war of the Russians. The exact orders for the surrender and the march into captivity would be rendered after von Dufving negotiated again directly with the Russians.

It did not take long to establish radio contact. At midnight, von Dufving would be picked up as intermediary at the Bendler Bridge. He was to ask for the honorable surrender of our troops, an immediate cease-fire, the protection of civilians against terrorism, each soldier's right to keep food and personal belongings, and the right of officers and men to remain with their units.

In the courtyard, fires were burning with all our papers and the files of the Supreme Command of the Army. I was especially sorry that all the personnel files went up in flames, because I had always taken great pride in my military record. But the years of being a professional soldier were now over.

When von Dufving returned from talking to the Russians, Weidling called all the staff together and told them that arrangements had been made for us to surrender the next morning.

I wrote a letter to Lilo and addressed copies of it to various relatives, since I could not know who might still be alive. I gave the letters to several women signal auxiliaries and Red Cross nurses, for whom the Russians had promised unimpeded travel. Then, for the last time, I ate a meal prepared by my orderly: tender green beans, boiled ham, and fried potatoes. I also had two glasses of champagne. To be on the safe side, my orderly filled my haversack with food and my canteen with cognac.

I then carefully took inventory of my personal things in order to decide what I might need most as a prisoner of war. The biggest question was whether to take my sleeping bag or my fur-lined overcoat. With my previous experiences with the cold winters in Russia firmly in my memory, the fur coat prevailed, even though summer had hardly begun. I exchanged my tailored uniform for a regulation uniform because it would not call attention to me and would be more comfortable. I pulled a pair of tanker's coveralls over that to cover the red general staff stripes on my pants in case they should prove to be a liability. My best shirts and underwear, some food, my photographs and letters, and a few packs of cigarettes for barter completed my luggage. In spite of my throwing away a great many things, my knapsack must still have weighed over thirty pounds. And on top of that, my heavy fur-lined uniform overcoat. But if necessary, I could always throw some things away later.

Of course, there was no thought of any sleep now. I had slept during artillery bombardments and I had slept knowing that attack was imminent—but now the uncertainty of what lay ahead drove sleep away. I wandered outside, into the Berlin night. The mild spring night contrasted with the flaming ruins around us. An almost ghostly silence lay about us. It seemed almost tangible after the constant noise of battle during the past few weeks. As I surveyed the ruins around me, the question "At what cost?" ran through my mind. The cost of this war had been far beyond the capacity of mere humans to tabulate. Did I feel in any way responsible for it on this night? Did I feel any moral guilt? Not yet, although it was to come later, when I learned much that I did not know on this night. For now, I regretted only that we had lost the war, and my first priority was surviving what lay immediately ahead of me.

A thousand questions about my destiny went through my head in the early darkness of that Berlin night. What would my new life as a prisoner of war of the Russian Army be like if I were not shot? How long would captivity last? How would it end? I knew that when we had recaptured German towns from the Russians, we often learned that they had murdered the German officers they had captured. I felt that I had to assume that my life was now over and I would be shot. The biggest question was how things were at home. Had everyone survived the fighting in Leipzig?

This question provoked another, more and more urgent: Should I try to avoid captivity? Should I now clamber on my own through the ruins and try to get home? I thought of the possibility of hiding in the rubble, taking enough to eat and drink to last several days until things quieted down, and then trying to escape to Leipzig. But I knew the Russians would be looking for people doing that. I was familiar with the ring of Russian forces around Berlin, and as the operations officer during the defense of Berlin, I knew the bottlenecks that had been created by the blown-up bridges everywhere. I knew, without any doubt, that there was no chance of my leaving Berlin without being caught.

I drew my pistol from its holster, disassembled it, and threw the pieces as far as I could in different directions. I did not want it to become a souvenir for some Russian soldier. This symbolic act was my final resignation and surrender.

I stood in the darkness and listened in amazement to the warbling of some thrushes nearby. I had not heard such sounds for so long, and it seemed incredible that they could have survived the final battle. It was spring, and the thrushes would be preparing to raise a new generation of themselves. Could there possibly be rebirth after such total destruction? In my present state of mind, I could not believe it. In any case, my world had ended.

7

SOON DAWN CAME, and we had to swallow the bitter pill of surrender to the Russians. At 5:55 A.M. on May 2, 1945, our arms were stacked and everyone was in marching formation in a gray Berlin drizzle. We were Weidling's corps staff and a number of communications people (radio and telephone technicians) who had remained at Bendlerstrasse when the headquarters of the Supreme Command of the Armed Forces moved out of Berlin. Devastation lay all about us. Much of the city was still burning in the drizzling rain, and the acrid smoke sharply assaulted our nostrils and eyes.

Weidling had already gone by car to the Russian General Chuikov's headquarters near Tempelhof Airport. I busied myself getting the troops into formation and making sure that none had weapons. Oberst von Dufving, Oberst Refior, Major Wolff, and I led the column to the end of Bendlerstrasse, about a half block away, where the Russians were waiting for us on the far side of the Landwehr Canal. The canal was about a hundred feet wide, with steep cement banks on each side. It had been used to move barges through the city. The bridge across the canal had been destroyed, but a huge bundle of cable that had been strung across the canal underneath the bridge was still intact. There were telephone and electric cables—thick cables, thin cables, cables of all different colors—that went into the ground on each side of the canal. Approximately three feet in diameter, the bundle of cables (all tied together) formed a workable footbridge, and the ranking

Russian officer crossed it to our side. Von Dufving saluted and reported to him.

The Russian officer spoke to von Dufving and then returned to the other side of the canal. About two dozen Russian soldiers with submachine guns waited on the other side of the canal, along with several American-made jeeps. Our column crossed the bundle of cables, walking upright in single file. When I stepped onto the other side of the canal, I thought of it as the symbolic end of my life. The Russian soldiers with submachine guns all had big grins on their faces when we reached the other side. One of them said, *"Hitler kaput!"* and they all giggled gleefully. They were enjoying their victory hugely, as any victorious soldiers would.

Von Dufving talked to the Russian officer briefly and then told Refior, Wolff, and me that we were to be taken to General Chuikov's headquarters about three kilometers away. First, however, we drove only a few blocks, to a Russian division headquarters, where we were put on display and looked over with a great deal of curiosity by the division staff. General Chuikov's headquarters was in a side street near Tempelhof Airport, in an upper-middle-class neighborhood.

Chuikov's headquarters was on the first floor of a large apartment building that had been built around the turn of the century. Some younger Russian officers led us through a corridor to a large room where General Weidling was awaiting us, and von Dufving reported the orderly surrender at the bridge. Finally, Chuikov's chief of staff came in, and a few minutes later Chuikov entered the room. We saluted, and he returned our salute. Chuikov instructed General Weidling to compose a written order directing those German soldiers in the city who were still resisting to stop fighting. A German typewriter was brought in, and I typed Weidling's order as he dictated it (the Russian writer Ilya Ehrenburg incorrectly reported in an article I read later that a blond female secretary typed the order—I was blond, but male and a major in the general staff). I made several carbon copies, at the directions of the Russians, and Weidling signed them all. The Russians kept one copy and gave the rest to Wolff and me. Weidling, von Dufving, and Refior were then invited to join the Russians in a big breakfast feast at Chuikov's headquarters while Major Wolff and I delivered General Weidling's order to the still-resisting German troops. The feast was apparently a victory celebration. I am sure Weidling, von Dufving, and Refior had no stomach for it, but they were hardly in a position to refuse the invitation.

I went in one of the American-made jeeps, with a Russian captain, to a Russian corps headquarters and then to a division headquarters. At both places, I was gazed at with great curiosity. German-speaking Russian officers at their corps headquarters asked about Hitler and Göring. I told them that Hitler was dead and I did not know where Göring was. I had the impression that they were having a difficult time realizing that they had actually defeated Germany and that Berlin lay at their feet.

One Russian officer at their division headquarters said to me in German, "What have you got to say about Auschwitz?" When I asked him what he meant, he said angrily, "What about Bergen-Belsen? What about Treblinka? What about Buchenwald?" He was turning red in the face with anger. I did not recognize the names, and I could not understand why he was getting so angry. He finally shouted, "Don't pretend you don't understand!" and stormed from the room.

The Russian captain and I then went to a Russian battalion headquarters at the Anhalter Railroad Station, where resistance was still taking place. I was taken to a group of German prisoners and instructed to select two soldiers from among them to deliver Weidling's order. I was told to assure them that the men delivering the order would be given written orders that would allow them to go home. I was later to learn not to believe such promises, but now I had no reason to doubt their sincerity. With such an incentive, there was no shortage of volunteers, and I selected two feldwebels. I gave them a copy of Weidling's order and a white flag to carry. They were to take it to the German commander at the Europa Haus, a huge office building nearby. I watched them disappear down the railroad tracks at Anhalter Station, in the direction of the fighting. Then the Russian captain and I went to a different battalion, where we repeated the procedure, and then to a third. I am certain today that the Russians never honored their promises to any of those men, because I learned quickly that they would promise anything they thought would get you to do what they wanted and then just ignore the promise once you had done it. And it was a dangerous mission, because the resisting Germans were probably SS troops who were determined to fight to the last man and who would shoot anyone who tried to interfere.

The Russian captain then returned me to Chuikov's headquarters. On the way, we passed through an area where there had been very heavy fighting the day before. The streets were filled with burned-out tanks, dead horses, and dead people. German and Russian corpses lay side by side. I especially remember two dead Russian soldiers on a balcony who stared down at us through lifeless eyes, streaks of their blood coloring the wall beneath the balcony. I had a terribly uneasy and queasy feeling, because I was in the jeep with the Russian captain, at the mercy of the Russians, and to some degree I was responsible for what had happened to these dead Russian soldiers; although I had not actually been out in the street fighting with the men, we staff officers were the ones in charge of the fighting and of oiling the fighting machine to keep it working. It was a most unsettling feeling for me, but the Russian appeared to pay no particular attention to it. In general, the Russian officers were behaving correctly. Of course, they saw how Chuikov and his chief of staff treated us, and they conducted themselves accordingly.

When we arrived back at Chuikov's headquarters, Weidling was no longer there, but Refior and von Dufving were. I was taken into the banquet room, where a huge table was loaded down with gourmet food, and was invited to help myself. There was champagne, caviar, tarts, every conceivable kind of meat and cheese, and endless other kinds of food. Major Wolff had already returned and was there also, and we took advantage of the food, because we could not know when we would have another meal. Then we were instructed to retrieve our knapsacks of belongings and were put in a jeep and taken to a column of marching German prisoners. We were told to join the column.

Wolff and I marched in the column of German soldiers the rest of that day. I had one scary moment when a Russian guard pulled me out of the column in a wooded area and motioned for me to give him my boots. Believing I would not be able to survive without them, I gambled and started shouting at him, dressing him down as I would a German soldier who had just misbehaved. It worked! He instinctively snapped to attention, just as if I had been a Russian officer, and I quickly slipped back into the column, before he could regain his composure. It was a terrible gamble—and possibly a stupid one as well—because he could have shot me and taken my boots and no one would have cared. But it had worked, and that was for the moment all that mattered.

That night we arrived at a big improvised prison camp behind a barbed-wire fence. It had been a cement factory and a large gravel pit. It was in a suburb of Berlin, in the general vicinity of Rüdersdorf. More than a thousand of us were lodged in the camp. The camp had several large buildings, and we could have got inside if it had rained. Wolff and I found a corner and just waited to see what would happen next. We had both brought food, so we had something to eat (the Russians provided no food the first few days).

The compound in which we were held was huge. All

we were provided at first was water and toilet facilities. It wasn't exactly sanitary, but the Russians did their best, because they were very much afraid of epidemics. Although we had no bathing facilities or soap, we had unlimited access to running water, and a fire was kept going at a central location so we could heat water.

Wolff and I inspected the entire prison compound. Then there was nothing to do. After the incredible pace of our lives during the past several months, such enforced idleness was almost nerve-racking. I had to keep fighting the urge to jump up and get busy; it was almost impossible to accept that there was nothing to do. I tried to suppress any thoughts about the implications of our having lost the war, about my immediate future, about what I was sure was to come.

Wolff and I got to know each other better on a personal level. He was in his late twenties, just under six feet, with thin brown hair, blue eyes, and a perpetual smile.

Wolff had also brought some coffee and a box of good cigars, so in the afternoons at four o'clock we would get some hot water and have a cup of coffee and smoke a cigar. It seemed so good that we decided we would do the same every afternoon as long as we were together there. We did not know what would happen, how long we would be there, or even how long we would live—so every afternoon at four, we got some hot water and had coffee and a Dutch Rittmeester cigar. That became our daily quiet hour, when we would talk about family, about home, about the future—what was likely to happen, whether we would ever go home again. I really did not smoke, but during those first days in prison, in this special hour, with all the reminiscing and talking about home and the future, this became something special. Otherwise, our life in this camp was very monotonous and boring. We spent our time talking with other prisoners, being counted, and so forth. We slept on the ground, but we could get inside if the weather turned bad. Having been relieved of the responsibility for making decisions constantly, I was suddenly overpowered by a craving for sleep and could not seem to get enough.

One day after we had been there about two weeks, my name was called out on the loudspeaker: "Major Knappe, report to the gate." I thought, "Well, this is it. Now I will be shot." I really felt nothing special at the prospect of dying. So many people had died, and I would be just one more. I shook Wolff's hand and took my leave of him. He had my address in case he got home. I got my bag and went to the gate. The camp commander and a Russian major were waiting for me with a jeep. The camp commander just said, "Go with the major." We got into the jeep and drove to Köpenick. In addition to the major and me, there was a driver and a guard with a submachine gun.

They stopped the jeep in front of a five-story apartment building. I was taken to the third or fourth floor, which proved to be something of a "gentlemen's prison" for German officers. I did not know any of them, but there were perhaps a dozen. Some were generals, some were general staff officers, and some were communications officers. Here we were treated quite well. There were beds and there were kitchens in the different apartments, and we got food to cook. This was much better than the gravel-pit camp with a thousand or so prisoners, with its dust and dirt and crowded conditions and little chance to wash.

We all had difficulty adapting to our enforced idleness after so many months of frenzied activity. We exchanged our stories of those last months, but there was little else to do except prepare our meals and get to know each other. Once each day we were allowed to walk around the backyard for perhaps an hour, with several armed guards watching us. I had taken off my Army trousers and wore my riding breeches with red general staff stripes. The Russian guards at the rear door always saluted me when I went out of and into the building, apparently mistaking me for a general because of the red stripes on my breeches. They must have been surprised by how young some of the German generals were!

One of the people here was an old general of perhaps seventy, who had retired many years before. He lived in Berlin, and someone in his neighborhood had told the Russians that he was a general, so they had made him put on his uniform and brought him here. It was fortunate for him, at his age, that they brought him here to this more comfortable place. But they seemed to treat generals differently anyway.

From our windows in this apartment building, we could see the street in front. The back of the building overlooked the Spree River, but between the river and the apartment building were gardens. The distance between the building and the river was a few hundred meters. The river at that location was perhaps two hundred meters wide. I decided to try to escape and swim across the river. I had no idea what would await me on the other side, but there was at least the possibility that there were no Russians. From there, I thought I might be able to hide during the day and move short distances at night (it was about two hundred kilometers from there to Leipzig). There were gardens on the other side of the river, and each garden had a little toolshed, and I thought I would be able to hide in one of the sheds the first day. I hoped I would be able to get civilian clothes from the people who lived there. Our apartment building happened to be the last in a row of apartment buildings, and the next building would have been built against the wall of this one. We had freedom of movement in the building, so I started exploring to see what I could learn that might help me escape. In the attic, I found a heavy clothesline that was long enough to reach the ground, and I discovered that from the attic I could remove some tiles from the roof—so I could anchor the rope in the attic and put the line down the blank wall at the end of the building.

I started watching the guards to see if I could establish

a pattern. They kept one guard in front of the building and one in back. I noticed that at times the two guards arrived at the end of the house at the same time, leaving the other end unguarded. I noticed also that they changed guards in front and back at the same time and that when they did the guards usually stayed there and talked for a few minutes. The guards patrolled the front and back of the house, but not the end. I watched them carefully and timed them. I decided that if I timed it right, I would be able to get down the rope, hide in the tall weeds at the end of the building until the guards were both at the far end, or until they changed again, and then get to the river, swim across, and hide there in a garden toolshed. It would have to be at night, and it would have to be a moonless night. Unfortunately, the moon was bright during this period. I could only wait for a dark night. Everything else was ready.

Finally the time arrived when I felt the next night would be dark enough. That morning, as we were having breakfast, the Russian officer in charge of the building came in with a happy smile on his face. When he saw me, his face brightened even more. "Major Knappe, you are a lucky man," he said. "You are going to Moscow!"

For a Russian, to go to Moscow was a wonderful thing; for me, however, it was not so wonderful. Instead of swimming across the Spree River to possible freedom that night, I would be landing in Moscow. He told me to be ready to leave at ten o'clock. I hurriedly wrote a letter to Lilo and gave it to the old general, who was going home and offered to take a letter for me.

At Tempelhof Airport, I was put aboard an American DC-3 cargo plane that was full of German loot the Russians were taking to Moscow. The passengers—a dozen or so Russian officers and soldiers in addition to me—sat on rolls of expensive carpet (I had to wonder if it could be the same carpet General Weidling and I had climbed over in the basement of Führer Headquarters). The Russian soldiers stared at me when they boarded the airplane, but ignored me thereafter.

The airplane lifted off the ground in the bright June sunshine and turned eastward, toward the vast Soviet Union. My heart was heavy with the realization that my last chance for an easy escape had passed, and it seemed that the higher the airplane climbed the more my hope for freedom diminished. My next stop was Moscow—and an unknown fate.

We flew over the same ground I had covered when we invaded Russia in June 1941—four years earlier to the month—as a young artillery battery commander, an ober-leutnant. In 1941, we had taken six months to cover the same area on horseback and on foot, an area we would now cover by airplane in a few hours. We had been fighting as we crossed the same territory then, of course, but the fighting had not become severe until we passed Smolensk on the way to Moscow.

I could not help wondering whether I would ever make the return trip, even though I felt certain I would be shot when the Russians had everything they wanted from me.

Yet it had all begun with such promise. My mind drifted back to 1936, the year I graduated from Petri Gymnasium, to a ski trip in the Sudeten Mountains that four friends and I had taken to celebrate our graduation. . . .

PART TWO

Sunny Times

1936–1939

8

THE ROAD WAS getting steeper and more curving, with the view around each bend becoming more spectacular than the last. The five of us in the car—Werner Friedrich, Hans Liebelt, Siegfried Ebert, Ernst Michaelis, and I —had graduated from gymnasium together just a week before, on March 6, 1936. We had all entered gymnasium together nine years ago, at the age of ten, and two years ago we began planning this ski trip to celebrate our graduation.

Friedrich was exuberant, as usual, challenging everyone to a race once we reached the ski area and assuring us all that we did not stand a chance. We were all anticipating the trip with great excitement. Finally, we rounded the last steep, sharp curve, and there, slightly below us, nestled securely in the lap of the Sudeten Mountains of Silesia, was our ski village. We found a place to leave our car—a sedan that belonged to Liebelt's father—and followed signs to the cabin check-in office in a running snowball fight. Our faces must have looked quite flushed, from both the cold air and the running, to the old man we startled when we charged through the door.

"Hello there," he said. "What can I do for you?" He peered at us over oval wire-framed glasses.

"We have a reservation for one of your cabins," Ebert said. "The name is Siegfried Ebert."

"Let's see. . . ." He flipped through what looked like scrap papers. "Here it is!" he said. "I am Hoffer." He extended his hand, and in turn we each shook it. His grip was firm in spite of his advanced age and his frail build. We each put our share of the money on the counter. He slowly counted the money and carefully placed it in an old wooden lock box, then sorted through a pile of keys until he found the one he wanted. "Here you are," he said. He smiled, his old eyes twinkling behind his glasses as he dangled the key before Ebert. "Have a good time, boys."

Ebert took the key, and we herded each other out of the office, eager to begin our adventure. We began to unload our gear from the car, which amounted to throwing everything into a pile.

"Here, carry this," came an order, followed by something thudding into my back.

I knew it was Friedrich without turning around. As usual, he was taking charge and dividing up the gear to be carried to the cabin. When we were all finally loaded to Friedrich's satisfaction, we trudged up the mountain, toward our cabin. Although the temperature was only 28 degrees Fahrenheit, the steep climb up the mountain made us sweat.

The cabin was one big rectangular room with two windows, one facing east, or front, and the other facing the slopes to the west. On the north wall was a huge fireplace, complete with a spit for roasting meat, a bar for hanging kettles, and a small iron grid for skillets, pots, pans, and other utensils hanging from the mantel. On the south wall were two sets of bunks. We had been instructed to bring sleeping bags and pillows.

"Let's *ski*!" yelled Friedrich.

In a rush, we got our skis out of the pile of gear. We had to go only a few paces until we were at a slope. Down we would go, then back up we would struggle, only to be unable to resist going down one more time. We one-more-timed until we could barely crawl. Finally, we'd had enough and made our way back to the cabin. We decided to eat in the village, because we were too tired to cook.

The aroma inside the café immediately provoked hunger rumblings in our very empty bellies. There were no customers, and there appeared to be no employees either. We were all fidgety from hunger. Friedrich and I leaned our chairs back on two legs.

"Take it easy on the furniture!" a familiar voice boomed as Herr Hoffer popped into the room as if from nowhere. Our chairs dropped to all fours promptly. "Hello, boys. Can't stand your own cooking, huh? No matter, Frau Hoffer will feed you." A second later she came bustling into the room and told us what we would be eating.

Knowing that our supper was on the way, we settled down. I looked through the window. From our table we could barely see the foot of the mountain, which was muted by the soft glow of the few streetlights. A gentle lazy snowfall had begun, with large aimless flakes wafting slowly to earth. In the warm café, with the aroma of food being prepared, we enjoyed a satisfied sense of being free and yet cared for. Outside, a farmboy about our age led a draft horse that was pulling a sled loaded high with hay slowly along the road. Old Herr Hoffer and another man about his age had begun a game of chess at a table near us, carrying on a constant conversation about politics as they played.

Frau Hoffer emerged from the kitchen pushing a cart laden with food. She deftly placed the bowls of food in front of us and handed us each an empty plate and the necessary silverware. Without further conversation, we ate every morsel she had placed in front of us. We all seemed to lean back and heave a satisfied sigh at nearly the same time. Frau Hoffer must have been watching us from the kitchen, because here she came again, with the empty cart. She quickly cleared the table and left us to ourselves for our own after-dinner discussion. Suddenly we were aware of Herr Hoffer's voice becoming louder.

"Hitler is going to get us into another war!" he said emphatically.

"Why do you say that?" his chess partner demanded.

"Because Hitler is a gambler, and gamblers will not quit until they lose."

"I do not know how you can say that," his chess partner responded. "He has provided people with jobs, he has restored the economy, he has stopped all the political brawling in the streets, he has built the autobahns, he has torn up the Versailles Treaty and restored national pride, he has even reclaimed the Rhineland." The old man finally ran out of breath.

"And how has he done all those things?" Herr Hoffer demanded. "He has provided jobs by building up the armaments industry. What do you think he is planning to do with all that firepower? Admire it? And he restored peace to the streets by putting all his political opponents—and a lot of Jews as well—into concentration camps."

We all glanced furtively at Michaelis, who was Jewish.

"So why do you say that Hitler is a gambler?" the other old man asked.

"What do you think would have happened if the French had resisted when our troops marched into the Rhineland?" Herr Hoffer asked. "Our pitiful force would have been wiped out. But Hitler was playing poker, and he gambled that his opponent would not call his bluff. He won that hand, and he may win more—but eventually he is going to overstep himself, because gamblers never quit when they are winning. They always keep betting until they lose."

"But he is just getting back what the Versailles Treaty took away from us," his friend protested.

Herr Hoffer rose and walked to the fireplace, where he knocked the ashes out of his pipe. "He won't stop there," he said. "He will continue until he gets us into another war. And at what cost?" He turned and waved his hand in our direction. "At the cost of these boys' lives, most likely, as well as the lives of millions of others."

"What an old grouch!" Friedrich whispered to the rest of us.

"I am not so sure he is not right," Michaelis offered in a quiet voice.

No one responded. Michaelis's being Jewish made us all uneasy in the context of the old men's conversation.

We returned to our cabin, where we got a new fire going quickly, because it was cold.

Up at daybreak the next morning, we made tea, had breakfast, and were hiking up the mountain with our skis on our shoulders in less than an hour. As we crested the mountain, the view into Czechoslovakia was as breathtaking as the view on the German side. We skied all day, speeding down the glittering pristine slope and then trudging back up with our skis on our shoulders. Then we skied the cross-country route we had laid out the evening before.

In late afternoon, we finally decided to call it a day and skied down the German side of the mountain to our cabin. After getting a fire going, we poured some beans into a kettle, covered them with water, and hung them over the fire. Then we peeled potatoes and did the same with them. Soon both were boiling busily and we waited patiently for them to cook. Half an hour later the potatoes were soft to the touch of a fork and obviously ready, but the beans appeared to be as hard as ever. We set the potatoes to the side of the fire to keep them warm as the beans continued to cook. An hour later the beans were still boiling briskly, but no more done than ever.

"What kind of beans did you buy, Knappe?" Friedrich demanded.

"Just beans. Why? Are there different kinds?" I asked sheepishly.

"I don't know, but are you sure these were meant to be cooked? They have been on that fire an hour and a half!"

"Let's eat the potatoes," Ebert suggested. "We will eat the beans whenever they are ready."

We divided the potatoes into five equal portions and devoured them with bread and butter and a fresh pot of tea. We felt better after eating, although the potatoes alone did not completely satisfy our appetites. Together, we slowly cleaned up the mess, checked the fire, and put fresh water over the still-boiling beans.

"Want some American popcorn?" Liebelt asked, rising to go get it from his gear.

"What is that?" I asked.

"I will show you," Liebelt said, returning with a bag of tiny kernels of corn and a skillet. "My uncle in America sent this to us from Chicago. You heat the kernels in a skillet and they pop open. They're good. Move those stupid beans off the fire; they're never going to be edible anyway." He put some butter into the skillet, melted it, and then filled the skillet half full of yellow kernels.

Liebelt rearranged the logs and laid the iron grill squarely on top of them, then carefully set the heavy skillet down on the grill. The popcorn was soon popping, slowly in the beginning and then with increasing rapidity.

"Grab a lid," Liebelt shouted as popcorn shot out of the skillet and into the flames. I grabbed one, but it was too late. Things were out of control—the corn was popping so fast that it had risen well above the level of the skillet and was spilling into the fire. Liebelt had evidently put too much popcorn into the skillet. As the popped kernels fell into the fire, they began to smoke and fill the cabin with a burnt odor.

"Open the door," someone said. Liebelt pulled the skillet off the grill, but the heated cast iron retained its heat and the corn continued popping and spilling onto the floor. Nonetheless, some was edible, so we set the skillet in front of us and began to dig handfuls from it.

"You're right. It really is good," Friedrich agreed.

A knock sounded at the door. It was Herr Hoffer.

"Frau Hoffer thought you might like these cookies," he said. When he saw the kettle of beans, a smile crossed his old face. "I see you tried to cook beans without soaking them," he said.

We stared at him. "Soaking them?" I asked lamely.

"You must soak beans overnight before cooking them," he said. "It is a common mistake."

We looked at one another and groaned inwardly.

The next morning we were up and on the German side of the mountain slope early. The day was one long competition. We staged downhill speed races, jumping competitions, competition to see who could get back up the hill fastest—and by the time the sun disappeared, we were exhausted but exhilarated. We fixed ourselves a supper of cold cuts and tea and relaxed in front of the comfortable fire in the fireplace.

"Do you realize that tomorrow is our last day already?" Ebert said a bit sadly.

We all stared silently into the fire a moment. One more day, and then we would have to take up our new adult lives. I would be leaving for Labor Service, Friedrich would be entering the Army (by agreeing to become an officer candidate after his first year in the Army, he had avoided Labor Service), Michaelis would be entering university (he did not have to serve in the Labor Service or Army because he was Jewish), and Ebert and Liebelt would be entering a university to study medicine, which also exempted them from Labor Service. Suddenly what the transition from child to adult meant was becoming real —we would be splitting up.

There were no competitions the last day. We each went our own leisurely way. I skied long, slow, curving swoops, trying to savor these last moments. At one point I stopped skiing to listen to some thrushes singing in the nearby pines, as they busily went about building their nests. Germany was truly a beautiful place. With all this splendor, how could Herr Hoffer possibly be right? How could anything go wrong? I took a deep breath and propelled myself on down the slope.

9

ON THE MORNING of Sunday, April 4, 1936, I woke early and with great anticipation. I was to be at Augustus Square at nine o'clock to be transported by bus to somewhere in Bavaria, where I would serve the next six months in Reich Labor Service.

I breakfasted with my family. My fourteen-year-old brother, Fritz, was excited about my impending adventure and seemed to look forward to it for me. My older sister, Ingeborg—tall, thin, blond, and sober—was convinced that I was making a big mistake by not going directly to the university instead of getting Labor Service and the Army out of the way first and she said so. My mother hovered maternally around me, alternately bubbly and teary-eyed. As we ate breakfast, she scolded Inge for her remark that I was making a mistake. Inge pouted a bit and said nothing. We all seemed awkward when I arose from the table.

"Well," my father said, not looking directly at me, "I guess it's time."

"Yes," I replied, noticing his discomfort and loss for words. My throat went dry, and I swallowed in the hope of finding the appropriate action. Finding none, I merely extended my hand; he slowly raised his and gripped mine firmly, then held my hand in both of his. In the background, my mother sniffled. Then she wrapped her arms around me. Few words were spoken. Few needed to be. I looked around for Inge, but she was no longer in the room. Fritz punched me on the shoulder. I picked up my suitcase and headed out the door. Once out in the street, I walked quickly away, my family calling goodbye.

At Augustus Square, I looked around at the milling crowd of young men my own age, hoping to see a familiar face, but I saw none. I did notice a figure in a Labor Service uniform standing near three parked buses. Shortly before nine o'clock, he bellowed in a voice of unbelievable volume: "All right! We are going to fill these three buses front to back. I want every seat in the first bus full before a man sets foot in the second. When I call out your name, get in the bus—on the double."

As we left Leipzig, the bus moved through the streets that I had known all my life. I felt as if we were rolling out of my childhood and into a new adult world. I had been away from home on vacations before, but never for as long as six months. I was looking forward to this new adult experience.

By the time we arrived at our destination at seven o'clock, it was almost dark. We were at the village of Burglengenfeld, near the Czechoslovakian border. The Labor Service camp consisted of several buildings. The main building was a large former villa that had been remodeled to house as many as 160 people. The buses pulled up in front of this main building and disembarked their passengers.

The Labor Service man ordered us all to gather around a porch in front of the building. The buses pulled away then, making me feel very much alone in the midst of 160 boys. As we grew quiet, the Labor Service man announced, in that awe-inspiring voice he had used in the square, "Gentlemen, the commanding officer of Burglengenfeld Labor Service Camp, Abteilungsführer Werner." He drew himself stiffly to attention as a middle-aged man in a fancier Labor Service uniform emerged through the door behind him.

The commanding officer appeared very straight and military as he looked out over us in his neatly tailored uniform, seeming somehow to look each of us in the eye. "Welcome to Burglengenfeld, men," he said, in a voice nearly as impressive as his subordinate's. "Now you are proud Labor Service men." He continued his brief prepared speech, informing us that our first four weeks would be training in military drill and only then would we be permitted to go to work for the Fatherland. He finished by saying, "I leave you now in the capable hands of your leader, Gruppenführer Brandt." Then he turned and disappeared into the building from which he had emerged.

After being assigned room numbers, we piled into the building. I was assigned to Room 7, which had four bunks, four lockers, and one big table with four chairs. The other three occupants of Room 7 were a fat boy named Dietl, a gangly farmboy named Fischer, and a little red-haired guy named Zimmermann.

The next morning, we were rudely awakened at five-thirty by THE VOICE, bellowing with an unbelievable volume: "On your feet!" He was standing in front of his room, which was next door to ours, projecting a volume intended to wake the whole building. We were jolted out of a deep sleep and looked at one another in wonderment. Brandt appeared in our doorway. Although short and stocky, he appeared much larger in the doorway.

"One person from each room go to the mess hall and get breakfast for your room," he ordered.

At promptly six-thirty, THE VOICE ordered us out into the square in front of the building. We were divided into four squads and introduced to our squad leaders. Mine was Squad Leader Krupp, who was about twenty-one years old, tall, broad-chested, with sandy blond hair and a pleasant expression.

Each of the four squad leaders selected a different spot on the soccer field, far enough apart that each could issue orders to his squad without causing confusion among the other squads. Krupp, who seemed at ease and calm about his duties and us, was a pleasant contrast to the constantly bellowing Brandt. He patiently taught us first how to stand at "attention," then how to space ourselves apart with an "eyes right" maneuver. That was followed by how to step off on our left heels at the command of "forward march," then how to react to a "squad halt" command. We finished by learning how to do "left face," "right face," and "about face."

Finally, we were marched to the supply building and issued uniforms. We were issued different uniforms for work, for parade, for exercising, and for sports. Then we were marched by squads to the mess hall for lunch. A half hour of free time followed, during which we admired ourselves and one another in our new uniforms. The little guy, Zimmermann, kept jerking himself to attention and saluting everybody, making a joke of it. His sense of humor helped relax everyone.

In the afternoon, we attended an hour-long class, mostly on the "New Greater German Reich." Herr Hoffer's warning crept into my thoughts during the lecture, but I forced it aside. We were learning discipline, order, and how to follow commands. These were all positive qualities, and I felt good about it.

Following the training session, we were marched back to the supply building, where we were each issued a shiny new spade. Krupp marched us back to the soccer field. I felt as if I were playing soldier, now that I had something on my shoulder as we marched. Krupp called us to attention to begin our spade instructions.

"Men," he began, "this is the Labor Service, and this spade is the symbol of work and toil. The spade you now hold will never touch dirt; it will be used strictly for exercise and parades. At all times, your spade must sparkle as if it were made of chrome. Since they are steel and not chrome, they will rust easily. Spot inspections are to be expected." Krupp then offered instructions on how to keep the spades clean by rubbing them with wet sand that was kept in a big bin in the courtyard, and he advised us to work on the spade every day rather than waiting until rust built up on it.

After another hour of drill in which we were taught to march properly with the spades on our shoulders, we were finally released to return to our rooms. We had an hour to get cleaned up for supper and get to know each other.

In the mess hall at supper, we were instructed to meet at seven-thirty in the Assembly Hall. That meeting was to give us the next day's schedule and any announcements that needed to be made. Following the announcements, one of the squad leaders led us in some organized singing. Then we had an hour to relax before the lights were turned out at ten o'clock.

We spent the following four weeks learning military drill and routine. An important function of Labor Service was to free the Army from having to do this very basic type of training. Everyone who went into Labor Service would also be drafted into the Army, and we would enter the Army already partially trained.

We were not permitted out of the camp the first four weeks. We had a library, however, and a recreation hall with Ping-Pong tables, card tables, and chess sets. Our four weeks of training passed quickly with drill, calisthenics, and classes; we were acquiring a general familiarity with military life. At the end of the four-week training period, we were inspected by the camp commander and then released to begin our work detail.

On our first work day following our training period, we marched forty minutes to a strip coal mine with "parade spades" on our shoulders. We fell out and stacked our parade spades, like rifles, in four-spade pyramids. I worried about my spade, because I kept it perfectly clean. I hated putting it in the stack with the others from my squad for fear someone would grab mine and leave his rusted one for me to clean. We were then issued working spades.

The work we did consisted of removing layers of dirt from veins of coal and loading the dirt onto lorries (small tip-bed freight cars) that were pulled by a narrow-gauge steam engine. Brandt did not accompany us on work detail, although we were warned that it was not unusual for him to pop in to check things out. We were given forty-five minutes for lunch. Late in the afternoon, we would march back to camp, arriving by five o'clock. We would wash and have dinner, followed by assembly, which would feature either singing or a history lesson. At times, we also had to do kitchen duty or guard duty, just as in the Army.

One of our first days at work proved to be especially tiring, because the weather was very hot and humid. The work spade had worn blisters on my hands, and sweat poured from my body, making it extremely desirable to gnats, flies, and mosquitoes. To make matters worse, Brandt rode up on a bicycle while we were eating lunch. He parked the bicycle and headed directly for the pyramid of parade spades.

"You call these clean?" he bellowed, kicking the pyramids over, all the spades spattering in mud.

I gulped, knowing that mine had been clean, and I had strategically placed it so I would know which one was mine. Now they all lay like identical matchsticks covered with mud.

"Tonight, we will polish spades from ten o'clock until midnight. And we will do it every night until all these spades are clean," he said.

A groan arose, because we were already exhausted and knew we had another half day of work in this heat and humidity.

At ten o'clock, as promised, we were called together to clean spades. My muscles ached, my blistered hands hurt, and I had someone else's grimy spade. As I scrubbed and scraped with wet sand, Inge's face appeared before me, laughing in an "I told you so" manner. I blinked her away, only to have Friedrich's face appear with the same look. The only good thing about the endless two hours was that I never saw Brandt's face!

In June, we received a five-day furlough to go home. We traveled again by chartered bus from Burglengenfeld to Leipzig. We were unsupervised this time, except for the bus drivers, and we knew each other for the trip home. Our conduct was a good deal more boisterous during the all-day ride, but by the time we reached Leipzig we had tamed down considerably. As we entered the outskirts of Leipzig, we began to see the familiar Leipzig trolleys, with their distinctive green-and-beige color designs that were unique to the city of Leipzig. I had not consciously felt homesick during my three months in Labor Service, but the sight of the first Leipzig trolley brought an unexpected lump to my throat, and I realized for the first time how much I had really missed my home.

The buses took us to Augustus Square, and I caught a trolley to my parents' apartment, arriving in early evening. I cannot describe the feeling of warmth and security that came rushing back when I was in the midst of my family again. My mother's face beamed from ear to ear, and she fed me until I thought I would burst. Fritz asked questions so incessantly that I hardly had a chance to answer them, and my uniform so impressed him that he could hardly wait to enter Labor Service himself. Almost in spite of herself, even Inge was curious about my experience. Her presence reminded me of the muddy-spade episode, which I did not mention. My father just smiled happily and was content to let everyone else have center stage.

After three days at home, we departed by chartered bus again from Augustus Square. The trip back to Burglengenfeld was not as lively or enthusiastic as the trip home had been. I did not know how a few days could make such a difference, but I felt that I was somehow older and more mature when we arrived back at camp that night.

We quickly returned to our old routine of calisthenics and jogging after breakfast, marching forty minutes to the strip mine, singing as we went, working all day, marching home, cleaning up, having supper, going to assembly, and going to bed.

On weekends, we were free from 4:00 P.M. on Saturday until 10:00 P.M. on Sunday. Three or four of us would go by train to a nearby city that seemed interesting to us. We would visit the cathedrals and museums and other noteworthy buildings. We would have lunch in a restaurant and go to a movie or maybe to a dance and meet girls. Our parents supplemented our pay, so we could afford to do these things. For our labor, we were paid a half mark a day, which was just enough for snacks and incidentals. We were paid each week.

The final leg of Labor Service occurred with the selection of those of us who would parade at a huge political rally the government was planning to stage at Nuremberg on September 8, 1936. The Army, the SA, the SS, the Labor Service, and the Hitler Youth were all to parade in a grand spectacle. Tens of thousands would be participating in the parade. The purpose of the political rally, called the Reichsparteitag, was to unify the German people and to impress the rest of Europe with our military strength and martial spirit.

Only those of us who demonstrated the greatest skill on the parade ground were selected. To my delight, I was among the 10 percent of my *Abteilung* to go, as was Fischer. Those selected to go to Nuremberg began to work less and do extra drill in preparation for the rally. We practiced drilling by ourselves for two weeks, and then we went to Amberg for two weeks of drilling in a company-size unit composed of elements from several different Labor Service *Abteilungen.*

We went to Nuremberg, which was not far away, by bus. We arrived the day before our parade and disembarked from the buses in the city. We marched the two miles from Nuremberg to a virtual tent city that had been erected for all of us who were taking part in the parades, through the traffic-cleared and flag-lined streets of the inner city. The sidewalks were packed with cheering people, and bands were placed at strategic locations—all playing martial music for us to march to.

More than fifteen hundred tents, each accommodating six people, were arranged in neat rows, with grass streets running between the rows of tents. Many tens of thousands of people were participating in the parades, which were to continue for five days. We had already been assigned tent numbers and even bunks in the tents. We arrived in late afternoon, and by the time we got settled in our tents, evening was beginning to descend. We were marched to a huge tent mess hall and fed. Then we were marched back to our tents and dismissed.

Fischer and I decided to walk around the tent city and see what was going on. It was almost a carnival atmosphere. Everyone was excited about being in Nuremberg on such an auspicious occasion. Everyone knew that Hitler, Göring, Goebbels, and all the other high party people would be in the reviewing stand watching us march. The excitement of possibly seeing them swelled in my chest.

Lanterns appeared in the tents as darkness began to smother daylight. Card games sprang up in some of the tents. Here and there, groups of young men would break lustily into marching songs. The smell of kerosene drifted through the air from kerosene fires that glowed atop ten-foot columns spaced approximately fifty feet apart in every direction throughout the camp. Everywhere, young men milled about in the grass-and-dirt streets, talking, laughing, practicing drill steps. Everyone was giddy with excitement and anticipation. I had never seen so many people in one place. We went to sleep that night eagerly anticipating the great honor that tomorrow would bring.

At ten o'clock the next morning, we performed a carefully timed march into the stadium. We stood at parade rest and watched a precision presentation by sports units consisting of teenage boys and girls who performed intricate maneuvers and then marched past the reviewing stand. Shortly before noon, the tension began to rise in us as our turn neared. We still stood at parade rest, facing the reviewing stand, with its enormous granite swastika below the German eagle.

"Achtung!" boomed over the loudspeakers, and we snapped to quivering attention. At one command, ten thousand spades went up, with the sun reflecting on them dramatically. The spades would turn with every move, the sun flashing on them. On command, we formed a series of large rectangles and then went through a series of maneuvers with the spades (turning them, putting them up, putting them down, presenting spades, etc.). We had to be careful not to bash the man in front of us with the spade; it was heavy, and a spade is more difficult to handle than a rifle. It must have been a tremendous spectacle, and from the reports we received, the Labor Service parade was the most impressive of the parades that year.

Then we were ordered to parade rest, and after some martial music someone made a speech. From my vantage point as one of ten thousand Labor Service men, I could barely see the reviewing stand, but we all knew that Chancellor Hitler, Generalfeldmarschall Göring, and all the important government figures were there watching us. That knowledge induced a peculiar tingle of excitement in us. We felt ten feet tall and indestructible! This was pageantry of the highest order, and it inspired enormous national pride in us. It was a jubilant extravaganza with the unmistakable message that Germany was being reborn. I felt extremely proud.

Back at the camp, we could hardly sit still. We wanted the feverish emotions aroused by the thrilling experience on the parade ground to continue. We were not allowed to leave the camp, however, because our leaders did not want to turn ten thousand keyed-up young men loose on Nuremberg. We were marched back to our buses and put aboard them for the return trip.

After the Nuremberg rally we returned to Burglengenfeld to finish our nearly completed tour of duty with Labor Service. The rest of it was anticlimactic after the glamour and excitement of Nuremberg.

Finally, on September 24, 1936, we had a discharge ceremony, and Abteilungsführer Werner thanked us for our service. We gave back our uniforms, put on our old civilian clothes, received our final pay, and were released to go home. Although we had been brought to Burglengenfeld by chartered bus, we were trusted to return on the train by ourselves.

10

THREE WEEKS LATER, on October 15, 1936, I boarded the train that would take me from Leipzig to Jena, some forty miles away, to begin my new life as a soldier in the artillery. My father had been a naval gunnery officer before and during the World War, and all during my childhood he had told me many thrilling stories about the big guns. Whenever I had thought of myself as a soldier, I had always thought in terms of those glamourous big guns. For two years our newspapers had been full of stories about the technological advances that had been achieved in mechanizing our modern Army, including the artillery, and I had volunteered for the artillery with visions of driving self-propelled mechanized artillery.

As the train neared Jena, I saw a large complex of barracks. Turning to the middle-aged man sitting next to me, I asked if he knew what they were. He looked up from his newspaper to tell me they were infantry barracks. A little closer to town was another barracks complex; my seat companion, who was a bit portly and starting to gray at the temples, told me this was the artillery. Then to my dismay I saw horse stables and horses, and my heart began to sink. I turned to my seat companion in consternation.

"You mean they still pull the artillery with horses?" I asked, hoping desperately that it was not true.

"Yes, I am afraid so," he said softly, sensing my disappointment.

Suddenly the artillery lost all its glamour and appeal.

Instead of driving massive mechanized artillery, I would be driving horses. I wanted to turn around and go back home.

At the Army barracks, an unteroffizier sat at a desk. He asked my name, found it on his list, put a check mark beside it, and said curtly, "Room 29." He was clearly bored with the routine. When I looked at him quizzically, he responded, "Second floor." The door to Room 29 was open, and a soldier in uniform sat at a table inside. When I walked up to the doorway, he stood and extended his hand.

"I am Oberkanonier Baresel," he said. "I'm going to be your Room Elder."

I shook his hand and introduced myself. He had me select a bunk, and I unpacked my satchel and stored my belongings in a locker next to the bunk. The room had six bunks and lockers and a large table with six chairs. My other roommates began to trickle in. The first was Ernst Rausche, who had been an assembly line worker in a factory. The next was named Peter Wohlthat, a farmboy. Next came Boris Weinreich, a tall, strikingly handsome specimen who was from East Prussia, the son of a schoolmaster. Our final roommate was a city urchin named Vogel.

I went to bed that night still disappointed that the artillery was horse-drawn, but I finally drifted into a sound sleep.

A whistle woke us rudely at five o'clock the next morning. "Out of bed!" Baresel shouted.

"God, it's still the middle of the night," Vogel moaned.

"Well, a little stable duty before breakfast will bring morning around." Baresel grinned. "You have exactly one minute to be assembled in front of the building if you do not want extra duty."

We all jerked our heads toward him, startled, and began frantically to pull on our clothing.

Shivering in the early-morning cold and darkness, we assembled in front of the building. Baresel led us to an area and arranged us in a formation with other men from other rooms. Baresel and the other uniformed Room Elders remained outside the formation. An obergefreiter appeared, called us to attention, and marched us to the horse stables. I still could not believe I was actually in the horse-drawn artillery. It all seemed so backward in this modern age!

"One man per stall," the obergefreiter instructed. We tentatively moved toward the stable. "Move it!" he shouted.

We ran to our posts, selecting our stalls at random. When we had taken up our positions, he called us to attention. "I am Obergefreiter Sebastian, and this is stable number one," he bellowed. He was a paunchy, older man in his thirties, with a mustache. "Note the number of the stall behind you when you are dismissed. This will be your permanent stall to keep clean. A shovel is clipped to the post behind you. You will not be trusted with pitchforks for a few weeks, until we can be sure you can handle them without stabbing the horses. The horse in your stall has been haltered and tied. Take careful note of how the halter fits and how the horse is tied to the ring in the corner of the stall. I will demonstrate it for you once."

He disappeared into a stall and reemerged with a horse in tow. He showed us how to remove and replace the halter and how to tie a quick-release knot on the lead rope. With his demonstration horse now tied, he showed us how to push the horse's body from side to side so we could clean the area under it. I only hoped that all the horses were as easygoing as the demonstration horse.

The stable had twenty-three stalls down one side of a large center aisle and twenty-three down the other. The horses were tied with their heads to the wall and their rumps to the center aisle. The "stalls" consisted of beams that hung from the ceiling to separate each horse from the one next to it. Only officers' horses had real stalls. Two wheelbarrows were now pushed into the center aisle by uniformed soldiers.

"When you clean your stalls, bring the manure to the wheelbarrows in the center aisle, then return the shovel to its attached position on the post," the obergefreiter instructed. "Anyone whose stall does not pass inspection will be assigned extra duty. Now fall out and clean your stall."

I turned and looked at the rump of my new ward. "Great," I thought. "Now I am going to be *hausfrau* to a plowhorse." I had never been this close to a live horse before. It obviously outweighed me by at least a thousand pounds. It seemed impossible that I could move this huge brute by simply pushing it. I hoped it was a tame one as I removed the small, short-handled shovel and entered the stall. I inched nervously toward my target, wondering what one says to reassure a horse. Stretching the short shovel as far as I could reach, I scooped up the offensive pile of manure and retreated hastily to the safety of the center aisle, depositing the contents of my shovel into the wheelbarrow. To my delight, the horse had simply ignored my presence. Recalling the obergefreiter's warning about extra duty, I returned to make sure I had left no traces. The horse turned his head to look at me, took a deep breath, and returned to munching hay. I returned my shovel and clipped it securely in place. We were called to attention again and the obergefreiter marched us back to the barracks building, where we were informed that we had one hour to clean up and have breakfast.

After breakfast, Baresel instructed us to form a line with the other recruits in the center hallway of the barracks, and we were led to another part of the building, where our hair was cut very short. Then we were issued two sets of uniforms—one for drill and stable work and another for everything else. We were also issued riding boots and riding breeches with leather seats, since we were in the horse-drawn artillery. We were especially proud when we were issued steel helmets and cartridge pouches. That made us feel more like *real* soldiers. They tried to give us the right sizes, but sometimes they could not fit us and we had to take what they had and exchange it later.

Although the first day was busy, it included nothing of real substance—mostly just getting us checked in. Things did not start in earnest until the next day.

Following stable duty and breakfast the next day, we were called into formation and introduced to Unteroffizier Max Krall. He was a very small man of about twenty-three, with dingy blond hair, a ruddy, scarred face, and pale blue eyes. He stepped up onto a portable platform, took a deep breath, puffed himself up to all the height he could achieve from his five-foot-four-inch frame, and stared down his now-raised nose at us for a long moment of silence.

"I am Unteroffizier Krall," he said finally through clenched teeth. The skin on the back of my neck began to crawl. "It is my responsibility to make soldiers out of the sad specimens I see before me," he gritted. "Obviously, they expect miracles of me. But I am going to do it if I have to work you day and night for the next three hundred and sixty-five days. From the looks of you, that is what it is going to take." He paused. Then, appearing to draw himself up even straighter, he asked, "How many of you are *Abiturenten*?" mispronouncing *Abiturient*, the German word for gymnasium graduate.

I raised my hand; I could see Weinreich's hand go up, and I thought I could see two others. "Take a good look at me," he growled threateningly. "I plan to take especially good care of *Abiturenten*."

Krall broke us into squads and turned us over to obergefreiters, whose styles and attitudes were not much different from his. They went to work on us, assuring us that, Labor Service notwithstanding, we not only did not know how to march, we did not even know how to *walk*. Then they went about teaching us, in their own way. It was beneath them to recognize our Labor Service training, so they taught us to march and drill all over again. We were issued rifles and taught how to clean and care for them, as well as how to disassemble and reassemble them. Our instructors disparagingly assured us that we were not carrying spades on our shoulders now. Although we would never have admitted it to our instructors, we were proud to have rifles on our shoulders now instead of spades. In the afternoon, we attended classes on Army ranks and on German history before returning to the parade ground for yet more practice and drill.

Our training began in earnest the next day with six weeks of infantry training. This included handling our rifles, shooting them on the firing range, moving on the ground under fire, and digging in. Of course, that was in addition to marching, drilling, and learning to parade. We kept cadence while marching by singing. We also had training with hand grenades and machine guns. This portion of our training was conducted primarily by Stabsgefreiter Weizsacker, who made a special point of riding the gymnasium graduates. All we could do was hunker down and endure his abuse. We received only six weeks of infantry training, compared with twelve months for the infantry soldiers. It was important, however, because the part of the artillery that accompanied the forward observation officer, called the battery troop, was always up front with the infantry.

During this infantry-training period, we would get up at five o'clock, perform stable duty, have breakfast, fall out, and begin a very full day that ended only when we fell into bed, exhausted, at ten o'clock. The training was interesting, well planned, and well organized. Lunch was our main meal of the day. The food was good, and it was well prepared. After lunch, we would get fifteen minutes or so of rest, then we would typically change uniforms (the clothing was prescribed for different activities) and get a lecture on espionage or German national history.

We stood guard in the stables at night. We had to keep a wheelbarrow handy, and whenever a horse at our end of the stable let something fall, we had to take the wheelbarrow and scoop it up so the horse would not lie down in it. Guard duty was boring and unpleasant, but it was only for two-hour stretches.

We had calisthenics regularly, as well as handball training; the batteries played handball against each other or against nearby infantry.

Around December 1, 1936, we ended our infantry training and began three months of basic artillery training. We were divided into two groups: those who would handle the horses (usually those from farms) and those who would handle the guns (usually those from the city), although each group had to be familiar with the other's duties. We had to learn everything about the horse side of the business and the gunners' side of the business. Basically, the horse handlers were learning equine care and how to bridle and harness horses. Those of us who were gunners practiced going through the motions of firing: taking the gun off the ammunition cart, placing the gun in the proper position, loading it with a dummy shell and bags of sawdust for powder, aiming it at a fixed point, making corrections, and firing on command. We went through these exercises every day in the training area, just going through the motions without live ammunition. The horse handlers (fahrers) and the gunners (kanoniers) exercised constantly but separately.

A guncrew consisted of one gun leader (an unteroffizier or unterwachtmeister), five kanoniers, and three fahrers. The direction gunner was the key kanonier, because he handled the sighting and the aiming of the gun. The others handled ammunition, loaded the gun, and helped camouflage the gun with branches. After a couple of weeks of the kanoniers and fahrers practicing separately, we came together for the first time. From then on, fahrers and kanoniers practiced together daily, and once a week all four guncrews would come together and practice as a battery.

Christmas was approaching, and we began looking

forward to a break in our training routine. Half of us were to get five days of furlough at Christmas, and the other half were to get five days at New Year's. Rausche, Wohlthat, and Baresel drew Christmas furlough, and Weinreich, Vogel, and I received our furloughs at New Year's.

When the first group left, just before Christmas, everything seemed suddenly very strange, because our total regimentation had been broken. We had to police the area and keep everything spic and span, but most of our routine training was discontinued until after New Year's, and we had free time to lie around and be lazy. Most of the higher-ranking noncommissioned officers had managed Christmas furloughs, leaving mostly stabsgefreiters in charge. Stabsgefreiters were a unique group in the German Army, because this was a rank reserved for losers: career soldiers who could not handle responsibility and would never hold a rank higher than stabsgefreiter. Christmas furlough was an opportunity for them to exercise authority, however, and they took full advantage of it.

The stabsgefreiter in charge of us in Krall's absence was Weizsacker, and we were more than a little apprehensive about him. He seemed to be a very sadistic sort who liked to throw his weight around when he had a rare opportunity. Since Weinreich and I were "intellectuals," we knew we would be in trouble if we ever found ourselves at his mercy.

Weinreich and I drew stable duty on Christmas Eve. At least we were trusted with pitchforks by now. Stable duty consisted of cleaning the stalls and sorting out the straw. The straw could not be too dirty, so new straw had to be placed on top of the old straw. The underneath mattress of old straw would already be pressed down and the new straw would be placed on top of that so the horse would not get dirty when it lay down. The stable had a cement floor, and we had to learn how much straw to take out and how much to leave. About every three weeks all the straw would be removed, the cement floor would be cleaned with water, and all new straw would be put down. An immense amount of new straw was needed to make the required mattress. After enduring the odor of removing the old straw, we found the fresh scent of new straw an unforgettable pleasure.

Weinreich and I drew the unenviable duty of removing all the soiled straw from a section of the stall and washing down the cement floor. We had hardly begun when Stabsgefreiter Weizsacker came marching Vogel into the barn, shouting at him about extra duty. Weinreich and I stopped our work and looked around to see what was happening.

The moment we stood up, Weizsacker pounced on us. "Ah ha! The intellectuals are loafing," he shouted gleefully, momentarily forgetting about Vogel. "Well, if you have so much free time, I have a perfect solution—especially designed for intellectuals and smartmouths." He grinned at Vogel. Weizsacker motioned for Vogel to get into the stall with Weinreich and me. "Now, let's see you guys clean this place out with your hands!" Our expressions must have reflected our shock, because he grinned even wider. "That's right," he said. "Hang up your pitchforks."

Vogel started to protest, but quickly thought better of it. Weizsacker's half-moon grin was topped by a round, bulbous nose and small close-set eyes. He was obviously enjoying his rare experience with authority.

"I will be back in thirty minutes," he said, "and this stall had better be empty and spotless." He turned and strutted importantly toward the door.

Vogel picked up a tiny piece of horse manure and flipped it at the departing Weizsacker, who fortunately never saw the defiant gesture. We began picking up large sections of packed straw with bare hands, trying unsuccessfully to avoid the overpowering stench of horse urine that arose as the straw was removed, and carrying it to the wheelbarrows. With nearly superhuman effort, we had our part of the stall completely cleaned and washed down when Weizsacker returned thirty minutes later. He came stalking into the stable, looking smug and self-important, like the Italian dictator, Mussolini, in newsreels I had seen. When he saw the empty stall, his face fell. He clearly had thought it would be impossible for us to do the job in thirty minutes and was looking forward to imposing more extra duty on us. He seemed confused upon finding that he had no excuse for further punishment.

"It is a damn good thing," he muttered, as a way to save face, and stalked out of the stable.

It was not exactly an ideal Christmas Eve, but we survived it, and actually in fairly good spirits once the filthy task in the stable was finished.

Five days at the mercy of the stabsgefreiters left me more than ready for my own furlough. Being home again was very pleasant, however brief. The total lack of regimentation seemed unnatural and strange at first. Having my mother hovering to serve my every wish made me feel that I must be in another world, a dream world. My father was interested in comparing my experience to his experience in the Navy twenty years earlier. Fritz, of course, was fascinated with both sets of stories and sat at our feet as we related them. Inge was friendlier than I could ever remember her being before, but still reserved. Grandma came to visit, of course, and to brag about her handsome young soldier-grandchild. My father had got out of the wholesale grocery business and was now operating a restaurant and nightclub.

I found Liebelt, Michaelis, and Ebert and learned from them that Friedrich was also home on furlough. I was delighted that we could all get together for an evening before Friedrich had to return to Dresden, where he was in training to become an officer. Of course, since he was a fahnenjunker-unteroffizier and I was but a lowly kanonier, he strutted about, playfully shouting orders at me.

"We should plan another ski trip to the Sudeten

Mountains when Knappe and Friedrich get out of the Army," Liebelt suggested.

"I wonder if old Herr Hoffer would still be there," Friedrich said.

"I don't know if I will still be in Germany," Michaelis said gloomily. "My father is talking seriously about moving to England. He does not trust the Nazis, because we are Jewish."

"God, I hope you're still here," Ebert said. "It wouldn't be the same without you."

"Let's toast the five of us, just in case," Michaelis suggested, raising his glass of wine. "To us, and to the future."

We all drank to Michaelis's toast.

Following the wonderfully nonregimented furlough, we quickly fell back into the old routine of training. Actually the routine felt good to me. Our whole first year was intensive basic training, with maneuvers in the field once a month. Practice sessions would include pulling the guns, first on the road and then cross-country, and getting into position. The battery commander, a hauptmann, would select the battery position for the guns and the leutnants would get the people into place, select the individual positions for the four guns, and camouflage the guns.

In late January 1937, Weinreich and I were selected for training in communications because of our gymnasium education. The battery troop (which was always up front with the infantry) and the gun crews communicated by both wireless radio and telephone. This required a radio operator and a telephone operator up front with the battery troop and another of each back with the guns. Wireless radio was cutting-edge technology in 1937, and I was very proud to become a radio operator, even if it was in the horse-drawn artillery.

My training as a communications man also included measuring angles, estimating distances, and all the things the forward observation officer had to know, so that I could do his job if he was killed or badly wounded. Fairly often in combat the communications man would have to assume these duties, and we practiced this constantly.

Now that I was a communications specialist, I had to learn how to ride a horse. As a city dweller, I had to get accustomed to handling these huge animals, but it did not take long. We had to learn to brush and feed the horses (each of us had two to look after) and to saddle them. We had riding lessons an hour a day for about ten weeks, under the tutelage of Obergefreiter Sebastian. It was winter, so we would lead our horses into the covered riding arena. The riding class was ten to twelve riders, and most of us were new and inexperienced with horses. Leading our horses, we would march into the riding arena and learn how to stand the right distance from each other in a straight line in the middle of the arena. Then we learned how to mount a horse, how to hold the reins, and what to do and not do.

In the summer, the battalion (all three batteries) came together for the first time, and in late summer we worked together with the infantry for the first time. For this, we had to leave Jena, our garrison town, and go to a military reservation at Jüterbog, near Berlin, where we could fire live ammunition. Working with the infantry was the highlight of our training.

We seldom practiced with the infantry in garrison because of limited space, with the farms all around. We could practice in the fall, after the crops were in, but even then a lot of damage was done and the farmers did not like it. We had to take the farmers' fences down and then put them up again. We had to be very careful with the fences, which was time-consuming and difficult.

We marched from Jena to Jüterbog. We were roused out of bed at 4:30 A.M. and had an hour to feed and water the horses and have our own breakfast. Then we hitched the teams to the guns and wagons and moved out. The infantry led the way, with the artillery following. The infantry marched on foot, and we in the artillery either rode horseback or rode on the guns or wagons. The guns were pulled backward, with their barrels pointing behind us. The battery commander led the Eighth Battery on horseback, followed by the forward observation officer with the battery troop. Then came the battery officer with the four gun crews and the ammunition and supply wagons.

Suddenly we received word that the infantry in front of us had encountered resistance and we were to deploy and support the infantry. The battery commander and the forward observation officer, with the battery troop, moved up to join the infantry. After being advised of the infantry battle plan, the battery commander rode back to instruct the battery officer and determine the gun positions, designating the exact spot for each of the four guns. The guns were unhitched and positioned by hand by the kanoniers. The ammunition was unloaded from the limbers, which the fahrers then took back to cover, where they dismounted and cared for their horses. The battery officer selected a reference point that could be seen from the gun position. The forward observation officer selected a target for sighting purposes and gave directions to the battery officer (as well as the position of his reference point), who then gave orders to the guncrew of gun number two, which did the initial sighting for all four guns. After each round, the forward observation officer called back adjustments. When gun number two was zeroed in, all the guns fired on the target—live ammunition for the first time—and the roar of the guns was deafening.

When we received word that the enemy resistance had been broken, the fahrers rode back to the gun positions and hitched the horses to the guns. We communications people restored our equipment to their containers and remounted them on our horses. We then resumed our cross-country march, but we were all flushed and excited from actually going through the whole coordinated action and firing live ammunition for the first time; we were considerably less disciplined than we had been before, but only for a short while. We were soon back in our disciplined routine.

While we were at Jüterbog, Hitler ordered a big parade for the benefit of Mussolini, who was visiting Germany and whom Hitler wanted to impress with German military might. I think this was one of the few times when a whole division went on parade. As participants, unfortunately, all we saw was dust, with an artillery regiment of four battalions totaling forty-eight cannons, each pulled by a team of six galloping horses. Nearly three hundred horses and one hundred cannon wheels raised so much dust that not only could we not see, we could barely breathe.

On the weekends back at Jena, we could get a pass to go to town unless we had stable or guard duty. Weinreich and I had become good friends and usually went to town together. As in Labor Service, my weekend passes were usually spent in a combination of cultural pursuits and meeting girls and dancing.

One day in the spring of 1937, I was instructed to report to Leutnant Badstübner's office. This was my first personal contact with an officer. I reported to him in his office as ordered, and he cordially invited me to take a seat.

"I understand that you plan to attend university after your Army service," he said.

"Jawohl, Herr Leutnant," I replied.

"What would you think about attending a military academy and becoming a reserve officer?" he asked. "Instead of two years, you would have to serve three, but then you would have no reserve duty obligations and would be completely free to attend university and study."

That sounded logical to me, and I was enjoying Army life, so why not? *"Jawohl,* Herr Leutnant," I replied. "I would like that."

Weinreich and two other gymnasium graduates had also been invited to become officer candidates. So we now had additional training, as well as some duties of noncommissioned officers. Leutnant Badstübner was responsible for our training and special duties. He was only a couple of years older than we were and not long out of the military academy himself.

Our military training was now stepped up. Normally, our second year in the Army would have been a repetition of our first except that in the second year we would have taken over some supervisory duties. But because we were in officer training, we began learning military tactics. We began to learn the observation officer's and battery officer's jobs.

We were put into command positions to learn leadership and how to use our voices to command troops. In training new troops, we did the same job as the noncommissioned officers. Some of the noncommissioned officers were friendly, but some of them resented us because they were older and they knew that one year later we would be leutnants and they would still be noncommissioned officers five years from now.

There were four ranks for officer candidates. The ranks were fahnenjunker-gefreiter (equivalent to gefreiter) and fahnenjunker-unteroffizier (equivalent to unteroffizier) before we went to the academy. Halfway through the military academy, we would become fähnrich, and at graduation from the academy, we would be promoted to oberfähnrich, which was almost an officer.

On June 1, as an officer candidate, I became a fahnenjunker-gefreiter (I would otherwise have qualified for gefreiter rank only after one year). Stabsgefreiter Weizsacker was bitter at the thought of a first-year recruit suddenly almost equaling him in rank, and he knew that I would outrank him in a few months. He, of course, would never be more than a stabsgefreiter regardless how long he stayed in the Army. I could sympathize with him, but he was still a little hard to take at times.

The fahnenjunker-gefreiters stayed in the same barracks, and we did the same things as the others, except that on certain days, at certain times, we came together and had special training. The special training made our lives more interesting. Those of us in officer-candidate training also had increasingly more contact with the officer corps. They had regular social events, to which we were occasionally invited. The dances were attended by daughters of the older officers and by local business and professional people and their daughters. The dances and social events provided us with excellent opportunities to develop and practice our social skills.

We went out with the other enlisted men to help the farmers with their harvest, during the latter half of July 1937. It was fun, it was a nice break in routine for us, and it was a great help for the farmers. Of course, we were all accustomed to working with horses, and many of the soldiers were accustomed to farm work. We sang as we went to work in the fields, and we thoroughly enjoyed helping the farmers out. They were very appreciative, and they fed us extremely well.

On September 1, 1937, I was promoted to fahnenjunker-unteroffizier. On October 1, after one full year in the Army, I received a ten-day furlough before reporting to the military academy in Potsdam. Weinreich and I were both assigned to Kriegsschule Potsdam near Berlin.

11

I ARRIVED AT KRIEGSSCHULE Potsdam in mid-October 1937, looking forward to an exciting new experience. I took a train to Potsdam, a relatively small town near Berlin, and then caught a bus to the school, arriving in late afternoon. Kriegsschule Potsdam was a very large and modern complex, surrounded by a wrought-iron fence on a concrete base. The whole complex looked very military and official.

A gefreiter at the gate inspected my orders and directed me to the administration building. There a clerk directed me to Room 1-C, where I found a leutnant seated at a wooden desk.

"I am Leutnant Breker," he said. "Welcome to Kriegsschule Potsdam. I am going to be your platoon leader while you are here." He sat back down at the desk, opened a folder, and began to look through some papers as I stood before the desk. A photograph of Chancellor Hitler adorned the wall in back of the desk, along with a photograph of Generalfeldmarschall von Blomberg, Commander in Chief of the Wehrmacht. "You established quite a good record at Jena," the leutnant commented finally. "I am sure you will do just as well here. You have been assigned to Barrack 3, Suite L. Your training will begin tomorrow morning."

I crossed a parade ground to four barrack buildings, where I found Barrack 3 and Suite L and learned that a suite consisted of a large study room with four desks and a large bedroom with four beds, four lockers, and four individual washing facilities.

Weinreich greeted me at Suite L, a big smile on his face. "Welcome to the manor, Herr Knappe," he said.

I looked at him with both surprise and suspicion. "Are we rooming together again?" I asked.

"No. I asked the leutnant if he would put us together," he said, with a shrug and a palms-up gesture. "He could not, because every suite must have people from different branches of the service. But I am in the suite next door."

My other roommates arrived during the afternoon. One was an infantryman named Hans Bottler, another was a cavalryman named Gustav Hoffmann, and I don't remember the fourth one.

Since we had no duties for the rest of the day, we all decided to explore the layout of Kriegsschule Potsdam. The parade ground was the center of the whole complex. On one side of the parade ground were the four barrack buildings, and on the other side was the administration building. To one end of the parade ground was the mess hall, which included a lounge where students could have a drink. Behind the barracks were the training area and the stables. Immediately behind the administration building were four classroom buildings, and beyond them were an indoor swimming pool, a large gym, and several tennis courts. Overall, the place was quite impressive, with its manicured grounds and neat new brick buildings.

After a breakfast the next morning, we were all called to an assembly, where we were greeted by the commander of Kriegsschule Potsdam, Oberst Wetzel. We learned that we were but one of four kriegsschules and that the others were at Munich, Hannover, and Dresden. Anyone who became an officer at that time had to graduate from one of them. Each had approximately a thousand students.

We were then divided into two groups of five hundred each, labeled Group A and Group B. Suite L was assigned to Group B. Each group was commanded by an oberstleutnant, Group A by Oberstleutnant Eduard Burkhardt and Group B by Oberstleutnant Erwin Rommel. Rommel's name meant nothing to us then, but we would soon learn that he had been quite a hero in the World War and that even today, at the age of forty-five, he was something of a celebrity in the German Army. His feats of bravery and effectiveness in combat were astounding. We learned that he had received the Pour-le-Mérite, Germany's highest decoration, during the World War as an oberleutnant in the Alpine Korps on the Italian front. He had been a brilliant tactician even then. He had just this year, 1937, published a book on tactics, called *Infantry Attacks*, which we were to use as a textbook. Once a week, we were to have an assembly of both groups, at which Rommel would teach tactics.

Within each group were sixteen platoons of thirty-two men each. Each platoon was commanded by a major, who was assisted by a leutnant. After the commander's presentation, Rommel was introduced and gave a little speech about the importance of a strong officer corps and what an honor it was for us to be selected to become officers in the German Army.

We were then separated into platoons and introduced to our platoon commanders. Mine was Major Kassnitz, a man of about forty, with thinning hair that was already turning gray. We got another short speech from him. He told us that at the academy we would be taught to lead an infantry battalion in combat. We would all be treated as infantry, even though many of us were in the artillery, the cavalry, and the panzers (tanks).

Our training began immediately and continued without letup until Christmas. We studied only military subjects, because we were all gymnasium graduates who had just completed thirteen years of intensive academic studies. Our major subject was tactics, and we spent most of our time on it. Other subjects included topography and reading maps, engineering (mostly building and blowing up bridges), basic artillery, horseback riding, drilling on the parade ground with rifles, cooperation with the Luftwaffe, and physical education. We spent six hours each day in the classroom and three hours in the field. We learned everything an infantry battalion commander had to know in any kind of precombat or combat situation. At the end of our training we would theoretically be able to command an infantry battalion in combat.

Every week we would have a test that was graded, very much as in gymnasium. We were not normally assigned homework during the week. In the evening, we would look over what we had studied during the day and go over it again so the next day we would be better acquainted with what had been discussed.

We got homework every second or third weekend. In an attempt to put us under stress similar to a combat situation, they gave us very little time to do the assignment. They would give us a situation in which we were a battalion commander. Our battalion was given a certain goal for the day and we were marching to meet that goal. Suddenly we would receive a message that the enemy had been spotted. Then we might get a contradictory message. Then we would encounter something else that would alter the situation. The problem was written out and we would read it as if we were seeing it. From all the information given us, we had to make our decision. Three or four possibilities might be equally correct. We had to judge the situation and make a decision on the basis of what we knew. We had to write the orders we would give to implement that decision. We had to explain why we made the decision; it was not so much that we had to make a patent decision as how we came to it, how we defended it, and how we executed it.

We would go out in the field and "play" battalion commander. One person would be designated as the battalion commander and the others would make up his staff. The staff would include an adjutant (an executive assistant to the commander, principally for administrative duties), three company commanders, a communications officer, and so on. An assault had to be prepared and orders issued. Major Kassnitz would make the assignments and distribute the rules for playing. Then he would keep notes on how well everyone handled himself. Sometimes the school commander, Oberst Wetzel, would also observe. After the exercise in the field, we would go back to the academy in a bus. Often the most warlike action of the day was the run toward the bus to get one of the better seats.

In tactics, we studied how to attack, how to retreat, how to march, and so on. We studied military history, mostly Prussian battles from the seventeenth and eighteenth centuries and battles from the great World War. We studied how tactics and strategy were used in the battles.

Often our three hours a day in the field would be infantry practice, for which we would wear our field uniforms, steel helmets, and gas masks. We would march about twenty minutes from the academy, with machine guns and the ammunition for them. We would march and then deploy. We marched three abreast; then when we "came under fire," one person went left, one went right, and one went straight down. We would practice attacking, defending, retreating, and so on. We did this to make sure that everyone knew infantry tactics even if he was in the artillery or panzers, because tactics usually determined the outcome of a battle.

We also did some basic infantry training, like target shooting, firing machine guns, throwing hand grenades, and so on. Sometimes in studying engineering, we would go out and lay barbed wire and put up antitank obstacles. We learned where to apply dynamite to a bridge so it would collapse and not remain usable. We also studied how to deal with mines. We studied all these things both in the classroom and in the field. We had to take riding lessons also, even those of us in the cavalry and artillery, who already knew how to ride.

Our lives were quite pleasant at Kriegsschule Potsdam. We could study in our room, which was equipped with four desks and chairs. The mess hall was not much different from the soldiers' mess at Jena: a large hall with tables for ten or twelve people each. The mess hall was used only for the noon meal. We were issued a two-pound loaf of *Kommissbrot,* or "Army bread," every other day, which we kept in a special food compartment of our lockers. For breakfast, we would have *Kommissbrot,* butter, jam, and coffee. Somebody had to go to the mess hall every morning and get the butter, jam, and coffee and bring them back to the suite. For our evening meal, someone would also go to the mess hall to get butter and either liverwurst or cheese to go with our *Kommissbrot,* and we would also eat this in our suite. We had a lounge adjoining the mess hall where we could go at night and on the weekends and have a drink if we had the time. We could order beer, wine, cognac, or any other kind of drink. On rare occasions, someone would get drunk, but learning to drink socially without getting drunk was part of the training. An Army officer who could not hold his liquor would present a bad image. Sometimes we drank a lot if we had something to celebrate, but almost everyone knew how to handle it.

As students, we sometimes made excursions away from Potsdam. Major Kassnitz would go with us on these trips, because he had to observe us in all kinds of different environments. Some of the excursions were for skiing (a skill considered necessary for winter combat), and others were to visit different battlefields. We made one early trip to East Prussia that lasted two weeks. On one trip we spent a week skiing in the Sudeten Mountains, and I thought often of my trip with Michaelis, Liebelt, Ebert, and Friedrich.

At each battlefield, we would study the campaign and then go and tour the battlefield to get a feel for how these battles were fought—flank attacks, retreats, defense, counterattacks. We would study the battle in the classroom, and then when we visited the battlefield, one of us would be designated to explain the battle. Then Major Kassnitz would criticize our explanation of the battle. It would be an all-day affair. On the way to a battlefield, we might visit a castle or a fortress. The excursions gave us some historical insights in addition to military insights. We studied the tactics of Alexander and Caesar, the battle of Hastings, and Roman and Greek battles. We learned why things went right and why things went wrong.

Sports were an important part of academy life. Tennis courts were available if we cared to play. Some sports were required, such as swimming, high-diving, boxing, fencing, and horseback riding. In addition to enhancing physical fitness, the sports were intended to test our courage and make us competitive. I started training for the modern pentathlon, which consisted of fencing, pistol shooting, horseback riding, ten-kilometer cross-country running, and thousand-meter swimming. Every day for some time I ran ten kilometers and swam a thousand meters before going to bed. It was terrific training. Others played tennis and swam, and some just went to the lounge and had a drink.

Sometimes on the weekends when we did not have homework, we rented horses and went sightseeing. Potsdam was both colorful and historic, and these excursions were always interesting.

Social affairs were arranged so we could practice our social graces and be observed and evaluated. We often had dances to which daughters of the older officers were invited. Anyone who had not learned how to dance properly had to learn now. There were dance schools in Potsdam for those who needed them. The dances were held in a large ballroom, with live orchestras. Many of the officers at the kriegsschule and their wives attended these dances. They were quite formal; the men wore dress uniforms and the women wore ball gowns. There were perhaps four dances during the nine months I was at Potsdam. Major Kassnitz was always watching and evaluating us. His wife and his two teenage daughters also attended the dances. At one of the dances, all the thirty-two men in my platoon were introduced to Rommel's wife. We had to kiss her hand properly and exchange a few words.

At Christmas, we got a furlough to go home. Liebelt, Michaelis, and Ebert were, of course, still at the university, and Friedrich was now a leutnant. Of course, he lorded it over me even more now that he was a full-fledged officer and I was the fähnrich. I was beginning to wonder if our relationship would remain this way the rest of our lives.

Shortly before graduation, I was ordered to report to Major Kassnitz's office. When I reported, he returned my salute with a smile and invited me to have a seat.

"Knappe, in the combined military academies, approximately four thousand new officers will graduate next week," he said.

"Jawohl," I said, a bit perplexed.

"Of those four thousand, your grades place you twenty-fourth from the top," he continued. "That is no small achievement, and you are to be congratulated."

"Thank you, Herr Major," I said.

"But in addition to your grades, your athletic achievements and your demonstrated leadership ability led me to submit your name as a candidate for the Inspector of the Kriegsschules' Award for outstanding achievement," he went on. He then stood and extended his hand across his desk. "I am proud indeed to inform you that you have won that prestigious award," he said. "Congratulations!"

I was dumbfounded, but extremely proud and pleased. "Thank you, Herr Major," I said, shaking his hand. "I am very flattered. I had no idea that you had submitted my name."

I titled my photograph album from Potsdam "Sunny Time at Potsdam." I had really enjoyed the experience. The school had been hard work, and it was challenging, but it was also great fun. We all had a lot in common: we were sports-minded and athletic, and we shared a certain intelligence level and a similar education. We were peers and very comfortable with each other.

Just before graduation, we were all asked if we would like to volunteer to join the Luftwaffe, which had only recently been formed as a separate branch of the Wehrmacht. I enjoyed the artillery now—had even fallen in love with horses—and preferred to stay with it. Since not enough people volunteered, a number of the new graduates were drafted into the Luftwaffe. Among them, much to my chagrin, was Weinreich. I had hoped until then that we would both be assigned to the same unit.

Tailor shops were all around the academy in Potsdam, and we all had tailored uniforms made for graduation. We were very proud to be graduating, and we strutted about in our new tailored uniforms. We could wear the officer's insignia on our hats now, but the epaulets on our shoulders were still different.

At our graduation ceremony, the commander, his staff, and the students met in an assembly. We heard a few short speeches. Oberst Wetzel made an impassioned speech in which he reminded us that we were part of a proud nation, a proud people, and a proud Army. We who were graduating, he said, were a class of destiny, and he expected us to hold our heads high and live up to our country's expectations. I almost shivered with nationalism at his words.

The ceremony was over in an hour. Then the platoon celebrated a little. Major Kassnitz was not quite as distant as he had been before, and we talked with Leutnant Breker on an almost equal basis. A camaraderie was there now, from both of them, that had been missing before.

Oberstleutnant Rommel signed my final school record, on which he wrote: "I agree that Knappe should receive the Inspector of the Kriegsschules' Award for outstanding achievement."

I graduated from the military academy at Potsdam on July 2, 1938, although I was not commissioned as a leutnant until September. The academy was a tremendous experience for me, and to have won the Inspector of the Kriegsschules' Award was a great honor.

Except for those assigned to the Luftwaffe, we all returned to the specialties from which we had come: infantry, artillery, panzer, engineers, or whatever, but we were assigned to different bases where nobody had known us as enlisted men.

I got a furlough to go home and arrived in time for my parents' twenty-fifth wedding anniversary. I wore the formal dress uniform of an oberfähnrich, complete with sword, and all were very proud of their splendid young soldier.

My new assignment was to the 24th Artillery Regiment.

12

HEADQUARTERS FOR THE 24th Artillery Regiment was at Altenburg, about thirty miles from Leipzig. Eight of us reported to the regiment from the various kriegs-schules. The next morning, all eight of us were introduced to Oberst Hartmann, our regiment commander. I knew him by reputation, since I had served under him at Jena, although quite remotely. He was known throughout the 24th Artillery Regiment as "the Ice-Gray One" because of his gray hair and stern manner.

After Hartmann's welcoming speech, we were given our assignments. The 1st Battalion was at Plauen, the 2nd Battalion was at Altenburg, and the 3rd Battalion was at Jena. I was assigned to the 1st Battalion, at Plauen, an industrial city with a population of about ninety thousand. I had been to Plauen before, but I had never been to the Army garrison there. I arrived early so I could familiarize myself with the facilities. The layout was very similar to that of the Jena garrison. The battalion administration building faced the main gate. Extending in a line behind it were three barracks buildings, each housing one battery. The three barracks faced a cobblestone assembly area. A huge training area lay behind the barracks. Behind the training area were two very long and narrow horse stables, and beyond the stables were indoor and outdoor riding arenas.

I was greeted by Leutnant Gerald Niebergall, the battalion adjutant, who told me that I was assigned to First Battery, commanded by Hauptmann Dörnberg.

Hauptmann Kurt Dörnberg welcomed me to First Battery. "Actually, you are arriving just in time to go on maneuvers," he said. "You will be our new observation officer, but you will hardly have time to get to know your people before we leave. I will introduce you to our battery officer, Leutnant Witzleben, at dinner. You and he will need to get to know each other well. You will be working very closely together while we are on maneuvers, as well as in training new recruits when we return from maneuvers."

Leutnant Erik Witzleben was about twenty-three years old, had short blond hair, a quick smile, and an easygoing look about him, and had been in the battery two years. "Glad to have you with us," he said when we were introduced. "You will like it here, especially when we get back from maneuvers. It is a good life."

I moved my gear into an officer's apartment in First Battery's barracks. The apartment was simple, but nicely furnished. I had a bedroom, a small kitchen, and a sitting room. Dörnberg was married and lived off post. The unmarried leutnants from the other two artillery batteries also had apartments in the barracks.

We went on maneuvers three days after I reported to First Battery. I was up at five o'clock to check out the battery troop and make certain everything was in order. The early-morning darkness still held sway at that hour, but the soldiers were stirring. The cook had already been up an hour, had built fires under the kettles on his field kitchen, and had made coffee and tea. The satisfying taste of a cup of hot tea, coupled with the smell of the horses and the clanking of the chains as the horses were being harnessed and hooked up to the carts, guns, and wagons, slowly ushered in the light of day. I checked out the equipment of my radio and telephone operators and their horses, as well as the rest of the battery troop. At seven o'clock, we received the order to pull out and begin the journey to Grafenwöhr, where the maneuvers would be held. It was going to be an all-day march.

The 18th Infantry Regiment marched on foot, followed by the 1st Artillery Battalion. Our battery had four 105mm guns and all the ammunition and equipment that went with them. Horse-drawn carts also carried supplies, the field kitchens, hay and oats for the horses, and food for the people. We had a blacksmith, with his wagon and field forge, to replace lost horseshoes and repair equipment. Three or four enlisted men looked after the health of the horses—they were like medical corpsmen for horses.

On the way to our destination, we moved on roads. On.an uphill grade, the men on the guns, carts, and wagons got off and walked in order to make it easier for the horses. Once every hour, we stopped for ten minutes to rest the horses and the marching infantry. At noon, we stopped for an hour to water the horses and feed the men. Each artillery battery and infantry company had its own field kitchen, on which a huge kettle over a fire was used to cook stew as we marched. We stopped again to water the horses and feed the men at about five o'clock. We then continued to march, reaching our destination just before dark.

We had to position the guns and other equipment, unhook the horses, remove their harness, rub them down, and feed and water them. Then tents had to be erected. It was midnight before we could finally turn in. It had been a very long day, and many men with aching muscles lay down to sleep in the tents that night.

Maneuvers involved two divisions, one designated Red Division and the other, Blue Division. The two divisions were to oppose each other in mock combat. Each division had three infantry regiments, and each regiment had three battalions of infantry supported by one battalion of artillery. The division commander, a generalmajor, would normally keep one regiment in reserve, use one to feint and try to draw the enemy out of position, and use the remaining regiment to conduct the attack. All the artillery, of course, would be assigned to the infantry regiment making the real attack. We did everything on maneuvers that we were later to do in combat, even to the extent of building pontoon bridges across the rivers. Umpires judged the battle. They decided which units had been put out of action, how extensive the damage was, and which units were victorious.

As much as possible on maneuvers, officers were housed in local homes in the villages (families would volunteer guest rooms and be paid for them). If we stayed very long at one place and a restaurant was nearby, we would provide the restaurant with food and pay its staff to prepare and serve it for us for our main meal each day. The soldiers would stay in barns, schools, churches, or whatever larger facilities were available; if nothing else was available, they would stay in tents. If no villages were in the vicinity, officers would live in tents and eat from the field kitchen with the soldiers. Once at the area of maneuvers, we moved cross-country, just as we would in combat, and the farmers were compensated for any damage to their fences or land.

I got to know Dörnberg and Witzleben better during maneuvers, because we all had to rely on each other so much. Dörnberg, as battery commander, had to approve my selection of my forward observation post and Witzleben's selection of his gun positions. If he did not approve, he would explain why and make the necessary changes.

Going to training camps such as Grafenwöhr on maneuvers was good for us because it was the only time we could use live artillery ammunition. Going through the motions of firing the guns in the training area at Plauen was fine, but eventually the men needed to know the exhilaration of firing live ammunition and living under field conditions. Of course, we had to be very careful that no "enemy" troops were really in the vicinity where the rounds would fall. Maneuvers lasted a week, and then it was time to return to Plauen.

Following maneuvers, I found that life at Plauen was

very pleasant. My bachelor apartment in the barrack was quite comfortable, and I had an orderly who kept it clean and did a little cooking if I had a guest.

We worked ten to twelve hours each day during the week. On Saturday, we worked until noon and then were free until Monday morning unless we had officer-of-the-day duties, which consisted of supervising the guards and in general looking after things. We had such duties about every fourth weekend, and on the other weekends we were free to do as we pleased. I was only about a hundred kilometers from home and went home occasionally, but for the most part I found it more interesting to stay in Plauen.

Soon after we returned from maneuvers, Witzleben offered to show me the town. We put on civilian clothing, got into Witzleben's car, and toured Plauen during the afternoon. As always in a new place, I wanted to see the historical places, cathedrals, and interesting architecture. Witzleben was an excellent tour guide, since he'd had two years to find all the out-of-the-way places of Plauen. We crisscrossed the whole city, stopping whenever we saw a remarkable building or anything else that caught our attention. Around five o'clock, Witzleben announced that he was going to show me his favorite afternoon café. It was common for cafés to play dance music on gramophones in the afternoon, or even to have two or three musicians playing live dance music. Young men and women would go to the cafés as a way of meeting each other. If a boy saw a girl he wanted to meet, he asked her to dance; then if he liked her, he would ask her to join him at his table. The cafés served tea, coffee, beer, wine, and some food. Witzleben drove to the café and parked the car near it. When we went inside, a three-piece combo was playing dance music. Witzleben immediately saw a girl he knew and led us to her table.

"Bettina, it's nice to see you again," he said to a tall, attractive brunette, who smiled prettily at him with dancing green eyes.

"Hello, Erik," she said. "Permit me to introduce my friend Gisela." Her friend was small, with short blond hair, blue eyes, and a quick smile. Witzleben introduced me, and the girls invited us to join them.

I found Gisela to be very attractive. I danced with her and learned that she was also witty and fun to be with. She was very outgoing, with a bubbly personality. Bettina was more reserved, although both obviously liked having a good time. We enjoyed their company and had a very pleasant evening.

On September 1, 1938, I was ordered to report to our battalion commander, Major Kordt. I felt sure that my commission as a leutnant had finally been approved. I reported as ordered and found the battalion's other two oberfähnrichs there as well. Major Kordt smiled and congratulated us on being promoted to leutnant. We had been functioning as commissioned officers all along, so all it really meant was that our shoulder epaulets changed from those of oberfähnrich to those of leutnant. It was nonetheless cause for celebration, and Niebergall, Witzleben, and I celebrated late into the night in the officers' mess, along with the other new leutnants and their friends.

There were many social events in Plauen we could attend. Plauen was an industrial town with a large upper class that had private clubs where we were always welcome. We were not members of these civilian social clubs, because we could not afford to be, but many of the wealthy families had daughters and were glad to have young officers to escort them. For most major social events in Plauen, we in the officer corps had a standing invitation to attend. A notice would be placed on the battalion's bulletin board, letting us know of coming events. We were part of the social life of the city. Army officers were considered part of the social elite because of a long tradition of the nobility being Army officers. Those of us who were not part of the nobility were accepted by association and long tradition. Because of this, we felt a special responsibility when we were in uniform. As soon as we put our uniforms on, we adopted impeccable etiquette. If we wanted to relax, we wore civilian clothing. If it was an official event or if the battalion commander was to be there, we always wore uniforms.

I attended my first social event in late September. Witzleben and I picked up Gisela and Bettina in his car and drove to the dance. Because it was a formal affair at one of the private clubs, and because Hauptmann Dörnberg and Major Kordt were going to be there, we wore our dress uniforms. The private club was on the outskirts of Plauen, a few miles away from the post, in a massive ivy-covered brick building. Large pillars with rounded pots on top supported kerosene-fueled lanterns that lit the walkway. As we entered the club we could hear an orchestra playing. Inside, Witzleben pointed out Hauptmann Dörnberg and Major Kordt. They were seated at a large round table and invited us to join them.

During the evening, I danced with both Frau Dörnberg and Frau Kordt. Frau Dörnberg was very proper and said very little. Frau Kordt was outgoing and talkative. At one point as we were dancing, she broke into a few steps of the Lambeth Walk, an English dance that was very popular with young people but had been forbidden by the government as "degenerate." I was startled at her indiscretion, but she smiled impishly and winked. She apparently enjoyed startling a young officer with her naughtiness.

Like young people everywhere, we liked music and we liked to dance. In addition to the Lambeth Walk, some music was also forbidden by the government as "degenerate," especially American and British pop music. We could not do the forbidden dances or play the forbidden music in public dance halls, but at the private clubs we would wait for the battalion commander to leave and then we would do as we liked. There was always a live band, and they always knew the music.

I took Gisela to many of the social events in Plauen.

As an attractive fun-loving eighteen-year-old blond and the daughter of a wealthy manufacturer, Gisela was very appealing to young officers, and I had a lot of competition for her attention. She and I rode our horses together on weekends and went to riding tournaments together. We also went to theaters and concerts. It was a very happy and carefree time.

My Army pay was enough to maintain a fairly good standard of living. A leutnant was paid 300 reichsmarks (about $71) per month, an oberleutnant 400 reichsmarks (about $95), a hauptmann 500 reichsmarks (about $119), and a major 600 reichsmarks (about $142). Our room and board were also provided. On our pay, we could afford to have an inexpensive car and a horse. I was learning that being an officer in the peacetime German Army was a very nice life.

The new class of recruits arrived in October. Last year's class received promotions to oberkanonier or gefreiter, and they would now help train the new class of recruits under First Battery's two senior wachtmeisters, Schmundt and Ritter, and their subordinate unteroffiziers, obergefreiters, and stabsgefreiters. The soldiers who had completed their two years in the Army and did not choose to remain in the Army for a career were discharged to go home. Leutnant Witzleben and I divided thep responsibility for training the recruits between us. I had the responsibility for fahrer training, and Witzleben had the responsibility for kanonier training. Witzleben and I did most of the classroom lectures, and the noncommissioned officers performed the field training.

I would go from one training group to the next during the day, either on horseback or on foot, and observe the training being performed by the noncommissioned officers. I would normally just observe, although occasionally, if called upon, I would participate. Once as I was observing a group on the pistol-firing range, the gefreiter conducting the training invited me to demonstrate for the trainees. I took a pistol and placed three rapid shots into the bull's-eye. Although I was a good marksman, this was pure luck; nevertheless, the trainees and the gefreiter were enormously impressed. Naturally, I did not confess that it was just a stroke of luck.

Each artillery officer had two horses and an enlisted man called a pferdehalter to care for them. In maneuvers or combat the officer rode one of the horses and the pferdehalter rode the other. When the officer dismounted in a combat situation, the pferdehalter took both horses to cover in a woods or valley or creek, where they were protected and could not be seen. If the stop was for a day or two, he found shelter for the horses.

Every year some officers and the veterinarian from each battalion went to horse auctions to buy horses. These were all experienced people who knew horses very well. The horses would be three to four years old. Each battalion had its own budget, and if we needed ten riding horses and twelve draft horses, we would try to get the best we could for the money we had to spend. The horses would be completely untrained, and the Army would then train them. We had unterwachtmeisters who did that constantly under the direction of a leutnant or a wachtmeister.

Officers spent a small part of their time training their own horses. We could buy our own horses, train them, and then sell them for a profit. Most artillery and cavalry officers did that each year. We could buy an untrained horse for about 1,500 reichsmarks and sell a well-trained horse for 4,000. It provided a nice extra income. We had the fun and gained the experience of training the horses, and the Army was happy with the arrangement as well. We did the training as part of our regular duties.

I did not really know enough to buy my own horse at this time, so I had a hauptmann who was an expert at judging horses buy one for me near Hannover. I just had to buy the horse and the saddle; the government would pay for its upkeep, and I would have a soldier to take care of it.

When my horse was led from the van, I was impressed. He was a four-year-old chestnut gelding named Schwabenprinz (Swabian Prince). Frightened from the strange experience of the train ride, he came off the van sweaty, wide-eyed, and snorting loudly. I talked to him in soothing tones and rubbed his neck and shoulders and calmed him somewhat. I stayed with him in his stall for some time, just talking to him and petting him.

During the training period, I visited him every day, talked to him, brushed him, and led him a little. I worked him on the line teaching him the basics, but I also added some small one-foot jumps. I wanted a well-schooled jumper, so I began the process early. Then several of us who were training our own horses would take them together into the riding arena so they would get used to other horses. When the time finally came for me to mount him, he accepted my weight without resistance even though he was obviously very nervous about the new experience. He knew me well and I had taken ample time to prepare him for this moment. Then I began a program of an hour of riding every day.

Then came the occupation of the Sudetenland, a part of pre-World War Germany that had been given to Czechoslovakia by the Versailles Treaty and that was still heavily populated by ethnic Germans. As early as May, while I was still at Kriegsschule Potsdam, the newspapers had been full of stories about the abuse of the ethnic Germans in the Sudetenland by the Czechoslovakian government. The stories had continued through the summer and become increasingly worse. We did not know, of course, that much of it was the creation of Goebbels's propaganda machine. The only news we received was from the controlled press, and it never occurred to us to question it. At the Nuremberg rally in 1938, Hitler had threatened to see to it that the Czechs gave justice to the Sudeten Germans. The British Prime Minister, Neville Chamberlain, had been negotiating with Hitler since mid-September. In a speech at the Berlin Sportpalast, Hitler had announced that he would have the Sudetenland by October 1, even if he had to take it militarily.

We received orders to be prepared to march and were moved up to the Czech border on September 26. I recalled Herr Hoffer's gloomy predictions of war barely thirty months earlier, as we now prepared to invade the Sudeten area near where I had met him. I had seen some of the Czech fortifications on skiing trips in the Ore Mountains (Plauen was only thirty-five kilometers from the Czechoslovakian border, and the best skiing area was just across the border). Then on September 29, Hitler and Prime Minister Chamberlain met again, along with Daladier of France and Mussolini of Italy. On September 30, the announcement was made that Czechoslovakia had accepted our peaceful occupation of the Sudetenland area of Czechoslovakia. The occupation was to begin October 1 and be completed by October 10. We all felt that we had righted a wrong that had been done to us by the Versailles Treaty.

We were ordered to be ready to pull out at 7:00 A.M. on October 1. I was up at 5:00 to see that everything was done properly and went smoothly. The cook's hot tea was a real bracer against the early-morning chill at this time of year. The horses were fed and watered, and then the men were fed. The big difference between this operation and maneuvers was that this time the men were issued live ammunition for their rifles. We did not expect resistance, but the issue of live ammunition had a sobering effect on everyone.

All the units were lined up, and precisely at 7:00 we pulled out. We followed the roads instead of going cross-country, which means that we went south first and then turned east into Czechoslovakia. Although we did not expect resistance, we had full equipment, were well trained, and could have gone into battle if necessary. As it turned out, the Sudeten Germans we encountered all greeted us enthusiastically, and we did not encounter any Czech Army units. They had apparently withdrawn from the Sudetenland prior to October 1. I felt comfortable in the Sudetenland because I had skied here so many times. We went into Czechoslovakia only thirty-five to seventy kilometers all along the border.

On October 5, 1938, we went into quarters in a village near Karlsbad, Czechoslovakia. Everything was quiet, and all the news was good. I was quartered with several other officers, including Niebergall, Dörnberg, and Witzleben. The four of us met at a village restaurant for our noon meal.

"Everything has gone perfectly so far," Dörnberg said with obvious satisfaction. "This is a good demonstration of the value of constant training. It has been just like a maneuver."

"I think we should celebrate our victory," Witzleben suggested, always ready for a party. "So far, not a single casualty!"

"Good idea," agreed Niebergall with a smile. "I nominate Knappe to find some champagne or good wine for the celebration, since the rest of us outrank him."

"I guess that is the price you must pay for being youngest, Knappe," Dörnberg said.

After lunch, I tried to find wine in the village and discovered that none was available. The village was too small, and I would have to go to a larger town to get champagne or wine. I decided to take a motorcycle and go to the next town, which was about a thirty-minute ride. I put some saddlebags onto a motorcycle, started the motor, and headed down a gravel road toward the next town.

The next thing I was aware of was being in a hospital room. I could not imagine where I was until a nurse came into the room and I asked her. I learned that I was in a military hospital at Grafenwöhr, back in Germany. I learned only later what had apparently happened. All that was known was that the battalion veterinarian later that day went down that same road and found me lying near a culvert, unconscious, with the motorcycle nearby. He returned and sent an ambulance for me. It took me to the military hospital at Grafenwöhr, about ninety kilometers northeast of Nuremberg. The nurse told me I had been unconscious for thirty-six hours. The last thing I remembered was leaving on the motorcycle. It was a gravel road, and I must have lost control of the motorcycle on the loose gravel. A cement milestone was on the road near where they found me, and I must have hit my head on that. Fortunately, I was wearing my steel helmet, or I would probably have been killed. I had no broken bones, no cuts, and just a few bruises. I did not even have a headache. I found it hard to believe that the incident had even occurred. I had felt worse after my first full day in the saddle.

The doctor refused to let me return to my unit, because I had had a concussion, and as standard procedure I had to lie flat for three weeks. Then I was allowed to return to Plauen, but not to active duty. I went to Leipzig for several days of convalescent leave near the end of October, once I was permitted to travel.

My brother, Fritz, seemed to be almost disappointed that we had not had to fight our way into the Sudetenland. "Didn't you see *any* Czech soldiers?" he asked incredulously.

"None," I assured him. "If I had not rammed my head into that milestone, there probably would not have been any violence at all."

Our regiment returned to Plauen around November 1 and held a victory parade. By then, I was out of the hospital and back in my barracks apartment, but I was still convalescing and had to watch the parade from my apartment window. I took some ribbing from Witzleben and others about that.

Just after my return to duty, Kristallnacht ("Crystal Night") occurred. A young German Jew whose family had been sent to concentration camps had walked into the German embassy in Paris and shot to death a minor German official. In retribution, the Nazi Brownshirts during the night of November 9 rampaged across Germany, burning synagogues and destroying stores, buildings, and apartments belonging to Jews. In a few places Jews were killed when they tried to resist, and many were wounded. The event was called Crystal Night because of the broken windows.

I hoped fervently that Michaelis was not among them. It was reported on the radio and in the newspapers as a spontaneous expression of moral outrage by the German people. It was nothing of the kind, of course, and everyone knew it. We did not talk about it in the barracks, because we were ashamed that our government would permit such a thing to happen. We did not want to admit it to ourselves, much less to each other, so we did not talk about it. Strong anti-Semitism had always been just beneath the surface in the German population, but no one I knew supported this kind of excess. We all felt that Hitler had been very good for Germany—solving unemployment, eliminating political street brawls, restoring national pride—but there was a coarseness about him that we silently abhorred. His hatred of the Jews made no sense to any of us, and we just wanted to distance ourselves from the ugly side of his character. Herr Hoffer's face appeared to me in a dream that night—a dream that was haunted by the refrain "At what cost?"

Saint Barbara's Day, on December 4, was always a festive time for us (Saint Barbara was the patron saint of miners and artillerymen). The officer corps staged a celebration with a sketch about the occupation of the Sudetenland that numbered me among the "casualties," along with a chicken and a young rabbit, both of which had been run over by ammunition carts. It was embarrassing, but it was also funny.

On Christmas 1938, I stayed in Plauen as duty officer

—another price I had to pay for being the youngest officer in the battery.

During my New Year's furlough, Friedrich, Ebert, Liebelt, Michaelis, and I got together again. But this one was not a happy meeting. It started off well enough, but as the evening progressed, Michaelis became more and more quiet. Finally I asked him why.

"We have to leave Germany," he said softly. "And it is the only home I have ever known."

"Why do you have to leave?" Friedrich asked.

"Because we are Jewish. The Brownshirts destroyed my father's medical office during Kristallnacht, and his patients are afraid to come to him now. They are afraid of what the Brownshirts might do to them."

Silence fell over the group. We avoided one another's eyes, trying to think of something we could say that would not sound hypocritical.

"That is awful," Ebert said finally. "It feels so different when it happens to someone you know."

"Let's not let it get us down tonight," Michaelis said, shaking his head and attempting to smile. "It will be my last night with my friends. Let's enjoy it."

It was the last time any of us ever saw Michaelis. His family went to England, where he probably continued his studies.

In February 1939, I received an order to report to Major Kordt.

"Come in," he responded to my knock. He returned my salute and motioned for me to take a seat. "This came for you today," he said, handing me a piece of paper.

It was an invitation to a reception being given by Hitler at the Reich Chancellery in Berlin!

"Your performance at Kriegsschule Potsdam has earned you this honor," Kordt said, smiling. "Only the top graduates from the four kriegsschules are invited. My congratulations!" Kordt was obviously pleased at having one of his officers going to the reception.

It was an exciting experience. We young officers all met in a foyer off the large reception room in the new Reich Chancellery and waited there. In a large coatroom for visitors was a generalfeldmarschall's baton and a big hat with a lot of gold braid that obviously belonged to Hermann Göring. One of the other young leutnants took Göring's baton, put his hat on, and started strutting around with his belly stuck out, imitating Göring. We all enjoyed that immensely and threatened to blackmail him at some future date. Nobody was there but us, of course, and we waited in this foyer until we were called into the vast main room, where we were served champagne.

The room was furnished with green leather chairs, and there was a lot of marble. It was tastefully done, with many sculptures and paintings. All the top Army brass were there, Göring, von Brauchitsch (Commander in Chief of the Army), and others. Himmler and other high-ranking politicians were also there. All the famous leaders looked just as they did in the newsreels. It was quite a heady experience for a twenty-two-year-old officer. We were standing around in groups, just chatting with each other, when Hitler came in. The room felt charged with his presence as he began drifting from group to group, making small talk. We gave our names to Hitler's military aide, a major, who then introduced us to Hitler.

"Leutnant Knappe," the major said to Hitler when they came to me.

Hitler smiled warmly and extended his hand. "Good evening, Leutnant," he said. "I am happy to meet you. Where are you from?"

"I am from Leipzig, *mein Führer,*" I said.

"And where are you stationed?"

"At Plauen, in the 24th Artillery Regiment."

"Congratulations on your performance at kriegs-schule," Hitler said as he moved on.

Hitler was at the height of his power. Everything he had done had turned out in his favor: the reoccupation of the Rhineland, the buildup of the armed forces, the annexation of Austria, the takeover of the Sudetenland. He radiated enthusiasm and energy to everyone in the room. Everything he had done except annexing Austria had been to correct an injustice that had been imposed upon us by the Treaty of Versailles, and Austria had been annexed by plebiscite of the Austrian people. He made us extremely proud to be young German officers, and I am sure he sensed that pride in us.

We leutnants enjoyed the reception greatly. Although we were really very proud to be there, we treated it like a joke among ourselves. A couple of the leutnants drank a little too much champagne, and the rest of us had to protect them because that would have reflected badly on the Army.

On March 15, 1939, the German Army invaded the rest of Czechoslovakia, unopposed, but my unit was not part of that operation. Now, for the first time, I experienced moral reservation about my government's action. The Sudetenland had been taken from us, but our subjugation of all of Czechoslovakia was unprovoked and I saw no justification for it.

In May 1939, a national riding tournament was held at Bad Elster, which was nearby, and so more of us went than would have otherwise. We could have our horses walked there the day before the event rather than having to ship them. It was a very social event, an opportunity for well-to-do riders to compare horses and talents. A two-day affair, it was planned throughout the year by the social elite. Although I was quickly eliminated, I enjoyed the event greatly.

In June, I received a letter from my brother, Fritz, who was serving an apprenticeship with a merchant in Hamburg, asking if he would be permitted to visit me for a weekend. I invited him to come and began to plan a weekend for him. I checked out a two-horse carriage, had my orderly drive it, and wore a dress uniform to meet him. He arrived at a little past noon on a Saturday. He was seventeen years old, and his whole face lit up when he saw the carriage, the horses, the driver, and my dress uniform. I took him to the stables to meet Schwabenprinz. He was impressed that I had trained Schwabenprinz myself and that I had participated in a jumping tournament.

We changed to civilian clothes after dinner that evening and drove to town with Witzleben and Niebergall. Fritz was impressed with all the girls there, and he danced every dance—although he managed to sip enough wine between dances to get just a little tipsy. We all enjoyed him, and he had a memorable time.

After lunch at the officers' mess the next day, I borrowed Witzleben's car and drove Fritz to the train station. We had both thoroughly enjoyed the weekend together.

There were now more and more warning signs that war was getting closer. The Polish Corridor, a strip of Germany that had been given to Poland by the Versailles Treaty in order to provide her with a port on the Baltic Sea, separated East Prussia from the rest of Germany, and Hitler seemed determined to regain it, as well as the former German city of Danzig, which had been made a "free city" by the Versailles Treaty. More and more, however, it looked as if an invasion of Poland would not be as easy as Hitler's earlier conquests had been. France and England were now publicly stating that they would fight if we invaded Poland, and events seemed to be leading inevitably to such an invasion. I recalled Herr Hoffer. Was Hitler about to take the gamble that would prove fatal?

We were all startled, if not shocked, by the announcement of a German-Soviet Nonaggression Pact late in the evening of August 21. The government had always preached against the Soviet Union, and suddenly—overnight—the countries were friends. We did not know what to make of it. Goebbels's propaganda tried to put a positive face on it by reporting the importance of the raw materials we were to get from the Soviet Union, yet nothing could logically explain such a total and abrupt reversal. We young officers were troubled by the strange behavior of our government, but we felt that it was not our place to question such political decisions.

On August 27, 1939, the government announced the rationing of food, soap, shoes, textiles, and coal. The German newspapers and radio were reporting extremely serious provocations by the Poles; they made it appear that Poland was about to attack Germany, and we had no reason to doubt what we were being told. It was getting very serious, and now we felt certain that war would come. We felt, however, that if it came we could deal with it; we were highly trained and ready.

I had grown accustomed to Army life, and I enjoyed it. I was no longer thinking about studies or going to a university as I had right after gymnasium. I had decided to make the Army my career.

Then late in August 1939, we were placed on war alert.

PART THREE

The Road to Destruction

1939–1944

13

THE AMERICAN DC-3 cargo plane on which I was being taken to Moscow landed at Minsk for a brief layover after three hours of flight. The Russian passengers and crew left the airplane after posting a guard with a sub-machine gun to guard me.

I sat on the rolls of carpet, and images of going through Minsk during our invasion of Russia in 1941 crowded my mind. If anyone had told me at that time that exactly four years later we would have lost the war to Russia and I would be on my way to Moscow as a prisoner of war . . .

By invading Russia in 1941, we had transformed her from a very poor and backward country to a world power! I sat lost in my thoughts as my guard and I waited for the Russian crew and passengers to return to the airplane. After an hour or so, the airplane took off again on the final leg of the flight to Moscow.

As we flew through the sky over the endless Soviet Union, my thoughts returned to the beginning of the war in 1939. . . .

Reserves were called up in late August, and the Plauen garrison was placed on alert on August 28—all furloughs were canceled and no one could leave his unit.

At eight o'clock on the morning of August 31, Major Kordt presided at a meeting of his staff, the officers of all three batteries that reported to him.

"Gentlemen," he began without preliminaries, "we

have received orders to load on trains this evening. I am sure I do not have to tell you what that means." He paused to let us consider the significance of the statement, then quickly continued. "Our battalion is as close to a perfect fighting unit as training can make it," he added. "Every officer, every man, and every horse has been trained for a specific function and has practiced that function until it is instinctive. I am confident that we shall acquit ourselves well in combat. However, we must leave twenty percent of our people behind to form the nucleus of a new artillery battalion. That means twenty percent of the men, plus one officer from each battery. Leutnant Niebergall will also stay behind to provide an experienced adjutant for the new battalion commander. New battery commanders will be drawn from the reserves that are being called up.

"Horses for the new battalion are being appropriated now from their civilian owners. Both the new horses and the reserve troops will begin arriving tomorrow. Those who are leaving must begin immediately to prepare for departure early this afternoon. Those who are remaining should help the rest of us prepare for departure today and prepare to receive the new men and horses tomorrow. I suggest we begin immediately." Kordt stood up. "Good luck to all of you," he said.

Almost immediately the post erupted with hectic activity. As the officer from my battery who was selected to stay, I helped Witzleben and Dörnberg separate the 20 percent of the men who were staying from the 80 percent who were going and helped get the horses and equipment ready for their departure.

Before dawn the next morning, September 1, one and a half million German soldiers crossed the Polish border and were soon engaged in combat.

Our new battalion and battery commanders arrived during the day. First to arrive was Major Raake, who was to replace Kordt as battalion commander. My new battery commander was a reserve officer in his forties named

Hauptmann Wimmer. He was well over six feet and slender, with dark hair and heavy dark eyebrows that made his face expressive.

In the afternoon, Major Raake called a meeting of all battalion officers. He looked us all over. "Gentlemen, we have exactly three days to get ready for a move," he said. "We will move by train, pulling out at seven A.M. on September 4. I realize that you do not know each other, and this is going to be a difficult operation. I suggest that you get to know each other quickly."

Leutnant Rehberg was our new forward observation officer. He was just out of Kriegsschule Dresden. Hauptmann Wimmer called a meeting of Rehberg, me, and our new hauptwachtmeister, Schnabel, that evening.

"Gentlemen, we are all new to each other, but we must become a smoothly working team very quickly," Wimmer began. He puffed on an elaborately carved ivory pipe with a curved stem of deer horn. "Not only must we receive approximately one hundred and fifty new men, but we must also receive an equal number of horses. The men are at least trained and need only to learn to work together as a battery. We will have to train the horses—if we are given time to train them before we are in combat."

A shiver ran over my body involuntarily at his statement. I had been practicing for combat for the past three years, but now that I was confronted with the prospect of facing it in a few days, the word "combat" almost seemed to take on a new meaning—a meaning with much greater intensity and urgency. But it also carried a sense of excitement, for I was young, and my nationalistic fervor was high.

"Get a good night's rest, gentlemen," Wimmer concluded, smoke from his pipe curling past his face. "We have some hard days ahead of us." His dark, heavy eyebrows seemed to add solemnity to the words.

The next morning, both horses and men began arriving. I mounted Schwabenprinz and took a look around in the breaking dawn. Horses were being led into the compound and tied in the stables randomly. The clomping of metal horseshoes on cobblestone sounded everywhere. Schwabenprinz sensed the excitement, and I had to rein him in. Reserve troops, who were arriving in large numbers, were milling around and waiting for orders, their conversation creating an incoherent murmur in the early-morning air. Leutnant Niebergall was trying to establish order in the barracks area, ordering troops to assemble in the mess hall until they could be assigned to a barrack. Wimmer and Schnabel began to organize the arrival of men and horses. I began attempting to form guncrews of the arriving men, and Rehberg began identifying and cataloguing the arriving horses.

We replaced all the men and horses that had been sent to Poland. The government even appropriated the horses we officers owned and paid us for them and the saddles they wore, although we were permitted to keep them. The purpose of this move was so that if a horse was killed in battle, the government would take the financial loss rather than the officer. I was very happy to be able to keep Schwabenprinz. I had trained him myself and we had been through countless maneuvers together, and it was a comfort to have my own familiar horse. Lammers, my orderly, was also staying, and I was equally glad that I would not have to adjust to a new one.

The process of getting ready to move out in such a short time was hectic. I spent my time overseeing preparations for moving the guns, ammunition, ammunition carts, ammunition wagons, field kitchen, blacksmith's forge wagon, and other equipment. Rehberg did the same for the horses. I was barely able to touch base occasionally with Wimmer, Rehberg, and Schnabel, who were all as busily engaged as I was.

On September 3, the worst news came: Great Britain and France had declared war on Germany. It was indeed to be another great war. Herr Hoffer had been right after all, and we would certainly not be able to deny that we had started this one. We had subjugated Czechoslovakia without provocation, and now we had invaded Poland, even though it was done to regain Danzig and the Polish Corridor, which had been taken from us by the Treaty of Versailles.

After checking out the horses and then the equipment that evening, Rehberg and I went to the officers' club to have a drink and relax before turning in. There we found Wimmer and Schnabel at a table, going over the plans for our departure the next morning. We joined them in reviewing the plans. After a while it dawned on me that no one had questioned, or even thought about, the presence of a hauptwachtmeister in the officers' club, deeply engaged in conversation with the officers of his battery. This, I thought, portended well for the future. An Army unit that worked together *that* closely should be a very good one, it seemed to me, and a hauptwachtmeister who accepted that much responsibility on his own initiative was surely an outstanding one.

The next morning, the entire infantry regiment was ready to move out by 6:00 A.M. The three battalions of infantry went first, on foot, to the train station. Trains were scheduled one hour apart, and each infantry battalion took up ten cars in a train. Although two trains could take all three infantry battalions, each artillery battery required a separate train because of the horses and equipment. The infantry was scheduled to depart from the train station at 7:00, and trains were scheduled for the three artillery batteries at 8:00, 9:00, and 10:00. The trains, and all other logistics, had been planned and scheduled by the division's operations officer. We had only to arrive at the designated times and the trains would be waiting.

Since my battery was scheduled for the second train, we pulled out of the Plauen garrison for the railroad station at 7:00 and arrived at the train station at 7:45. Predictably, loading the horses proved to be the biggest problem, because most of them were farm horses that had never seen a train and were frightened by all the noise and commotion. I helped Rehberg and his men with their loading. Some of the horses were so frightened that we had to blindfold them and have two men lock arms behind them and physically shove them into the railroad cars. Getting the horses loaded without injury was tedious work. We finally got everything and everybody aboard, and the train pulled out at 8:00 A.M. Our train had twenty-four cars: fifteen for horses, three for troops, and six for guns, carts, and wagons.

Once the train was rolling, I was finally able to take a deep breath and try to review the frenzied activity of the last two days. The future quickly pushed the past out of my mind, however, and I found myself thinking about all the training we had to do once we arrived at our destination, which I now knew was our border with Luxembourg—*if* the French and British would give us time for it. The horses would have to be evaluated quickly. Having pulled plows and farm equipment hardly qualified them to become part of a six-horse artillery team. Our human resources were also a concern. Having been on maneuvers many times, I knew only too well how many things could go seriously wrong if a team did not function well as a unit. If we were attacked, however, I felt that the men were well trained and would be able to fight defensively.

Arriving at the Mosel River, near Koblenz, at 6:00 P.M., we found unloading to be much easier than loading had been. Even frightened horses were easier to get out of a railcar than into one. We disembarked in the Mosel Valley, at Cochem, at the foot of the Eifel Mountains. We would march the rest of the way by roads tomorrow after spending the night in tents. We tethered the horses after watering and feeding them, posted guards, pitched tents, and fed the men before turning in at approximately 10:00 P.M. We bedded down under the stars, to the musical gurgling of purling water in the nearby river and to the chirping of crickets and the croaking of frogs. Here and there fireflies announced their presence in the darkness. The familiar sounds of the horses, the snorting and stomping and chomping, as well as the smell of them, made us feel at home as we drifted off to sleep in the night air.

We were up at 5:30 the next morning. After our usual morning ritual when we were on the road, we pulled out at 7:00. Although the Eifel Mountains were not high, the roads were nonetheless all uphill with rough terrain, and the men walked instead of riding on the guns and carts. The mountains were pretty, but they could make maneuvering difficult because at certain points the road was quite narrow.

It would have normally been a three-hour climb, but one of the lead ammunition carts broke a wheel after we had been on the move about two hours. I sent a messenger ahead to tell Hauptmann Wimmer we would all be delayed, since nothing else could get past the broken-down cart. Then I sent to the rear for the blacksmith, Obergefreiter Max Knecht. While Knecht and his assistant worked on the ammunition cart, I went to the field kitchen for a cup of tea to pass the time. Our cook was Unteroffizier Josef Boldt, who had heavy dark eyebrows that ran together to form one long eyebrow.

We were on our way again in a little less than an hour. We continued our march uphill for another hour before being stopped again. I sent a messenger ahead to find out why and learned that some trees had been felled across the road a couple of days earlier to block an invasion by the French and British. We waited the best part of another hour while the people ahead of us cleared away the barricade.

We finally arrived at our destination around noon. We were about five kilometers east of the Luxembourg border, just northwest of Bleialf and Winterspelt, in a heavily wooded sector. A stream that we could use for washing and watering the horses ran nearby. Hauptmann Wimmer issued orders to set the guns into firing position, pointed toward the border, and to camouflage them. We ordered the horses taken back to Bleialf and telephone lines laid between the forward observation post and the gun positions.

We had not been given any information about the big picture: how many divisions strong we were or how many French and British divisions might be opposite us. Luxembourg and Belgium were between us and France, but we did not doubt that the French and British would march through those countries if they were to invade Germany, just as we had during the World War. That would be a sensible thing for them to do, because if they tried to come over the Rhine River, the Luftwaffe would be an added worry for them (they would be vulnerable crossing a wide river over which bridges would have been destroyed; they would be trapped in a bottleneck and become perfect targets from the air). We thought combat was imminent, and we went about our duties very grimly in that expectation.

We established a guarded perimeter area and immediately began digging in. The smell of freshly dug earth mingled with the natural odor of the decaying leaves of the forest in the warm September afternoon. Soon the odor of sweating bodies was added to the others. After digging foxholes, the men began building bunkers. We had no idea how long we might be here, but nobody liked living in a foxhole or a tent. The men cut down small trees to build bunkers. They trimmed the limbs off the trees, stood the trunks on end, side by side, and chinked between them with mud. The odor of the chinking mud had an unpleasantness about it. The men built a bunker for the forward observation post first, then bunkers for the officers, and then bunkers for themselves. The bunkers were usually dug into the side of a hill, with a door and a window in the front. The men rigged bunks with pole frames for themselves in the bunkers, seven or eight men to a bunker.

Rehberg moved into our forward observation bunker. As battery officer, my bunker was about three kilometers back from the forward observation post, with the guns. Of course, the guns and the bunkers were all camouflaged so they could not be detected from the air. It took us only two days to get our field position battle-ready. Lammers made my bunker quite livable under the primitive circumstances. Major Raake came by to inspect our position and complimented us on our fast work.

He also brought word of the first casualties in Poland among the men who had served with us at Plauen. One was a forward observation officer who was badly wounded by fire from his own battery when a round fell short and hit his observation post. The news had a chilling effect on me, not only because I knew him but because it could just as easily have been me had fate sent me to Poland with my old battery. The news made war considerably more real for us.

We immediately began a vigorous training program to train the horses and to get the men accustomed to working together. We practiced all day, every day, to try to achieve the cohesiveness necessary to fight in an offensive operation if that should be ordered. The stress of not knowing when we might be attacked was incentive enough to drive the men to work hard to become an effective fighting unit. We had trained for combat, and with a confidence born of youth and innocence, I did not consciously think of the possibility of dying or being mutilated in combat.

Our daily routine was constant training. The mountainous terrain made training particularly difficult; level ground was all but nonexistent and both men and horses had to work harder. At least the late-summer weather was dry, so we did not have to deal with rain and slippery footing. Days passed, and the French did not attack. Wimmer, Rehberg, and I—as well as a great many others, I am sure—were grateful that the French and British were giving us time to get our horses and troops ready before they attacked. Each day of training raised our confidence level. More days passed, and still no attack. By the time that two weeks had passed, the troops were beginning to make jokes about it.

Niebergall came by one evening and joined Wimmer, Rehberg, and me for a drink. He gave us the latest news from Poland. Things were going great there. "They are calling it 'blitzkrieg,' " he said, "The panzers break through and get behind enemy lines, where they begin to disrupt the enemy's communications and supply lines. The sight of enemy tanks behind the lines also panics the enemy. It is apparently working perfectly in Poland." Niebergall was ecstatic about the success of the new strategy.

"Good," Wimmer said. "Anything is better than the trench warfare we got bogged down in during the last war."

On September 17, Russia invaded Poland from the east. By then, the Polish Army had all but been defeated by the German Army, and the Russians encountered hardly any resistance. Apparently, this was a part of the price for our new relationship with the Soviet Union. It all seemed very cynical to me. My attitude toward my government was beginning to be a little less trusting.

Our troops were now calling our present status guarding the border against the French and British "sitzkrieg," a term the gossiping supply wagon drivers carried from unit to unit. In other sectors, the French or German artillery would occasionally lob a shell across the border, but not even that much occurred where we were, because Belgium and Luxembourg had not fortified their borders, since we were not at war with them.

At the end of September, we received orders to pull back to villages a little farther from the border where we could be more comfortable, living in homes and barns instead of bunkers. Apparently, the Supreme Command of the Army had decided that the French were not going to attack, even though they had declared war on us.

My battery pulled back to the village of Eisenschmitt.

It was arranged for our horses and troops to be housed on the Bismarck estate, which was just outside the village. Bismarck, the "Iron Chancellor," had been Chancellor of the second German Reich before the turn of the century. The estate had been inherited by Bismarck's grandson, but he had been drafted and his wife and two-year-old son were the only members of the Bismarck family remaining on the estate.

Our officers stayed in homes in the village. Having the Army quartered among them was a new experience for the villagers, but it was a poor area of Germany and they were glad to have the extra money we brought into the region. Rationing was also imposing a hardship on the local population.

I received a letter from Fritz and learned that he had been drafted. He was at Jena, just as I had been three years earlier, although he was in the infantry instead of the artillery.

On October 6, Polish resistance ended and the war in Poland was considered to be over. Although France and Great Britain had declared war on us, they had made no effort to attack us, and we all happily assumed that the fighting was now over.

Leutnant Niebergall came by one evening with a very grave expression.

"We have just learned that Dörnberg was killed in Poland," he said. "He was up front with the infantry, directing the fire of his battery."

Even though I knew the fighting was really happening, I still had not experienced battle, and I found it difficult to realize that Dörnberg was dead. The image of him and Frau Dörnberg at the dance in Plauen played through my mind all evening.

The village of Eisenschmitt staged a street celebration to mark the end of the fighting in Poland. Our troops really enjoyed that, because the beer flowed freely, the band played late, and after weeks of nothing but rigorous training from morning until night the men were ready to relax and have a good time. On our part, I think we may have subconsciously been celebrating the fact that we had not had to fight the French as much as an end to the fighting in Poland. Every time I began to enjoy the celebration, however, I would think about Dörnberg and the celebration would seem inappropriate.

The next day, Major Raake and all the officers reporting to him received an invitation to the Bismarck estate for cocktails to celebrate the victory in Poland. The invitation was from the wife of Bismarck's grandson. It was an interesting experience. We were given a tour of the mansion, which even had a bowling alley in the basement. Frau von Bismarck was a beautiful and vivacious young lady in her middle twenties. An excellent hostess and a good conversationalist, she made us all feel at ease, even introducing her two-year-old son to us individually.

As time went by with no sign of an attack from France, we relaxed our training schedule slightly and gave the troops a little more free time. Even though we were technically at war with England and France, everyone assumed that the war was really over with the defeat of Poland. October and November passed without event, except that the winter weather was more severe than normal. We conducted winter exercises, to keep the soldiers sharp and occupied. We practiced to become smoother and smoother at cooperating with the infantry and the other batteries. As Christmas neared, the decision was made to let the troops go home for a few days to celebrate the holidays. The high command now apparently saw no threat of an attack from France. Half the troops were to get five days at Christmas and the other half five days at New Year's, as usual.

Niebergall drew Christmas leave, and I was chosen to fill in for him as battalion adjutant, an administrative assistant to the battalion commander. The adjutant had to interface with all the battery commanders and therefore needed to be able to get along with people well.

I had a surprise visitor during this period. Liebelt, my gymnasium classmate, showed up in my office one day in the uniform of an infantryman.

"Liebelt!" I almost shouted when I saw him. I jumped up and pumped his hand. "How good to see you!"

"I am assigned to one of your neighboring units," he said, smiling broadly. "I hoped I would be able to find you."

He and Ebert were still at university studying medicine, but every so often they were called to active duty as medics for a few weeks. Liebelt had recently been called up, but he was soon to return to his studies.

"What do you hear from the others?" I asked him.

"Friedrich was wounded in Poland," he said.

"How serious is the wound?"

"Quite serious," Liebelt responded sadly. "There is some question whether he will survive it."

My heart sank, and Herr Hoffer's image flashed through my mind once more.

On Christmas Eve, those of us in the battery who had not gone home got together in a large wooden building with long tables and benches. Each soldier received a bottle of wine and a small *Weibnachtsstollen* (Christmas cake). We sang Christmas songs, and Hauptmann Wimmer gave a little talk about the importance of our being here to defend our borders. The same thing was happening with other artillery batteries and infantry companies all along Germany's border with Luxembourg, Belgium, Holland, and France. Our purpose was to spend a few hours together and enjoy Christmas Eve. I wandered among the men, wishing them a merry Christmas. I found myself at one of the tables sharing a glass of wine with a group of them that included Boldt, Lammers, Schmitt, and Knecht. These men made my life so much easier, and I told them that I appreciated them. They laughed and kidded me about being lost without them. Except for guard duty and caring for the horses, there were no official duties on Christmas Eve or Christmas. It was so beautiful and peaceful in the Eifel Mountains that the setting seemed almost idyllic.

After the battery party on Christmas Eve, Major Raake served drinks in his quarters in an industrialist's hunting lodge for the officers reporting to him.

"Gentlemen," he toasted, "here is to peace. If the French did not attack us while we were preoccupied with defeating Poland, surely they will not dare to attack us now."

I went home on a five-day leave during the New Year's holiday. It was the first time I had been home since the war in Poland began. Fritz was home also, and it seemed strange to see him in uniform. He playfully saluted me and teased me about not outranking him at home. I assured him that as the older brother, I would always outrank him. My mother was worried about both of us, but I tried to reassure her with Major Raake's logic: if the French had not attacked us when we were preoccupied with Poland, they surely would not dare attack us now. Fritz was full of bluster.

"If they did, we would give them a taste of the same thing the Poles got," he assured her.

My father just looked on and offered no comment, although he seemed uncomfortable with Fritz's bravado. Inge frowned and said nothing.

January 1940 passed with our same routine training. In February, we received orders to board trains and go to central Germany, probably as part of a strategic reserve. Having boarded trains with horses once before made it easier this time. The horses now knew their handlers, had been in maneuvers, and were much more cooperative in loading. We unloaded at Magdeburg and marched to Leitzkau, a small village nearby, where we resumed our training.

The winter weather was very cold, but the men were dressed for it. We had to break the ice to water the horses on most days, and later in January the men could ice-skate in their free time without danger of breaking through the ice. Although 1939–40 was an exceptionally cold winter, we had comfortable quarters. Leitzkau was a pleasant village, and we all liked it there. We had moved from one of the poorest areas of Germany in the Eifel Mountains to one of the richest. Although food was rationed in Germany, the local farmers had plenty of meat, milk, eggs, and butter.

We officers ate at a local inn, providing the food to the innkeeper, who prepared it and served it to us for a fee. The innkeeper, Willy Kurtz, was a very tall man who was around fifty years old. He was a bit heavy and almost bald, with just a ring of hair around the edges of his head. He was a very easy-going person with merry blue eyes. His father had been an innkeeper before him, and he had never known anything else except for a two-year enlistment in the Army during the World War. He and Wimmer often exchanged experiences of trench warfare.

"There were times when my feet were never dry for weeks at a time," Kurtz said once. "My whole body was wet most of the time. We just sat in misery day after day, hating the life we were living, yet fearing the dreaded order to charge."

From listening to the two of them, I began to appreciate Wimmer's fear of trench warfare.

Our division commander, Generalmajor von Studnitz, came to Leitzkau on an inspection tour in March. He seemed to be an interesting man, although as a leutnant I had little direct contact with him. During his inspection trip, he had dinner with us at Kurtz's inn. I was not at von Studnitz's table, but I could see that Kurtz was flustered to be serving a general. He very nearly overlooked the other tables altogether.

On April 3, we moved again, this time to Overath near Cologne, just east of the Rhine. So once more, we loaded aboard trains. By now we had learned how to do it efficiently. We continued our training at Overath, practicing crossing rivers, defending our gun positions against attack, and other operations.

On May 1, 1940, I was ordered to report to Major Raake's office. Raake returned my salute and motioned to a chair.

"Niebergall is being promoted to battery commander in another battalion," he said without preliminaries. "How would you like to become my new adjutant?" My answer was automatic, of course, since becoming battalion adjutant was a big step in the right direction for me.

"I would be honored, Herr Major," I assured him.

I was thrilled and pleased. My career was moving along nicely. In the normal scheme of things, a young artillery officer would progress from forward observation officer to battery officer to battalion adjutant to battery commander. The next step would then be adjutant to the regiment commander—or the General Staff College for the really outstanding.

As Major Raake's adjutant, I got to know him much better. He understood and admired blitzkrieg, as it had been practiced in Poland. Even though he was quite familiar with the trench warfare that Wimmer was so afraid of, Raake was able to see how blitzkrieg rendered it obsolete. I was favorably impressed with Raake and tried to model my own conduct after his.

During this period, I won a pistol-shooting competition that we put together at Overath. Early in May, very shortly after I became battalion adjutant, we started planning an equestrian tournament within our division. Generalmajor von Studnitz was an avid horseman, and very supportive of our plans. This was plainly going to be quite a tournament.

Except that it never happened. On the morning of May 10, 1940, Germany invaded France instead.

14

A T MY LEVEL, I had not been aware that the invasion of France was imminent. Our being moved to Overath, closer to our western border, did not arouse my suspicion because it was normal for us to move frequently. It was not good for troops to be too long in one place, because the soldiers would become complacent and would not take the training seriously. In a new place we had new terrain and new situations that we could exploit during maneuvers. In this case, however, our move was part of a large strategic plan, even though those of us below the level of division commander did not know it.

Major Raake received orders during the evening of May 9, 1940, to be ready to march at eight o'clock the next morning. He called me into his office.

"Be ready to issue an alert at five A.M.," he said. "This is not an exercise. It is the real thing. We are invading France tomorrow. Prepare orders tonight, to be issued in the morning. The unteroffizier who types the orders is not to leave the office where he types them until the orders are issued at five A.M."

"*Jawohl,* Herr Major," I responded. Although very surprised by this turn of events, I snapped into action. My job, as Raake's adjutant, was to make sure that all the details were worked out and that everything went according to plan.

I was out on Schwabenprinz before the alert was issued, checking the batteries to make sure that the cooks had their fires going and the men were being roused out of bed. Everything had to be timed exactly, because the trains were tightly scheduled. Since this was a full alert, we were to leave nothing behind.

By the designated time, each battery was in position and ready to move out. We waited for orders from our division headquarters to move out—but we did not receive them that day. We just waited. Over the radio, we learned that Germany had invaded France. I spent the day talking to Major Raake and the battery commanders while we all waited for the orders that never came. We assumed that the sheer number of troops, tanks, mechanized artillery, and other units taking part in the invasion was so huge that we were just waiting our turn in the sequence of things.

Major Raake was sure this would be another blitz-krieg operation, just like Poland. Wimmer was equally sure that we would get bogged down in trench warfare again, just as we had in the World War. Hauptmann Witnauer, commander of Second Battery, and Hauptmann Wagner, Commander of Third Battery, tended to agree with Raake. Since both were in their late twenties, neither had Wimmer's dread of trench warfare.

It was a very long day, just sitting and waiting for orders to move out. Raake's office, as the nerve center of our battalion, bustled with activity as the leutnants from the various batteries checked with us periodically to learn the latest news. All the news we received was positive. Our troops were progressing nicely in Luxembourg, Belgium, and Holland. I accompanied Raake in the afternoon as he visited the batteries to mingle with the troops and gauge their morale. We found their spirits quite high, especially with all the positive news, although, like us, they were tired of waiting and eager to move out. If they were afraid of the prospect of combat, I could not detect it. They were joking and playing around, just as they would have if they had been back at Plauen. All the reserve officers we talked to who had experienced trench warfare during the World War were very concerned about what was going to happen. All the young officers, on the other hand, assumed that the invasion of France would be similar to the invasion of Poland.

On the next morning, May 11, 1940, we finally received orders to move. I felt a little frustrated once again at being horse-drawn artillery instead of mechanized artillery. We were obviously going to be at least one full day behind the fighting, and with horse-drawn artillery we would probably fall farther and farther behind. We hooked the horses to the carts, guns, and wagons and marched about twenty-five kilometers to our designated train station. The planning for the move had all been done by our division's operations officer. It was my job to have the batteries at the designated places at the designated times, to determine which battery went first, and in general to be responsible for logistics.

Loading the train took about forty-five minutes for each battery, since we had now done it enough times to become fairly efficient at it. We boarded the trains in a suburb of Cologne. With three batteries, three trains were required to move the battalion. We were on the trains for only eighteen kilometers, which included crossing the Rhine River. We were probably moved by train because the road bridges were being used for the tanks and mechanized artillery. We unloaded at Euskirchen, southwest of Cologne, where we hooked the horses to the equipment again and marched toward the Belgian border.

We were part of Army Group A, commanded by Generaloberst von Rundsted; Fourth Army, commanded by Generaloberst von Kluge; and 8th Army Korps, commanded by General Heitz. We crossed into Belgium on May 13. The infantry regiment we supported marched ahead of us, which was the normal marching order, because we had to be ready to fight at a moment's notice. We went through the Ardennes Forest, where the terrain was heavily wooded rolling hills. We marched for seven straight days before getting a day off to rest.

We had to be ready to move out at 6:00 A.M. In our battalion, the horse people, the cook, and one officer from each battery got up at 4:30. At that early hour, it was still dark. It was always cold, and it was usually wet with early-morning dew if not with rain. The birds would soon begin to protest our disturbing their sleep as the cook started fires under the coffee and tea kettles and the two huge cooking drums on their field kitchens. The cooks would put everything for a thick stew in the large drums and build fires under the drums before we left at 6:00. The stew would continue to cook on the field kitchen wagon as we marched. The smell of the smoke from the cook's fires mingled with the odor of the earth's dampness.

A hot cup of tea usually helped me fight off the chill of the early-morning air. The men would begin to stir, their grunts and slow-motion movements bringing the area alive with activity as the dawn chased away the mystery of the night. The men would make their way to the field kitchens for coffee or tea, bread with butter and jam, and sometimes a can of liverwurst or an equivalent. Then the clanking of chains, the clunking of heavy wheels on rough terrain, and the creaking of leather harnesses would fill the early morning as the batteries moved into marching position. At 6:00 we would move out, and another day would begin.

After four hours or so, we would stop for the main meal of the day. We always stopped where there was water for the horses, even if it was only a small creek. We would feed and water the horses and check them for saddle or harness sores and loose shoes before we ate. Since there was no enemy resistance, the field kitchens were set up and the cooks dispensed the hot meal that had been cooking as we marched. We had forty-five minutes to eat. This was usually our only hot meal of the day, although the cooks might prepare a soup for the evening meal. They also served coffee and tea at breaks. After lunch, we would march until 5:00 or 6:00 P.M., or until we reached our objective for the day. Of course, weather would sometimes affect our pace. We averaged forty kilometers per day, but it varied from twenty to fifty depending upon the weather and the terrain.

Our division staff assigned our goal for each day, which was where we would spend the night. If possible, we tried to make it to a village, where water and quarters would be available. If we could not make it to a village, we slept on the ground or in tents. The first thing we did upon stopping was to post ten to fifteen sentries (more in villages and wooded areas, fewer in open areas) and arrange all the guns and vehicles so we could fight or move out immediately if that should prove necessary. We knew where the front was, so we positioned the guns against attack from that direction. The horses were watered and fed, and then the men were fed.

Each battery commander would then gather most of his 185 men around him and explain what was happening at the front, where the enemy line was, and so on. It would be at least 7:30 by then, and the men would rest and talk for a while or write letters before turning in. Most of the officers had sleeping bags, and the soldiers had horse blankets. We would find the most comfortable place we could and just bed down. After twelve hours in the saddle and then another hour checking to see that everything was in order, I never had any trouble falling asleep.

When it rained, we tried to get into a house or a barn if we were in a village. If we were in the open, everyone had one part of a tent (which doubled as a raincoat), and four people could put their parts together to make a tent in which four people could sleep. Each battery commander always had a tent because he had to have a place that was secure against rain and wind where he could do his map work. Usually he shared his tent with one of his leutnants.

We could not hear the battles that were being fought ahead of us, because we were now two days behind the invasion force, but we could see the evidence left behind.

As we marched we saw the battlefields—the burned tanks, blown-up bridges, and dead livestock. Trees would be felled across our path every few hundred meters; most had been cleared, but sometimes we would have to clear them away. Where bridges were blown, the engineer units had built pontoon bridges.

At Bra, Belgium, we had to leave the first horse behind because of exhaustion. We had bivouacked in a park, and the next morning the horse simply could go no farther. His wind was broken. I wondered at the time whether Stabs-Veterinär Lützow, our battalion veterinarian, was not as exhausted as the horse. He not only had to ride all day, but had to care for the horses who needed his attention at night. He was getting so little sleep at night that I often saw him sleeping on his horse as we marched during the day.

Other candidates for exhaustion were the battery blacksmiths. Things were not bad for them in the beginning, but when we reached Bomal, Belgium, we crossed the Ourthe River on a pontoon bridge. On a steep bank on the far side of the river, one gun's wheel was damaged and we had to wait while the battery's blacksmith fixed it. From then on, the equipment began to break down frequently, and we had many stops while the blacksmiths and their assistants fixed things.

Bonsin, Belgium, was dusty and hot. South of the village of Houx, we crossed the Maas River on a pontoon bridge. On May 17, our division's reconnaissance battalion took seven hundred prisoners. On May 18, we learned that Brussels had surrendered to us. At Osternerée, we bivouacked in a beautiful park on the estate of the Belgian king. Here, on May 19, our whole division finally got a full day of rest. The men spent the day bathing, washing clothes, and writing letters. Many of them spent a great part of the day just catching up on sleep. We resumed our march on May 20 and advanced to Rance, Belgium, where we had to blast away many large trees that had been felled in our path. We also passed trucks here that were loaded with French officers being taken to Germany as prisoners of war.

On May 21, 1940, we finally crossed into France. On that date, we were also unexpectedly detached from Army Group A and assigned to Army Group Kleist (named for Generaloberst Kleist). We then went almost in a straight line to the Somme River.

So far, things had been very much like maneuvers for us, except that we were following in the wake of real battles, covering the same ground where the battles had occurred a few days earlier and seeing the residue of real war. We were familiar with the dust and the smells of burned powder and gasoline from maneuvers, but this was our first exposure to the smell of death. Dead cattle and other livestock were everywhere, the victims of bullets, mortars, artillery shells, and bombs. Their bloating carcasses lay in the fields with their legs sticking up. I learned that the smell of rotting flesh, dust, burned powder, smoke, and gasoline was the smell of combat. This was my first exposure to it, but it was an odor that was to become all too familiar to me during the next five years.

My first sight of a dead soldier was an unexpected shock. We had been trained to deliver death quickly and efficiently, and we knew that in war people get killed. But "knowing" it intellectually was entirely different from seeing and experiencing it. We had known officers from our own regiment who had been killed in Poland, of course, and we felt a sense of loss—but the word "killed" still had a clinical connotation about it compared to its meaning when you saw lying on the ground before you a bloodied, mutilated, foul-smelling corpse that had previously been a vital, living human being. Now the former human being was just a gruesome, lifeless thing on the ground.

The first dead soldiers I saw were French Moroccans. They had been killed in a cemetery, and they lay where they had fallen, their limbs in grotesque positions, their eyes and mouths open. The experience was impossible to forget. This was what we were doing to people and what they were doing to us. It was devastating to realize that this was what we had to look forward to every day, day after day, until the war was over. From that moment on, death hovered near us wherever we went. We had been trained for combat, however, and we had to learn to accept the ever-present nearness of death.

We marched from Englancourt to Guise, which had been virtually destroyed. Burned-out tanks littered the streets, and the road exiting the town was steep and narrow and congested with abandoned French vehicles. We crossed the Oise River at Proix, the Somme Canal at Morcourt, and then we bivouacked on a large farm at Omissy. Then to Moislains, and from there to Hénencourt.

Maneuvers had not prepared us for the refugees and the empty houses. We did not go through big cities with our horses and cannons, but stayed to the countryside. The farms had been abandoned, and we often encountered the refugees from them. They had left their homes because they heard the sounds of battle coming toward them. Because they did not know what else to do, they had panicked and run away. It was sad to see them: women, children, and old men with bicycles and horse-drawn carts loaded with whatever they could carry, going they knew not where. People jammed the roads with their carts and wagons loaded with whatever personal belongings they had hurriedly thrown together. Actually, a blitzkrieg attack was like a tornado that would pass quickly, and the best thing they could have done was to go into their cellars and wait for the battle to pass them by. We always told them to go back, that the battle had passed on and there was nothing left to fear, but they often seemed dazed and uncomprehending. I felt sorry that we had to do this to them. They were paying a terrible price because France had declared war on us.

We were amazed at the speed of our breakthrough in

Luxembourg, Belgium, Holland, and northern France. On May 25, we approached the Somme River, where the French Army had built fortified positions and was apparently determined to stop us. Our tanks had gone all the way to the coast of the English Channel at Dunkirk with their blitzkrieg operation, but the German Army as a whole had progressed no farther than the Somme River. It was now massing there for a huge assault to break through the fortified French line and then move on to Paris.

As we approached the Somme River, Raake, Wimmer, Wagner, Witnauer, and I went ahead, along with our regiment's infantry commanders, to look the area over. Our sector of the line had been assigned to us on the map by our division staff, but specific locations for infantry companies and artillery batteries could not be determined until the commanders could look over the terrain in person. Our infantry regiment commander, Oberst Haushofer, made specific assignments within our sector to each infantry battalion, and a battery of artillery supported each infantry battalion. The artillery battery commanders then found the best observation points and the best positions for the guns in their sectors. When we had made specific assignments for all units, we sent wachtmeisters back to lead the units to their assigned emplacements.

We had a good position on a high ridge on the north side of the river. Conveniently, a road ran along the ridge, above the river. Opposite us, across the river, the bank rose slightly, and we could see for four or five kilometers. The French had only their forwardmost positions in this exposed area, hidden among the trees at the intersections of some small creeks that fed the Somme. The small village of Proyart was there, fortified by trenches. Their main line of defense was four or five kilometers farther back in a series of hills that lay before the French village of Villers-Bretonneux. The fact that we were on high ground just above the river and their main line of defense was about five kilometers on the other side of the river would make our job easier when it came time to attack. We knew we would not encounter determined resistance until we reached their main line of defense close to Villers-Bretonneux.

The Somme River was about a hundred meters wide where we were. Our men dug in and began to build bunkers. We did not know how long we would be here, but it was obviously going to be a major operation when we moved out, so we guessed it would be at least several days. Living conditions for the men were even more primitive than they had been in the Eifel Mountains, but they accommodated themselves as best they could. We set up our battalion headquarters in an abandoned country home just behind the ridge. As battalion adjutant, I was able to sleep in the house instead of in a bunker.

It was here that we fired our first round of the war and experienced our first direct combat. In the afternoon of the day after our arrival, the French attacked us with a heavy artillery barrage. The sound of the exploding artillery shells was nerve-racking at first, but I was surprised at how quickly I got used to it. The duel between their artillery and ours continued for what seemed an eternity, during which our world was filled with explosions, the smell of burned powder, trembling earth, and frenzied activity. Our guncrews, pumped full of adrenaline by fear and excitement, hurled shell after shell at the French. When it was over, we were almost in a daze—from exhaustion, from excitement, and from the sudden silence following the incredible roar of combat. We actually felt light-headed.

I began to check with the batteries to determine casualties and found everyone extremely excited. We had taken casualties, however, and Hauptmann Wagner, battery commander of the Third Battery, had been seriously wounded by shrapnel. He was treated by medics at a field station and then sent to the rear for hospitalization. As soon as his physical condition permitted, he would be returned to a hospital near his home in Germany. Wagner's battery officer, Oberleutnant Karl Schumann, moved up to become Third Battery's new battery commander.

When Wagner was hit, I began finally to be seriously aware of my own mortality. It was clear that it could just as easily have been me, or any of us, and that in fact any of us could be next. It was difficult for me to realize that I was not immortal.

It began to rain heavily that evening, and the soldiers in foxholes abandoned them and put up their tents. I was very glad to be inside a dry house where I could listen to the patter of the rain on the roof and not be out in it. Our motorized artillery kept up harassing fire on the French all during the night. The next day was quiet except for our nuisance artillery fire directed at crossroads and any other known strategic targets behind enemy lines—and the French nuisance artillery fire attempting to do the same to us.

On May 28, the French hit us again, this time not just with artillery but with bombers, fighter planes, and armored vehicles as well. The artillery opened up on us first, and we immediately began to respond. The crashing of shells and the constant roar of combat began again, and the adrenaline flowed again. Suddenly we became aware that the explosions occurring around us, sending dirt and debris high into the air, were considerably more than the French artillery could be firing, and we realized that a few French airplanes were bombing us. As we continued our artillery barrage, the French bombers were followed by a dozen or more fighters making strafing runs on us. The sounds of the airplanes just added to the roar and confusion of battle. About twenty armored vehicles tried attacking us next, but they were no match for our artillery and quickly scurried back toward Proyart. We determined after the action that our battalion had fired 361 rounds to help stop the attack. We took heavy nuisance artillery fire during the night, and we answered with three salvos of our own every hour. We were becoming so accustomed to the sound of artillery that the lack of it would have seemed abnormal. How quickly the definition of "normal" can change in just a few short days.

I was finding combat to be both exhilarating and frightening. It was exhilarating because while the noise and action were going on we lived in a high state of excitement. It was frightening because at any moment an exploding shell could blast us into eternity. No one could know one minute whether he would be alive the next.

Since the French tanks had gone to the English Channel just as ours had, the only combat occurring was artillery exchanges, only occasionally accompanied by airplanes and armored vehicles, and infantry patrols sent out to probe the four or five kilometers of level ground between the river and the hills. The purpose of the patrols was to find out what was there, to try to take prisoners, and to clean out the area so the French could not see us building pontoon bridges across the river and try to disrupt the work of the engineers. The patrols would vary in size from five or six men to a whole company of 180 men, depending on the purpose of the patrol. From captured prisoners the division determined that opposite us were the 4th French Colonial Division with Senegalese infantry regiments and the 7th French North African Division with the 10th Moroccan Regiment and the 31st Algerian Regiment.

My job was to be in contact with all the batteries, to handle logistics for the battalion, and to be ready to issue orders to the batteries to move up if the infantry should break through. If our infantry broke through, the artillery would have to move out also to prevent the infantry from moving out of our range so we would not be able to support them. We could not move all three batteries at once, however, because artillery had to be available at all times to offer assistance if the enemy should counterattack our infantry. The batteries would move out one at a time, and the battalion staff would go with the first battery so they could determine where the other two batteries should go into position.

Meanwhile, we continued to duel with the French artillery. We would select strategic targets to disturb the enemy, to give him no rest, to disrupt road crossings or bridges or communications. We would sometimes fire 100 to 150 rounds along a two-kilometer stretch. We would often fire at the French rear echelon just to keep the personnel there off balance. Mostly, such fire was for nuisance value, but occasionally it could do real harm to the enemy.

Altogether, we were at the Somme River nine days before launching our attack against the fortified French positions. When the operation at Dunkirk ended with the evacuation of much of the British Army to England and our tanks were free for further action, we prepared an attack to break through the French defenses and proceed south toward Paris.

The night of June 4 was filled with tension. The men were obviously restless. Major Raake came to the makeshift desk where I was working in my office and sat down. He lit a cigarette and smoked in slow, deliberate puffs, inhaling deeply and exhaling slowly.

"Working late, Knappe?" he asked finally.

"Catching up on my paperwork," I said.

"The French are burrowed in like moles," Raake said, speaking what was really on his mind. "And they obviously have no shortage of artillery. This will not be an easy assault. My hunch is that they know tomorrow is the date for our attack."

"We should be able to help the infantry a great deal," I suggested. "We know exactly where they are, and we are zeroed in on them." I felt confident that our assault would be successful.

"Proyart is well protected by those hills in front of it," Raake countered. "The French will be firing down on our infantry from those heights, and their Moroccan and Senegalese soldiers are fierce fighters. We would make a bad

mistake to underestimate them." He stood and snuffed out
his cigarette. "Good night, Knappe," he said. "It is going
to be a short night and a very long day tomorrow." With
that, he left. It was disturbing to see Raake worried. He
was normally unflappable.

The village of Proyart was the infantry's goal for the
first day. We opened our artillery barrage on the French
defensive lines at 5:00 A.M. We knew the exact distances
and the sight corrections to make to hit almost any target.
We knew where the roads were in back of their lines, and
we knew where all the crossroads and sensitive places
were.

When our infantry attacked, we shifted our fire to the
enemy artillery and mortar positions. We knew where
those positions were from our own observations and from
aircraft observations. Major Raake determined the targets
for each battery and the number of rounds to be fired at
each target. The Luftwaffe also bombed the French positions. Our infantry took the hills before Proyart, but then
they were stopped by heavy French artillery fire and were
unable to take the village. When they were unable to
achieve their objective the first day, they dug in; they had
to try again, of course, but they were exhausted and decided to try again the next day. We had to know where they
were dug in so we would not fire on them. We continued
with heavy fire during the day and on through the night.

In the evening, as I prepared the report of the day's
activity for Raake's signature, Hauptmann Wimmer suddenly appeared in my office. It was immediately evident
from the look on his face that something was terribly
wrong.

"Herr Hauptmann, what is it?"

"Rehberg," he said. "He is dead. I thought you would
want to know, since he was your friend."

I heard the words, but their meaning did not sink in
immediately. "What do you mean?" I asked stupidly.

"Hill 84, west of Proyart," he added, as if filling out a

statistical report. "A sniper got him. The Senegalese like to hide in the trees and shoot down on us. One of them killed him."

It was beginning to register, and I felt oddly as if I were in a daze. I felt myself grow cold in spite of the early-summer warmth. Wimmer stood in an awkward position, looking at me with a pained expression.

"After more than twenty years, I had really forgotten what it was like," he said. Then, suddenly, he turned and disappeared as quickly as he had appeared.

I finished the report, although my mind was hardly on it. Then I went out in the evening air to try to calm the turmoil in my mind. The flashes of the artillery, and the crashes that followed a split second later as our batteries continued firing during the night, seemed to punctuate Rehberg's death. *People get killed in war,* I told myself. It had to happen sometime that I would lose a close friend in combat.

I decided to talk to Raake about it. Maybe he had experienced it before and could help me adapt. I went back inside and into Raake's office.

"What is wrong, Knappe?" he asked when he looked at me.

"Leutnant Rehberg is dead," I said simply.

Raake stared at me for a moment. "I think you need a drink," he said finally, reaching into a drawer. He poured me a cognac and I took a sip. The strong liquor had a surprisingly calming effect on my nerves. Raake lit a cigarette and took a long drag.

"The price of war is very high," he said as he stood and walked to the window, staring out into the darkness. "Germany cannot regain the position it should have in Europe without war, because our enemies in the west will not permit it. And we cannot fight without suffering casualties and fatalities." He turned away from the window and faced me. "Leutnant Rehberg's life is one price we have to pay to restore Germany to its rightful position in Europe."

"Of course," I said. For a brief second, Herr Hoffer passed through my mind's eye. He, in a way, had predicted Rehberg's death.

"We will all lose close friends before this is over, Knappe. Probably the most effective solution is not to make friends, but that is not practical. We are going to need all the friends we can get to endure what is ahead of us. We cannot stop with France. We will have to deal with England as well. We just have to learn to take the loss of our friends like men."

"Yes, you are right," I said, finishing my drink. "Thank you, Herr Major."

I shed tears for a friend in the still darkness of that night. Death had hovered nearby for some time, but this was the first time it had touched me so closely. Hauptmann Wagner had been badly wounded, but he had gone home alive to convalesce. Rehberg would not go home. Ever. He had vanished from the face of the earth. He had been a friend, and his death brought the utter destructiveness of war home to me as nothing else could have. This was not a game, as maneuvers had always been. Combat meant having the lives of those you cared for snuffed out in an instant.

Rehberg's body was brought back during the night, under the cover of darkness. We buried him at seven o'clock the next morning, in a cemetery from the World War. I attended his funeral, along with Wimmer and fifteen of the men from the battery. His body was not mutilated. Although he was only twenty-two years old, he looked even younger in death—as if he should be at home, in the first flush of young adulthood, instead of lying there as a cold and cadaverous victim of war. My own mortality became a part of my mind-set from that moment on. Seeing the dead Moroccan soldiers had been a terrible experience—but they had been the enemy. When the body lying before you is someone you have known and worked with, someone you liked and admired, someone whose life was just beginning . . .

Army life could never again be the carefree existence it had been during my garrison duty at Plauen. But we had to learn to accept facts and try to go on with our duties. One thing that made it just a little easier was that we buried Rehberg and several infantrymen who had been killed at the same time in a cemetery from the last war—and the relative numbers of graves demonstrated that the World War had been much worse. We could see that hundreds of World War dead had been buried in the cemetery, and we were burying just a few. Our method of warfare obviously caused fewer casualties. Still, that knowledge offered little comfort.

Rehberg was replaced by Leutnant Jaschke, a small man with thinning blond hair, blue eyes, and a fair complexion. He proved to be competent and capable.

At five-thirty the next morning, we opened up with fifteen minutes of concentrated annihilation fire on Proyart. Then we lifted our fire and the infantry attacked again. Our forward observation officers tried to watch where our infantry was and where the enemy was and direct our fire on the French lines. We also continued our nuisance rounds on the enemy's rear echelon, on bridges, on crossroads, and on anything of strategic value to the enemy. But our priority was always to support the infantry.

In moving our batteries across the Somme River, we discovered while investigating potential gun positions that the French had mined the roads, so we stayed off them. Before we could set up all of our guns on the other side of the river, we learned from our forward observers that Proyart had fallen to us, so we just kept going. We turned south, toward Paris, and resumed our marching formation. Our infantry took 314 Moroccan prisoners at Proyart, whom we passed as we moved forward.

During the nine days we had spent at the Somme River, the French had prepared bridges to be blown up on all the roads to Paris, and now they blew them up as they retreated. On June 8, at the Avre River, the enemy took advantage of the natural defensive position on the far side of the river to turn and make another stand. This time, our entire artillery regiment went into position—all thirty-six 105mm cannons and twelve heavy 150mm howitzers—and laid down a withering barrage of artillery fire on the French position on the opposite side of the river. The enemy withdrew, and we crossed the river on pontoon bridges.

At Sacy le Grand, we went into position at the Oise River. The French had once more turned to fight at the natural defensive position provided by a river with all its bridges blown. Here we could set up some of our guns close to the river and fire point-blank into the enemy machine-gun nests across the river. Our infantry then sent a patrol across, followed soon by the rest of the infantry, which deployed on the opposite bank. By 9:00 P.M., our engineers had finished a pontoon bridge, and we sent one artillery battery across the river. During the night, our division intercepted a message from the French Fourth Army headquarters instructing their troops to disengage. We held our fire and let them withdraw in order to keep our casualties to a minimum, although the French kept up some rifle and machine-gun fire to make us think they were all still there. When we sent our remaining artillery batteries across the pontoon bridge, one of the pontoons sank and we were held up for four hours while the engineers were called back to repair the bridge. Then we finally crossed in full force and resumed our march toward Paris, although the French felled a lot of trees across the roads to impede our march. Our infantry lost twelve men during the fight at the Oise River.

We went into position again at Verneuil and Fleurines. On the evening of June 11, 1940, the French attacked us at Senlis at 10:00 P.M. The attack continued through the night and the next day. The constant roar of combat—a sound that incorporated the explosion of artillery and mortars, the stutter of machine guns, and the crack of rifle fire all packaged together like the sound of a hurricane—seemed an inherent part of life now. Three times during the battle, we had to change our observation posts when they came under heavy enemy artillery fire. At 5:00 P.M. on June 12, we moved our batteries back to the woods north of Senlis while our infantry regrouped, and the French immediately attacked us there with aircraft and artillery. At 4:00 P.M. on June 13, our infantry launched its second attack on Senlis. We took heavy enemy artillery fire on our own guns, our observation posts took light-machine-gun fire from French Senegalese troops in trees, and French airplanes strafed our rear-echelon positions. We moved our observation post back one hundred meters into a large basement, and during the night the vacated observation post took a direct hit from the French artillery. We finally captured Senlis and resumed our march south toward Paris. It had been a fierce and bloody battle, with heavy losses on both sides, but it was our last big battle on the road to Paris.

On June 14, from 8:00 A.M. until 3:00 P.M., we marched forty-five kilometers in one nonstop dash and went into position just short of the Marne River, in a beautiful park about thirty-five kilometers northeast of the center of Paris. We could see the Eiffel Tower from the park. We had marched a total of eight hundred kilometers from Overath to Paris. We had a chance to relax for a few hours here and to wash up, which had become very important to us by now because hygiene had been taking a backseat to daily combat.

At 9:00 P.M., however, we suddenly had an alert and were ordered to move into position just south of Tremblay, at the Ourcq Canal, which lay between us and the Marne River. Paris had been declared an open city (meaning that the defenders would not resist in order to prevent further damage to the city) the day before, but some French troops firing from the other side of the canal were sailors who had been drafted for the defense of Paris and apparently had not received word that they were not to resist. A bridge over the canal had not been blown, and these French sailors were defending it with machine guns.

It was a heavily wooded area, dotted with little villages. The canal was at the south end of one of these villages. A street ran through the village, flanked on each side by stores and houses. About thirty yards beyond a sharp bend in the street was the bridge. Our infantry had been pinned down at the bridge by the French machine guns firing from the other side of the canal, which was about twelve meters wide. After trying and failing to silence the machine guns with mortars, the infantry asked the artillery for help. We could not shoot from behind with an observer up front, as we normally did, because it was in a wooded area and the distance was too short. The only way was to bring a gun forward and fire directly into the machine-gun positions, as we had at the Oise River.

I was up front with the infantry, and when they asked for help I called for a 105mm gun from the First Battery to come up. The infantry commander showed me a house across the canal, to the right side of the bridge, from which the French machine guns were firing. I went to the gun and guncrew to get things ready. We had to have the gun ready to fire, push it around the bend (behind which we were protected by a building), aim, and fire at the machine guns about twenty-five meters away before they could get us with their fire. It was not my job to do this, but I wanted to do it to make sure it was effective. Seven of us manned the gun. The crew was headed by a wachtmeister instead of the usual gefreiter, apparently because the wachtmeister also wanted to make certain that nothing went wrong. The crew loaded the gun, and I checked to make certain nothing had been overlooked and everything was ready.

"At my command, we will push the gun around the corner, and I will aim the gun and give the order to fire.

Everyone understand?" I looked around, and all the six men nodded.

"Let's go!" I ordered.

We pushed the gun around the corner of the building at the bend. Pinpoints of light flashed from the machine guns in the basement across the canal as we aimed the gun and jerked the cord. The French had got their rounds off first, and by the time our gun fired, all seven of us were sprawled on the ground. I knew I had been hit in the left wrist, but I peered across the canal to see if we had knocked out the enemy machine guns. Only smoke now came from the basement where the machine guns had been located, and our infantry was already dashing across the bridge.

I ducked back to safety around the corner of the building to examine my wrist. A bullet had entered through the back of my hand and exited through my wrist. Blood was oozing out of the wound. It felt numb now; the pain would come later. I quickly inspected the rest of my body. Although no other bullets had touched my flesh, I found a hole through the side of my jacket, one through my sleeve, and one through my map case. I silently counted my blessings that I had only been hit in the wrist. The machine gunner was obviously a good shot, especially for a sailor! Although three of the other men had also been hit, no one had been killed.

The bridge was now open to us, and the next morning the division was in Paris.

15

INFANTRY MEDICS IMMEDIATELY tended to those of us who had been hit, bandaging our wounds as well as possible. They put some medication on my wound and then wrapped gauze around my hand and wrist. The wound still felt numb; the pain had not yet started. The infantry brought up an ambulance and loaded us into the back of it, where we sat on benches. The wachtmeister had been hit in the shoulder, and the kanoniers had been hit in the thigh and right side respectively. Despite our wounds, we left with the knowledge that our efforts had cleared the way for the infantry.

The ambulance took us to a field hospital a few kilometers behind the lines, where a doctor looked at our wounds. They put on better dressings, gave us tetanus shots, and gave us some medication to prevent infection. We were then loaded on a bus with other wounded soldiers and taken to a hospital at Noyen, where we were to catch an airplane to Bonn the next morning. The bus trip was not especially pleasant, since we were all beginning to recover from the shock of being wounded and the pain was beginning. There was very little talk, just an occasional groan from someone. The jolting bus had no concern for painful injuries. Pain can rob the sweetness from the taste of victory.

Arriving at the hospital at Noyen around midnight, we were quickly processed and assigned to beds. We were given pain medication to enable us to sleep, and I went to sleep thinking what a foolish thing I had done to take such a needless risk. It could easily have cost me my life. I wondered for a moment if I had subconsciously done it to prove my bravery. I shuddered involuntarily at the thought. I could have been killed so easily in that hail of bullets. But many men had been killed during this campaign, and I would have been just one more. I went to sleep very glad to be alive, even with pain.

Medics woke us early the next morning, gave us breakfast, and loaded us back aboard the bus to be taken to the transport airplane that would fly us to Bonn. By now my wrist was throbbing painfully and my hand was beginning to swell. The airplane had no seats, but the crew gave us each a cushion to sit on. We made ourselves as comfortable as possible on the floor of the airplane for the flight to Bonn. We were all able to walk; apparently the more seriously wounded were kept in hospitals in France.

Conversations sprang up among the wounded men as the flight droned on, mostly about the action in which people were wounded. Laughter was sprinkled throughout the conversations now. I was beginning to learn how the human mind tries to cope with the horrors of combat.

We landed at Bonn, where medics once again put us on a bus and took us to a hospital. A doctor inspected my wrist, put a fresh dressing on it, and told me he would have to wait until the swelling went down before putting a cast on it. I learned here that my division had held a parade in Paris and I had missed it, just as I had missed the parade at Plauen after the Sudetenland operation. I called my parents to let them know I was on my way home and that I was not badly hurt.

I stayed in Bonn nearly three weeks, just waiting for the swelling to come down. On June 19, while at Bonn, I was awarded the Iron Cross Second Class and the Verwundeten-Abzeichen in black (equivalent to the American Purple Heart; it was black for the first time a soldier was wounded, silver for the third time, and gold for the fifth time). Since I was not restricted to the hospital, I spent the days resting, going to restaurants and movies, and exploring the city. Bonn, the birthplace of Beethoven, was just a sleepy little town at the time.

Finally, after almost three weeks, the swelling had almost left my hand and the doctor put a cast on it. I asked to be transferred to a hospital in Leipzig, and the hospital administrator wrote me a train ticket to Leipzig.

I checked into the hospital in Leipzig on July 9, 1940. The doctor there removed my cast and inspected my hand. The machine-gun bullet had smashed some small bones in my hand and severed the sensory nerve for several of my fingers. The artery and the motor nerve were undamaged, however, so I was lucky. The doctor put a new cast on my wrist. The wrist had to heal itself. All the doctors could do was try to prevent infection.

I was not restricted to the hospital, and my parents' home was only twenty minutes from the hospital by streetcar. The familiar green-and-beige streetcars of Leipzig made me feel at home. I climbed the stairs to my parents' second-floor apartment feeling that it was very good to be home again. The happiness in my mother's face when she saw me was almost worth getting wounded for.

I was more aware of the apartment and little details of my family's appearance than ever before. I assumed this was a result of my close brush with death. I visited my father at his restaurant and nightclub that first day, rather than waiting for him to come home. He was as surprised and emotional as my mother had been, and we sat at a table and talked for two hours. Inge returned home in late afternoon from the hospital where she was a nurse. Even she seemed glad to see me and concerned about my wound. It felt very good to be back home with my family, except for Fritz, who was in the Army at Jena. My father was extremely proud of all that Germany had achieved, and he was proud that I had been part of it.

I looked forward to seeing Liebelt and Ebert while I was in Leipzig. I did not have to wait long, as they heard I was in town. I met them at a nightclub. They were there waiting for me. It was pure joy to be with old friends and to be entirely safe. It was as though we had never been apart.

"How is Friedrich doing?" I finally asked.

"You do not know?" Ebert asked, his voice dropping to a whisper.

"Know what?" My eyes darted from Ebert to Liebelt. Then the significance of their silence slapped me in the face. They both took deep breaths at the same time.

"I thought you knew," Liebelt said.

The same desperate, unhappy feeling I'd had when Rehberg was killed washed over me again. So Friedrich had died of the wounds he had received in Poland. I remembered Raake's counsel when Rehberg was killed. Friedrich's life was another price we had to pay for our success.

I learned where Friedrich was buried and visited his grave the next day. I stood in a drizzling rain, on wet, soggy ground by his grave, under an ugly overcast sky, just feeling empty. Poor Friedrich. He had been so full of life, and so sure of all the good things life had in store for him. Our ski trip after graduating from gymnasium came rushing back. Could it really have been only four years ago? So much had happened since then, and I felt so much older. I decided it was best not to dwell on such things, but to try to concentrate instead on what had been accomplished in that time.

I went home from the hospital every day, and I was even allowed to stay at home on the weekends. Most days I went to a movie or to one of the afternoon cafés that had dancing. Public dancing had been banned while the fighting was going on and while our soldiers were dying in France, but now it was permitted again. I did not dance, because my arm was in a sling, but I enjoyed watching other couples.

One afternoon in a café, I watched a naval officer at a table with two girls. The more attractive girl did not appear to be the one who was with him, although he danced with both of them. When the music was over there, I went to another café after getting something to eat. After a while, the naval officer and girls came there as well. Since these were the two nicest places in Leipzig, it was not a great coincidence. They recognized me when they came in, and I smiled at them. They sat down a few tables away from me, and I found it difficult to keep my eyes away from the prettier girl. She had beautiful brunette hair, a petite but shapely build, and a pretty face with high cheekbones.

When the musicians played the last dance, I was determined to ask her to dance in spite of my sling. Her blue eyes sparkled as she smiled. "Of course," she said, rising. She did not even deign to glance at my sling.

Dancing was just a little awkward with one arm in a sling, but we managed. We danced and talked, and she was friendly and witty. I was quite taken with her. I mentioned a piano concert that I planned to attend the following week and asked if she planned to go. She was coquettish and noncommittal, but I felt I had reason to hope she would be there.

At the piano concert the next week, I watched for her even though there were several hundred people there. I saw her come into the lobby and went up behind her and tapped her on the shoulder.

"Hello there," I said when she turned around.

"Well," she said, smiling impishly. "What a surprise!"

We sat together during the concert. From then on, we were together practically every day until I returned to duty. Her name was Lieselotte, abbreviated Lilo, and she was a nineteen-year-old photographer who managed a portrait studio.

Lilo and I spent our evenings going to dinner, to the theater, to concerts, and to dances. I would pick her up at the studio when she got off work, and we would spend the evening together. She was great fun to be with, light-hearted and gay, with a quick smile and a ready laugh. She loved life. We had about a month together before I returned to duty.

The mood of all the people I met during my convalescence was very positive. The surrender of France was a great victory for Germany. We had a friendship treaty with Russia, so England was the only remaining hostile power. But we recognized that England could be a real problem for us. Although we had just thrown the British Army out of Europe, we knew we would not be able to invade England without heavy losses. At this time, everything was pretty normal in Germany except that a declared state of war existed between Germany and England. Of course, rationing was still in effect, but the people were relaxed, and it was a time of great national pride.

The doctor at the hospital told me I could not return to duty until I could make a fist. As much as I was enjoying my convalescence in Leipzig, and especially Lilo's company, I was ready to return to military life. I started then to work my hand wherever I was, at the movies, in restaurants, everywhere. By September 1940, I could make a fist and the doctor released me to return to duty. I had now been in the Army four years.

I left Leipzig the morning of September 5, 1940. Lilo went with me to the train station to bid me goodbye. I hated leaving her. Meeting Lilo had been the highlight of my convalescent leave, and meeting her had helped offset the sadness of Friedrich's death. Thinking of Friedrich made me shudder, and I concentrated on thinking about Lilo instead.

I had been away from my battalion approximately three months, from June until September. I went first to Plauen, which was my home base when I was in Germany (every Army unit in the field had a home base in Germany). Plauen looked exactly as I remembered it. I had been gone from there only a year. Why did it seem so much longer? So much had happened during that year—in the Eifel Mountains, at Leitzkau, at Overath, at Proyart on the Somme River, at all the other towns and rivers where the French turned to fight on our march through France. I felt different and much older than I had when I last saw the assembly area by the barracks. I looked over the parade ground where we had staged so many parades and exercises. Maneuvers and exercises had been so textbook-logical then. We had staged mock battles, debated tactics and logistics—*and then had dinner and relaxed.* What a huge gulf existed between theory and reality—not physically, because combat was remarkably similar to maneuvers, but in the realization of the price that had to be paid in human lives and suffering. I wished almost desperately that I could erase from my memory the image of Rehberg's face before we buried him, and the faces of my friends when I learned of Friedrich's death.

I reported to the commanding officer of my old battalion at Plauen, a Major Brundt.

"You are to report to your old battalion in France," he said. "Only this time, you will be reporting as an oberleutnant." He smiled. "Congratulations!"

"Thank you, Herr Major," I said, pleasantly surprised.

I checked into my assigned room and went to the officers' mess for dinner. I knew no one there. After dinner I went into Plauen. As I walked through the door of a café, I saw people at tables, drinking tea and laughing and chatting. I just stood and enjoyed the sight of them for a moment. It seemed like such a long time. Had it been only a year since I too had felt that carefree? Time seemed to have stopped in Plauen. The war seemed not to have happened! People here seemed blissfully unaware of the price that was being paid in France for our successes. They all seemed exactly the same, while I felt so much older and . . . used, or sad, or something. Dörnberg . . . Rehberg . . . Friedrich. The cost of war was indeed high.

I left the next day for France and arrived in Paris on September 7, 1940. I stayed there a couple of days to enjoy the famous city. I went to the opera and I visited the Panthéon, Notre-Dame, the Arc de Triomphe, the Champs-Élysées, and even *climbed* the Eiffel Tower. While I was in Paris, I reveled in the architecture of the beautiful city and its cultural wealth.

I joined my old battalion at Montlhéry-Linas, about thirty-five kilometers south of Paris. Raake and Wimmer invited me to dinner my first night back. They filled me in on every detail of the grand victory parade that was staged down the Champs-Elysées after the capture of Paris. Altogether during our drive from Cologne to Paris, we had marched approximately eight hundred kilometers. I had experienced every moment of our drive from Cologne to Paris except the victory celebration. Someone had taken my place as battalion adjutant during the victory parade while I was in the hospital at Bonn. I resolved that I would not miss the victory parade in London.

Raake and Wimmer had other news as well. Wimmer had been released to go home. Apparently the Army did not feel that England would be such a demanding chore that we would need the reserves. I was happy for Wimmer. He was a good battery commander and a conscientious soldier, but he was a civilian at heart. Then it occurred to me that First Battery would be getting a new battery commander.

"When will the new battery commander arrive?" I asked Raake.

"He just arrived," Raake said, smiling. "Not only have you been promoted in rank, but in responsibility as well. You are First Battery's new battery commander. Congratulations."

I was elated. When I went to bed that night, my mind whirled with the news. So much had happened so quickly that I could hardly adapt to it all.

Leutnant Jaschke, who had replaced Rehberg at the Somme River, was still forward observation officer of my old battery. The battery officer was Leutnant Steinbach, a giant of a man at six foot six and 250 pounds. It was almost comical to see Steinbach and Jaschke together, because the difference in size between the two men was about a foot in height and a hundred pounds in weight.

After the fall of Paris, France had been divided into two sectors. The north was occupied by the German Army, and the south was administered by the French Vichy government. When I arrived, our battalion was ready to move just north of the demarcation line south of the Loire River. We were moving into the Blois area, probably as security against something happening at the demarcation line. The battalion had fully recovered from the campaign through France and had been replenished with replacements for lost people, horses, and equipment. We were fully prepared for whatever was in store for us, which we assumed would be the invasion of England.

Each unit within our division was assigned an area of administrative responsibility in the occupied zone. Within our battalion, our batteries were each assigned a different village, with battalion headquarters in a centrally located village. Candé-sur-Beuvron, a small, picturesque community of about 2,500 people, was assigned to my battery. It was located about eighteen kilometers southwest of Blois, where the Beuvron River emptied into the Loire River.

I had no idea what to expect from the people of Candé. As the battery marched into the village, we could see the villagers out in force awaiting our arrival. I halted the battery, dismounted from Schwabenprinz, and handed the reins to my pferdehalter. An older man with a cane approached me. Short, a bit portly, and gray, he wore a formal black suit.

"Monsieur Leclerc, mayor of Candé," he said in French.

"Oberleutnant Knappe, assigned by the German Army to administer your village," I responded in French.

If Monsieur Leclerc had the same apprehensive feelings I did, he certainly did not show them. I told him I would need a place for my headquarters, stables for our horses, and housing for our troops. He was very accommodating and told me that he had been fully instructed to prepare for our arrival.

He took me to a château near where the Beuvron and the Loire rivers met. It had been built long ago by a nobleman, and the present owner had fled the country when the fighting came near. It had stables and barns for our horses, troops, and equipment. It was an excellent site for our headquarters. I thanked him and invited him to have dinner with me that evening. He agreed and left us to settle in.

The château had fifteen fully furnished rooms. I used some of the rooms as headquarters offices and assigned some as quarters for Leutnant Jaschke, Leutnant Steinbach, and Hauptwachtmeister Schnabel. I chose a small cottage close to the Beuvron River as my quarters. It had a living room, a bedroom, a bathroom, and a kitchen. Lammers, as usual, fixed it up very nicely for me.

I sent word to Mayor Leclerc, via Lammers, to meet me at 7:00 P.M. for dinner. Lammers returned with the message that we would be dining at Leclerc's home. Apparently this was going to be a cooperative effort. We dined in his quaint house, with his wife serving us like a maid rather than joining us for dinner. It was a pleasant meal and a pleasant experience. I explained to Leclerc that he should continue in his job as before, that he would continue to handle civil matters. I instructed him to have all the villagers surrender their firearms to my headquarters the next morning. I also informed him that travel outside the village would be restricted, although I would issue travel permits on request for legitimate reasons. He agreed to everything, and the next morning the collected firearms were delivered to my headquarters, as instructed.

The French people in Candé were living quite well, considerably better than the German population in big cities. We lived better in Candé than I had at home on convalescent leave. In Germany, everything was rationed—food, clothing, gasoline, etc. But in Candé, we could go to restaurants and get anything we wanted without ration cards. We could buy any food we wanted from local farmers. I was even able to go to a tailor and have riding breeches made and buy the best riding boots without a ration card— and they had the leather to make them. This was both because France was less densely populated than Germany and because the French population was less regimented and controlled. For example, a German chicken farmer had to give a certain percentage of his eggs to the government; nothing like this was being done in France.

I quartered most of my battery on the château property, which was a very convenient arrangement. Jaschke, Steinbach, and Schnabel had their offices in the château as well as their living quarters.

We went back to our old precampaign schedule of training. Our philosophy was that soldiers had to be kept occupied. In addition, we had to be prepared for whatever might happen. We planned a full schedule for every day, from 5:00 A.M. until 8:00 P.M. Even though these were the same troops we had marched into France with (except for replacements), we kept them active and practicing. We wanted to keep their skills sharp and to train them in other functions so that if someone was wounded, we would have someone else who could do that job. The soldiers spent a lot of time keeping the equipment clean and in good working order. We had learned during our march across France that equipment can break down very easily on the march.

We did not feel the war was over, because England still had not been defeated. Although we expected to invade England, horse-drawn artillery could have no part in an amphibious operation. We would go over only after the beachheads had been firmly established. We did not take the expected invasion of England lightly. We knew the English Channel would be a very big problem for us, and we had a healthy respect for the fighting ability of the British Army, because it had acquitted itself very well in the last war. We also knew England had a formidable navy and air force. We did not know that the Luftwaffe was losing the Battle of Britain, because our controlled press did not report it—we learned only much later that the German press reported only victories.

Occupation duty was a pleasant interlude. Candé and the area for which I was responsible were quite peaceful. We had no instances of resistance or sabotage, although we received reports of that sort of thing happening in other areas and were cautioned to be on guard against it. It may be because ours was a rural area. The mayor and I retained an amicable working relationship. He came to me only when he needed help. If a farmer wanted to go to Blois to sell his produce, for example, the mayor would come to me and ask for a travel permit for the farmer and I would issue it. For the most part, I worked only through the mayor, although on rare occasions a villager would come to me with a problem.

I went home at Christmas that year for the first time since I joined the Army (I had always before gone home at New Year's). It was a nine-hundred-kilometer train ride from Blois to Leipzig. The trains and train stations were crowded with people going home for Christmas, a great many of them in uniform. Everyone seemed happy and in the spirit of the season. I spent Christmas Eve, the traditional time to exchange gifts in Germany, with my family. Fritz was also home from Jena, and we enjoyed rehashing our experiences there. He was enjoying the Army in spite of its rigors and discipline. I joined Lilo and her family on Christmas Day. Lilo and I spent as much time together as possible, and I returned to Candé more taken with her than ever.

Although the battalion's batteries were in various villages, we cooperated closely with one another. Once each month, Major Raake hosted a dinner for all the officers under his command. Some of us also occasionally went pheasant hunting along the Loire River, using some of the shotguns we had confiscated from the local population. I got to know some of the officers in the other batteries well.

On some weekends, two or three of us would go to Paris by train. We would get Raake's permission to go and have someone drive us to the railroad station in Blois. It was just over an hour to Paris by train, and the train was free to German soldiers. We would leave on Saturday morning and come back Sunday evening.

Blois and Orléans were also interesting in their own right. They were historic places, with beautiful large medieval castles that had not been damaged by the fighting. The area boasted many good restaurants, and the famous French cavalry school of Saumur was but a short distance from Candé.

In early March, I received a sixteen-day furlough. Lilo and I had been writing letters back and forth, sometimes in French just for the fun of it. We made arrangements now to meet in the Austrian Alps for a skiing holiday. We enjoyed being together for several days, we enjoyed the beautiful weather, and we enjoyed the skiing. We would sleep late, have a leisurely breakfast, and then hit the slopes. In the evening, we would have dinner in a nice restaurant and go to a movie. Then we would walk back to our hotel hand in hand, sometimes singing and laughing and sometimes just enjoying the beautiful scenery bathed in moonlight. We felt that it was a wonderful time to be alive and together.

Then we returned to Leipzig together and I visited my family and Lilo's. I looked up Liebelt and Ebert while I was home. We agreed that events had proved old Herr Hoffer's prediction accurate, but that events had certainly not hurt Germany as Hoffer's prediction had seemed to imply.

Shortly after I returned to Candé, our division was ordered to move—not toward the English Channel, but to East Prussia. I could not help wondering if we were abandoning the plan to invade England. If so, it seemed strange to me, because England had declared war on us and that state of war still existed.

For whatever reason, we had been ordered to East Prussia, away from the English Channel. As a battery commander, I was just concerned with my battery and my immediate responsibilities of making the move and getting established in East Prussia. The move was more than 1,200 kilometers, and more than a hundred trains were required in order to move the whole division of 18,000 men plus 2,500 horses and all of our artillery and equipment.

France had been very pleasant, with its beautiful countryside, good food, and friendly population, and we hated to leave. But East Prussia was also nice. It was an agricultural area, hilly, with sandy soil that was good for growing rye and potatoes. The area had a lot of lakes, beautiful beaches, and forests of white beech trees. It was a prosperous horse-breeding area, with rich farms and pleasant villages.

We unloaded at Osterode and marched to Marwalde, a village nearby, about 270 kilometers from the Russian border (the former Polish border). From time to time while we were there, we moved out to live in the field and practice the mechanical things, such as how to secure the horses, how to put together a tent, how to camouflage the guns, how to get the guns into position, and so on. It was practically a peacetime existence, with lots of practice and maneuvers in the field. As an oberleutnant and battery commander, I had two leutnants and about 180 soldiers. We practiced constantly with our guns. During practice exercises, the men would take the horses to the river to water and wash them—and as often as not, to have a swim in the river. They would sing as they rode the horses to and from the river. It was a happy time for us all.

We shared an Easter festival with the local population, with our regimental band playing for everyone. We staged soccer games and wrestling matches for everyone's entertainment. There was a dance hall in the village, where dances were held on Saturday night, and our men dated the local girls.

During the couple of months we were in Marwalde, we were often invited into homes and had many conversations with the village population. They had not suffered so far, because, like the people in France, they were farmers and they had enough to eat. They were not bothered by rationing, because they had all the eggs and meat they wanted, even though there was some control. They had to get permission to slaughter a pig or a cow, but they did not report all the livestock they had. So food was never a problem here the way it was in the city, where you could not have a dinner party unless you got some extra ration cards.

There was not much worry as far as the war was concerned either. So far, everything that we had been told about by the German press had been victorious. When we were less than victorious, such as in the air war over England, the German press did not report the battles. So it was a good time as far as we knew.

In early June, 1941, we received orders to move to Prostken, another East Prussian village that was only a few kilometers from the present Russian border. Prostken was not as large as Marwalde, and living conditions were more fieldlike because not enough housing accommodations were available and some of the soldiers had to live in tents. We had also left friends in the old village, and we were not very happy about this move. However, we accepted it—not only because we had to, but also because we knew that soldiers get complacent if they stay in one place too long. Any Army unit loses its punch if the soldiers are too comfortable for too long.

When we moved into the new village, we investigated the terrain for practice exercises as we would normally do when we moved into any new location, and we began our usual training routine. Then one day Major Raake summoned Schumann, Witnauer, and me—his battery commanders—to his office. He had a greatly enlarged map of the area posted on his office wall.

"Gentlemen," Raake said, "study this map carefully. We must determine the best position for our guns in the event of an attack on Russia."

We stared at him, speechless. We had a friendship treaty with Russia, and we were at war with England. Things were not adding up.

"Why would we attack Russia?" I asked.

"It is just an exercise," Raake said. "A hypothetical situation."

We studied the map and, with Raake, determined the best positions for the guns of each battery. We then went out and found the positions assigned to us. It *could* have been just another exercise, but none of us really believed that. We did not have orders to move our guns into the positions, only to be familiar with our assigned locations and *ready* to move our guns into them. This had formerly been the border between East Prussia and Poland, but now that Germany and Russia had divided Poland between them it was the border between East Prussia and Russia. The Russians had created a no-man's-land on their side of the border by removing everything that was there in order to provide an unobstructed view. Then they had installed a barbed-wire fence and sentry towers to keep watch. There were no changes on our side; rye and potato fields, as well as patches of birch and fir trees, almost bordered the fence.

Schumann, Witnauer, and I were then summoned to Raake's office again. Raake looked very serious and tense this time.

"You are each to send a work detail of men in civilian clothing to load three hundred rounds of ammunition for your guns into farm wagons and take the rounds to your assigned gun positions," he said. "Your men are to look like farmers doing farm work, and your ammunition is to be camouflaged after you unload it."

We did not look at each other. It was evident that we

were going to invade Russia even though we had a friendship treaty with her.

"When are we going to invade, Major?" Schumann asked.

"It is only an exercise, Schumann. A purely hypothetical situation. But we have to make it look as real as possible."

"*Jawohl,* Herr Major," Schumann said. Raake apparently was still not at liberty to tell us the truth and was obviously very uncomfortable with the position he was in.

I returned to my office and called Schnabel in.

"Select a work detail of twelve men, Schnabel," I said. "Have the men borrow civilian work clothing from the local farmers who are stabling our horses. They must also borrow wagons from the farmers. The detail is to move three hundred rounds of ammunition up to the gun positions for an exercise. They are to look to the Russian sentries like German farmers going about routine farm work. Of course, the rounds are to be camouflaged in the wagons and when they are unloaded."

"*Jawohl,* Herr Oberleutnant," Schnabel said.

We had been in Prostken about three weeks by now, and the horse handlers knew the farm families where their horses were being kept. Getting civilian clothing was no problem for them. They simply asked the farmers to lend them civilian clothing and farm wagons. This assignment was something of a holiday for them because it was different from normal Army routine. The rather comical-looking crew loaded the ammunition into the farmers' wagons and then, pretending they were farmers doing farm work, they hauled the ammunition to the designated positions, unloaded it, and covered it with brush.

The next day, June 21, 1941, battery commanders were finally officially informed of what was about to happen.

"Before daylight tomorrow, we will invade the Soviet

Union," Raake said simply. "I was forbidden to tell you until now."

"Why are we invading Russia?" Witnauer asked.

Raake shrugged his shoulders. "We are soldiers," he said. "We do as we are told."

It seemed inexplicable to me that we were getting ready to invade the Soviet Union. We were at war with England. We had a friendship treaty with the Soviet Union, and there had been no government propaganda against Russia. However, the propaganda started almost immediately, even in the official Army order we received: "The communist regime in Russia is imposing cruelties upon the Baltic and other ethnic minorities, as well as the Russian people; therefore, we must destroy this cruel government and the communist commissars." The justification was simply that they were communists and we had to fight them. The German government at that time used the word "communist" to excuse anything it wanted to do to Russia, just as the Soviet Union and the western powers later used the words "Nazi" and "fascist" to justify anything they wanted to do to Germany.

I did not know a lot about the Soviet Union at the time: I knew it was a backward country, I knew the communist government had persecuted landowners, I knew about the fighting between the Red and White armies during the Russian revolution, I knew about the forced collectivization and the mass starvation of large segments of its population, and I knew about the purge of the officer corps in the Soviet Army. I did not think the Red Army could be very effective, not only because of the purge of its officer corps, but because they had a political officer in every unit who could overrule the orders of any military commander —and I could not see how that could possibly be made to work. (Ironically, something similar was initiated in the German Army in 1944, after the assassination attempt against Hitler, except that the political officer could not overrule the military commander.) I also knew that trains were moving back and forth daily between Germany and the Soviet Union, carrying goods that were being exchanged between the two countries in agreement with the trade terms of the friendship treaty. The whole thing seemed almost dreamlike in its lack of recognition of existing reality.

Although I was deeply troubled about invading a country with which we had a friendship treaty, I assumed there were things that I did not know. I also found the very thought of communism repulsive and honestly felt that the Russian people would be better off if we removed their communist government. Perhaps I was rationalizing, or perhaps it was just the innocence of youth. I do not think it even occurred to me or anyone else that we would fail to defeat the Soviet Army. Our confidence was absolute.

Our guns were still in the village several kilometers away. When darkness descended, we moved the guns from the village to their designated positions. The noise of bringing all our guns into position and bringing the infantry into position had to be clearly audible to the Russian sentries in their watchtowers. Their towers were no more than four kilometers from our gun positions, and the infantry moved even closer, to within three hundred meters of them. Of course, they might have been sleeping. It is a very boring job to sit in a sentry tower day after day. There was no major road, railroad, or anything else of special importance nearby, and they had been watching for two years with nothing happening.

We then laid telephone wire between the guns and our forward observation post and went into full combat readiness.

16

I SPENT THE night checking out my battery, making sure that everything was in order and everyone was in the right place. I realized only now that the same thing must be happening for hundreds of kilometers along our border with Russia. The woods along the frontier were surely swarming with German troops who were resting, sleeping, waiting to go into battle.

A bright moon shone over the forests of East Prussia, spreading its light through the trees. It was the same moon that had watched countless other battles through the ages; the same moon had shone when the Persians marched into Greece, when Napoleon marched into Russia, when the Kaiser's army fought in France. A few kilometers away, the village that would be our first objective lay sleeping, bathed in the comfort of soft moonlight. The scene looked like a beautiful painting, but I knew the reality would soon be very different. War was about to fill the new day with noise, fire, smoke, rubble, lead, corpses, and the bloodstained bandages of the wounded. Those who lay sleeping now would not soon go to sleep again with the sense of peace they now knew.

The strong scent of pine needles permeated my consciousness as I wandered among the 180 men of my battery, checking things out. From somewhere in the moonlit night came the slow mournful hoot of an owl. I became more aware of the men as individuals than I had ever been before. Some were timid, others brash; some were gloomy, others easily amused; some were ambitious, others idlers;

some were spendthrifts, others misers. The diverse thoughts that lay behind their helmets as they waited for battle only they could know. Love of country and sorrow at the prospect of dying in battle were surely common to all of them. One soldier was humming softly to himself in meditation. Some were no doubt full of foreboding, and others were thinking of home and loved ones.

The men were strong and sure of themselves. They had practiced constantly, and they knew they could do their job well. Their confidence was total, like that of a diamond cutter taking a chisel to a priceless gem. Now they sat about in groups, joking bravely about everything except what lay immediately ahead of them. I was confident the world had never seen anything like them. Their native intelligence, their conditioned bravery, and their practiced skills would flow into one channel and coalesce, and when that happened they would be unstoppable. Leutnant Steinbach was circulating among them, joking with them and trying to relax them.

I checked our forward observation post, where Jaschke and his battery troop were waiting. Jaschke seemed a little edgy, so I tried Steinbach's approach of joking and laughing with him and his men. His radioman, Gefreiter Seldte, and his telephone man, Oberkanonier Hugenberg, seemed more relaxed than Jaschke was.

At the designated time in the very early hours of June 22, 1941, my battery opened fire on the small village of Sasnia, a few kilometers from our guns. I was not in the front line with the infantry but at a little hill about a half kilometer away, which I thought would be a good place from which to watch the effectiveness of our fire. I could see our shell bursts clearly from my observation post, as well as the oily black-and-yellow smoke that rose from them. The unpleasant, peppery smell of burned gunpowder soon filled the air as our guns continued to fire round after round. After fifteen minutes we lifted our fire, and the soft pop-pop-pop of flares being fired replaced it as red lit up the sky and the infantry went on the attack.

As the infantry moved forward, the morning darkness was filled with the sounds of shouting, the crack of rifle shots, the short bursts of machine guns, and the shattering crashes of hand grenades. The rifle fire sounded like the clatter of metal-wheeled carts moving fast over cobblestone streets. Our infantry overran the barbed wire the Russians had erected on each side of their no-man's-land and stormed the guard towers and pillboxes the Russians had built immediately beyond the death strip. Although we met with some resistance, the Russians had been taken by surprise in spite of the noise of our preparations. Our infantry had short but bitter firefights with the surprised Russian troops. Our men took as prisoners those Russians who surrendered and killed those who resisted. Some of the Russian soldiers in Sasnia tried to pull back and got caught in a bottleneck at a bridge, where Stuka dive-bombers decimated them. They lay where they had fallen, in earth-brown uniforms, the first combat dead I had seen since the invasion of France. Although I was no longer shocked by the sight, I had not become accustomed to it either.

We took Sasnia and Grajewo the first day, and then we started the long march to Moscow. We were part of Army Group Center, Ninth Army, 87th Infantry Division. We were led in our march by panzer divisions and panzer grenadier divisions (motorized infantry). Army Group North—and with it my brother, Fritz—moved out toward Leningrad, and Army Group South moved out toward Stalingrad.

We followed behind the panzer and panzer grenadier divisions, because we could not keep up with the tanks and motorized infantry. Because of the length of the Russian front, horse-drawn artillery was part of the attack group in Russia instead of being reserves as we had been in France. We did not have enough mechanized artillery to man a 2,500-kilometer front, so horse-drawn artillery had to be used; however, the units that advanced quickly were mechanized. This was blitzkrieg, but not as it had been in Poland and France, where the whole front advanced quickly. In Russia, the mechanized forces were like arrows that went out ahead of the rest of us.

After our first battle at Sasnia, I stayed close to the infantry battalion commander I was supporting, Major Kreuger, so we could both see what was going on and coordinate our actions on the spot. From that day on, whenever we went into action, I was at his side. In addition to Sasnia and Grajewo, we took Osowiec, Bialystok, Grodno, and Lida the first week, covering well over two hundred kilometers. When we went through Bialystok, which had formerly been part of Poland, Polish civilians in a church service applauded us; they were very happy because they had not been permitted to conduct church services under the Russians and they felt liberated.

As our tanks and motorized units moved far out in front of the horse-drawn artillery and nonmechanized infantry, the 87th Infantry Division virtually became a reserve division, although we were not designated as such. When the mechanized units ran into heavy resistance, we would catch up and help crush the resistance. (The Russians generally resisted only when they reached high ground or a river.) When our mechanized forces encountered no resistance, we fell behind again. The Russian Air Force had been practically destroyed on the first day of the invasion, so we could march unmolested during the day.

Our forward scouts—usually motorcycle troops, although we had some cavalry—went ahead of us, reconnoitering. When they drew fire, the point battalion would immediately spread out. The troops behind the point battalion would also spread out from the road on which we were marching. Once we knew how strong the resistance was, we would prepare an attack. We would have an idea how strong the resistance was from the type of fire we received. The first fire would always be rifle fire and some-

Gymnasium graduation. Center row, from right are Ebert, Liebelt, and Michaelis. Top row right is Friedrich, and I am top row center. Top row left is a man wearing a Nazi Brownshirt uniform.

Loading dirt on a lorry during Labor Service.

Pulling guard duty with a spade as a Labor Service man. The medals are for sports.

At the conclusion of an infantry competition in 1936 in the market square in Jena.

Helping with the harvest near Jena in 1937.

A party at the home of General Hartmann. Second from right is General Hartmann's daughter. I am third from left.

At right, Oberstleutnant Rommel; at left, the othe group commander at Pots dam. On board a steam- ship returning from an excursion to East Prussia.

Field exercises at Potsdam. Note the barbed wire in the foreground.

Graduation in Kriegsschule Potsdam. First row center is Major Kassnitz. (Those wearing neckties had joined or been drafted into the Luftwaffe.) I am in the front row, left.

A social event in Plauen in 1939. At left is Gisela.

Field exercises near Plauen in 1939.

Fritz visiting me at Plauen.

Schwabenprinz in training at Plauen.

The riding competition at Bad Elster in 1939.

A field kitchen in the Sudetenland in 1938. I am second from right.

Our battalion preparing to leave for the Polish border in 1939.

Marching up from the Mosel River into the Eifel Mountains in 1939.

Christmas in the Eifel Mountains, 1939. Note the cakes and bottles of wine in the background and the fruit on the tables.

My bunker as battery officer in the Eifel Mountains.

Bismarck's great-grandchild with the baby's mother near
Eisenschmitt in 1939.

Major Raake and Hauptmann Wagner at the Somme River in France
in 1940.

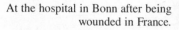
At the hospital in Bonn after being wounded in France.

Leutnant Rehberg, our first fatality.

French prisoners taken in Belgium near the Maas River in 1940.

Some of my men dressed in civilian clothing to bring ammunition up to the Russian border in preparation for the invasion on June 22, 1941.

A corduroy road in Russia in 1941.

The rowboat fight. Our men relax on a day of rest during the invasion of Russia.

In the former Russian-occupied part of Poland during a day of rest. I am in swimming trunks. The other man is my battery officer.

Russian prisoners on the post road. They do not seem unhappy about being prisoners.

In field uniform during the invasion of Russia. Note the flashlight attached to the left shoulder epaulette.

A peasant village in Russia after the fighting.

In dress uniform during artillery school in
Berlin in 1942. The upper decorations are
the Iron Cross Second Class and the medal
for the occupation of the Sudetenland.
Below them are the Iron Cross First Class,
the medal for hand-to-hand combat, and
the wound medal directly below the Iron
Cross First Class.

With Lilo in Berlin during artillery school.

At the rail station in Leipzig, preparing to return to the front near Smolensk in early 1942. At right is Lilo.

Fritz's grave in 1942.

At Lake Constance, near the German-Swiss border in 1942.

At our wedding reception in Leipzig in 1943.

The locket I wore during my captivity.

One of my fellow prisoners made this chess set.

Yet another talented prisoner made this beautiful fold-out picture frame.

Another prisoner made this cigarette case out of aluminum and awarded it to me when I became chess champion at Krasnogorsk Prison Camp.

times machine-gun fire, but the type of fire that followed—
mortar, tank, artillery—would tell us a lot about how
strong the resistance was. We would then make decisions
on the basis of that information.

Interestingly, the forward scouts were rarely killed,
and far more often than not they were not even hit. The
Russian soldiers firing at them were usually not there to
fight, but only to stop us momentarily and then very
quickly get back to report to their superiors what they had
seen. These Russian soldiers would be very nervous and
eager to run, because they knew that as soon as they fired
and disclosed their positions we would open up on them.
They were actually more likely to be hit than our scouts
were. Because of their eagerness to fire quickly and run,
their aim was rarely accurate.

When we encountered a prepared line of defense, we
would not only spread out but also dig in. Then we would
probe to see how long the defense line was and how strong
the resistance was. We would study our maps to see if there
were rivers and bridges, or what the terrain might present
in the way of obstacles or advantages. The corps staff
would also get reports from the divisions to the right and
left of us, so the big picture would start to form. If it
proved to be a line we had to break through, the point
battalion would be reinforced and an attack would be prepared. We would launch the attack at dawn the next morning. The prepared defensive position would usually be several successive lines of trenches. When our attacking force
overran the first line of trenches, the surviving Russians
would stand and raise their hands. The second wave of our
attacking force would collect the survivors and the
wounded and send them to the rear. This process would
continue until all the successive defensive lines had been
taken.

When night fell during a fight, whether the battle
stopped or continued into the night depended on whether
there was enough moonlight to continue, as well as upon

the weather and terrain and our intelligence gathered through reconnoitering. Sometimes we would deliberately stage a night attack, if our infantry was familiar with the terrain from the day's fighting and if we in the artillery had directed fire during the day and knew where our targets were so we could shoot blind. Usually, however, the fighting stopped at night. With the fall of night, the infantry would send out probing patrols to locate the enemy's latest defense line and try to take prisoners so we could learn from them the enemy units that were opposing us. They would move forward until they drew fire, and then they would try to flank the position that had fired at them. If they were lucky, and if they did not get hit when they were fired upon, they might surprise an enemy soldier and take him prisoner. The prisoner would be sent back to the division, where an interpreter would interrogate him and try to find out the identity of the units facing us, how well equipped they were, and how long they had been in combat.

We covered thirty to forty kilometers a day at first. I was in the saddle every day, from dawn to dusk, during this period. If there was no resistance, we would have three or four people on bicycles or motorcycles go ahead of us to the village or *kolkhoz* (collective farm) that was our goal for the day and prepare for our arrival. The infantry would be in the villages ahead of the artillery so that if an attack was planned for the next day everything would be in the correct order.

We would post sentries around the village so no one could approach without being detected.

Sometimes instead of stopping for the night, we would stop in the evening for a rest break of an hour and then keep marching through the night, because it kept the enemy troops on the run and did not allow them to regroup. Our troops would become lethargic after a while, but they woke up quickly enough if we ran into resistance. It did not happen often that we marched through the night, but when it did everyone would give his best, because we all knew that it saved lives in the long run.

While we were still in the Russian-occupied area that had formerly been Poland, an event occurred that demonstrated to me what the years of Nazi party propaganda had done to otherwise decent German people. While doing some of my paperwork one evening, I was distracted by shouting. I recognized the voice as Hauptwachtmeister Schnabel's and went to investigate. I found him in a school building with a middle-aged Polish civilian. He was not only shouting at the man, he slapped him in the face!

"Schnabel!" I shouted.

"*Jawohl,* Herr Oberleutnant," he responded, coming to attention.

"What do you think you are doing?" I demanded.

"But he is a Jew, Herr Oberleutnant," Schnabel assured me.

"I don't care what he is or who he is, as long as you are under my command you will not mistreat *anybody*," I ordered.

His actions were obviously the result of the incessant anti-Jewish propaganda of the Nazi government. He undoubtedly was doing what he thought was expected of him, but the incident enabled me to establish to my men that I would not tolerate such behavior, and it never happened again in my unit.

Burning villages, the bodies of dead Russian soldiers, the carcasses of dead horses, burned-out tanks, and abandoned equipment were the signposts of our march. The infantry had to move on foot, but we rode either on horseback or on the equipment being pulled by our horses. Occasionally, when there was resistance up ahead, Ninth Army would send trucks back to rush the infantry forward more quickly.

A supply column followed us to provide ammunition, hay and oats for the horses, food for the people, and fuel for the motorized equipment. If we outran our supply column, we had to live off the land, but most of the time our supply column kept up. Unteroffizier Boldt supplemented our rations by foraging in the evenings and bringing back chickens or a pig or whatever he could find. He always managed to keep us fed.

We had a day of rest occasionally, because the men and horses were only flesh and blood, and they would become exhausted and simply unable to continue. While we rested, the tanks and mechanized forces would continue putting pressure on the enemy. We got our first day of rest in a Russian village at the end of June after fifteen days of hard pushing. The weather was very hot, and it felt good to sit around in swimming trunks, with no boots, and just rest. We had our guns in position, but the Russians were running away and there was really no danger.

During rest days, the men got a chance to wash their clothes and write letters home. We also got better food, because there was more time to prepare it, especially if Boldt could find a loose pig or some chickens. At one point during a day of rest, the troops found some boats on a river and staged a boat fight. The boats were little rowboat-type things and had oars with paddles on each end. One man would paddle while his partner stood with another double-paddled oar and battled another pair in another boat, each pair trying to dump the other into the river. The rest of us stood and cheered them on. That sort of diversion was very relaxing for them. They would always find a way to relax and have some fun.

Once during a day of rest, we had a ceremony at which decorations were awarded. I was awarded the Iron Cross First Class on this day, for helping to break enemy resistance during the first week of the invasion. Major Kreuger recommended me for this because he felt that my willingness to risk my life to direct the fire of my battery from the position of his point infantry company had saved the lives of many of his men.

We had started taking prisoners from the first day of

the invasion. The infantry brought them in by the thousands, by the tens of thousands, and even by the hundreds of thousands. As we advanced farther into Russia, the stream of Russian prisoners going in the opposite direction, toward Germany, swelled. I wondered at first whether we were prepared to care for so many of them, and as the numbers continued to grow I was sure we were not. Our supply line did well just to keep the German Army supplied, and we could not possibly have anticipated so many prisoners. They seemed apathetic and expressionless. Their simple uniforms created the impression of a huge, dull mass.

They could not be cared for properly, in fact, and many of them died of starvation. They were given grain from the *kolkhozes* and meat from the horses that were killed in battle, but it was not enough to sustain them. It was a terrible situation, but it was not that they were neglected—it was just not possible to feed them in such numbers and still feed our own troops.

We had been informed about the now-infamous "Commissar Order." The communist commissars in the Russian Army were considered especially dangerous people who would instigate and incite others, and we were therefore to separate them from other prisoners and turn them over to the division. (What we did not know was that the division was to turn them over to the Nazi Party, which would execute them.) I did not give it any special thought, because as artillery my battery was unlikely to be taking prisoners.

One evening in mid-July, my battery was assigned to spend the night in the same village where the division staff were staying the night. They were assigned there because it had nice houses, and I was assigned there because it had good facilities for my horses. Apparently, Generalmajor von Studnitz's operations officer told him an artillery battery was quartered in the same village, and he sent someone to invite me to have dinner with him that evening.

He was in his middle fifties and a little on the heavy side. He was an impressive professional soldier who understood the art of warfare and was an effective practitioner. He was an intellectual, a political and philosophical thinker, and an avid reader. He was highly respected by his men and subordinate officers.

"Oberleutnant Knappe, commander of First Battery, 187th Artillery Regiment, Herr General," I reported to him in his log house.

"Good evening, Knappe," he said, smiling broadly and offering his hand. "Have a seat." He motioned to a table, and waved to his orderly to pour wine for us. "How are things going for you?" he asked.

"Just fine, Herr General," I responded.

"How is the morale of your people?"

"Excellent. They are fine soldiers, and their attitude could not be better."

"How are your horses holding up?"

"They are doing well. As long as they get a day of rest now and then and are well cared for, they will do fine."

"Are you getting all the food you need for your horses and men?"

"*Jawohl,* Herr General. We are well provided."

He was investigating how his supply functions were working. We were his forces, and he had to use us to achieve his objectives. I gave him an honest and objective picture of my situation. Up to that time, I'd had few losses, and he was pleased with that.

He looked pensive for a moment. "How do you think the campaign has gone so far?" he asked.

"Great," I said enthusiastically. "Everything seems to be going according to plan."

He did not respond for a moment, his thoughts seeming to be far away. "I was in Russia during the last war," he said finally. "I have experienced the Russian winter. It is savage, like nothing we have ever experienced. It will come, and it will come soon. We are just in this little part of Russia. We have a vast empty country ahead of us, and if we do not take Moscow before the weather turns bitter cold, I worry about what will happen."

He was clearly not optimistic. I was amazed, because it could not have been easier up to now, but I knew he was intelligent, experienced, and capable, and I began to tone down my own optimism after that. If someone had overheard our conversation and reported it to the Nazi Party, it could have cost General von Studnitz his career. His remarks could have been interpreted as defeatist, and the Nazis dealt severely with defeatism.

During this period, we spent most of our time marching, only occasionally meeting resistance. As we marched, we moved over deeply rutted dirt roads, through patches of loose sand and clouds of dust. Our feet sank into the sand and dirt, puffing dust into the air so that it rose and clung to us. The horses coughing in the dust produced a pungent odor. The loose sand was nearly as tiring for the horses as deep mud would have been. The men marched in silence, coated with dust, with dry throats and lips. Such conditions exhausted the horses and men if we were not extremely careful.

In some villages, May Day decorations were still up, and we wondered at first if the villagers were celebrating our arrival. We had heard of Russian peasants welcoming the German Army as liberators, especially because the Soviet government would not allow them to conduct church services. We passed burned-out German and Russian tanks and downed airplanes.

As we marched through Russia, we began to acquire an appreciation for the vastness of the country. In some forested places, the earth was squeaky and springy beneath our boots. The leaves on the surface were light and brittle, but underneath them lay leaves that had withered many years before and created a brown spongy mass in which many tiny insects scurried. In other places, dead, brittle underbrush crumbled beneath our feet. The forest smelled musty with old leaves, and the trees were full of noisy birds. The living trees usually smelled fresh and damp, and the odor of the dead trees was dry and rich.

In the open, the sun warmed the earth, as well as buttons, belt clasps, harness rings, and anything made of metal. Yellow butterflies, blue-black beetles, and small brown ants were common. Grass snakes rustled through the grass, practically invisible. Grasshoppers were plentiful and could not seem to tell a moving soldier from a stationary tree, often hitching free rides. Swarms of gnats plagued us, and darting flies were everywhere.

As we marched, low hills would emerge from the horizon ahead of us and then slowly sink back into the horizon behind us. It almost seemed that the same hill kept appearing in front of us, kilometer after kilometer. Everything seemed to blur into uniform gray because of the vastness and sameness of everything. We traversed treeless plateaus that extended as far as the eye could see, just one vast open field overgrown with tall grass. We encountered grainfields of unimaginable vastness that sometimes concealed Russian infantry. Fields of sunflowers stretched for kilometer after kilometer after weary kilometer. In other places we encountered immense forests that were like jungles in the density of their tangled underbrush. We struggled through marshes in Byelorussia that were as large as two German provinces. The rivers all seemed to run north and south, so we had to cross them, and they provided the retreating Russians with natural defensive positions.

Shortly after my dinner with Generalmajor von Studnitz, we arrived at Minsk, the capital of Byelorussia and a large city. A square in the center of the city contained a statue of Lenin that had been about ten meters high. It had been pulled down and Lenin's head had broken off. We did not know whether our troops had pulled it down or Russian civilians had done it when their military retreated. Minsk was deserted, like a ghost town. The only sign of life was German military traffic. We did not stop.

From Minsk on, we were on the post road that ran from Warsaw to Moscow, through Grodno, Minsk, Smolensk, and Vyazma. This was the same post road Napoleon had taken to Moscow. The road gave me an eerie feeling, perhaps because of its age and the fact that Napoleon's army had walked on the same cobblestones that we now marched on. It was a two-lane highway with deep drainage ditches on each side. It had a cobblestone surface, which was not the best thing for the horses' feet, because it was so rough and would cause stone bruises on their heels.

Altogether, we would be on the post road for approximately seven hundred kilometers, from Minsk to Moscow. Over two hundred years old, the post road was just wide enough to allow two vehicles to pass. A car could do no more than forty-five kilometers per hour because of the cobblestones. Since we were horse-drawn artillery, however, we had no problem. Even trucks and tanks had no problem if they went slowly. We could not get off the road except at intersections with country roads, because of the deep ditches on each side. All the other roads were dirt roads that would become mud in a rain. The bridges were usually destroyed, so we had to ford the creeks and rivers —which was why we needed six-horse teams to pull the guns and ammunition carts.

At the Berezina River, we got into a very tight spot. The bridge over the river had been destroyed, and we had to wait for the engineers to build a pontoon bridge. This made me more than a little nervous, because I knew that a blown-up bridge on the only hard-surfaced road in the area would be a natural place for routine interdiction artillery fire—they would just fire artillery shells at such a target every so often on the chance that they might catch a unit bottlenecked there. And now our entire division of eighteen thousand men was in the bottleneck! If we were to be attacked by artillery, the infantry would be able to get off the road and take cover, but with horses hooked up to the guns and wagons the artillery would not. We would have to just stand and take our casualties.

As we waited, it happened. The dreaded whining noise assaulted our ears and swelled rapidly to a fearful roar before a heavy artillery projectile exploded nearby with a shattering crash. A fiery blast of wind swept along the ground, carrying with it the ugly scent of burned gunpowder. Before we could gather our senses, the air was immediately rent by another piercing scream, followed by an explosion that shook the earth and produced a cloud of black smoke and a shower of rubble. It was the heaviest artillery we had encountered so far; the explosions were enormous and oppressive. The vehicles of my battery were on the road leading to the blown-up bridge, and we could only stay there. Although the fahrers had to stand to try to keep the horses under control, the gunners tried to protect themselves by lying down beside the road.

It was probably railroad-mounted guns thirty or forty kilometers away that were firing at us. We did not know whether they knew we were there or whether it was just lucky timing for them during routine interdiction fire. Fortunately, it did not last too long, so they must not have known we were there. We lost three dead and twenty-one wounded. Our losses, as bad as they were, could have been much worse.

The Russian villages varied considerably in size. The smallest was perhaps thirty peasant huts and the largest was several hundred. In many cases, they were just strung out in two rows along a road. They were very primitive wooden huts, with thatched or sod roofs. On the inside of many of them, newspapers were used as wallpaper. The furniture was extremely primitive as well, made by the peasant himself, and the huts always had earthenware pots and wooden tubs. A wooden box usually served as a small cupboard. Cradles were suspended from the ceiling on ropes. Illumination was provided by kerosene lamps or paraffin candles if at all; only the wealthier rural areas had even that, and in poorer areas the peasant lived in darkness between dusk and sunup—and in the winter, darkness accounted for seventeen hours of each day! A typical fence was just straight sticks or whatever the peasant could find. The poverty in which these people lived was very depressing. The ordinary peasant lived little better than his livestock. We seemed to be encountering a primitive past in human history, a virtual time warp of centuries.

The huts were normally occupied by workers on the collective farms that had been established since the communist revolution in 1918. The typical peasant hut had one big brick or stone stove—sort of an enclosed fireplace—in the center of the only room. The top was very thick, and the stone or brick would get warm by absorbing heat during the day. The stove was big enough that a family of six could sleep on top of it in the winter and keep warm from the heat stored by the bricks or stones. It had an opening for cooking, but it was used mainly for heating the room and for sleeping on.

Most of the Russian peasant huts had been built before the communist revolution; since then, few new houses had been built. Before the revolution, there had been some relatively wealthy farmers, so there were usually one or two larger houses in these villages. Most, however, were extremely primitive one-room huts. Behind each hut was an outhouse and a toolshed. A hut typically had a few very small windows. In addition to the stove, they also used snow to keep the hut warm by piling it up against the outside walls as insulation, up to the windows or even higher. The livestock were kept at a central location within walking distance of the village, although it could be up to an hour's walk. The only livestock they kept in the village were chickens.

Unfortunately, many of the village houses we stayed in had lice, and we got them. Once we got lice, they stayed with us until we could be deloused, and in a fast-moving situation such as ours there was no time for delousing.

Only when our advance stopped would delousing facilities be set up. The lice were a torment that was to stay with us for months. We scratched with increasing zeal. We scratched arms, legs, stomach, the small of the back, and it was a constant burning in the armpits. It was worst at night, and the men would thrash restlessly in their blankets.

On the post road after we reached Minsk, a railroad line ran parallel to the highway, so we always had a railroad to bring supplies up; however, as the Russians retreated they tried to destroy it, and repairing the railroad was a constant job. Because of this, the trains were always at least twenty-five kilometers behind us, even if the railroad was repaired quickly.

Somewhere between Minsk and Smolensk, we ran into resistance, and our infantry regiment commander called for a conference of his battalion, company, and battery commanders in a wooded area to plan what to do. It was not a wise thing to do, because we had all the regiment's key officers together in one small area. He should not have done that, especially in the woods, but the resistance was unexpected and it had been a long time since we had received artillery fire. As about fifteen of us were planning our response to the resistance, a chilling howl sent us all diving to the ground, pressing our faces into the earth. Then came the frightful blast of the explosions. A salvo of artillery shells exploded about ten meters above us, on making contact with the trees, and shrapnel slammed into us like machine-gun fire from heaven. I was unharmed, but I had seen the man lying next to me jerk with one of the explosions and I knew he had been hit.

"Medic!" I yelled. I reached for him, but it was immediately evident that he had to be dead. He had serious wounds in both his head and his back. Beads of sweat popped out of my skin and a sudden chill made me shiver.

We spread out quickly, because we did not know whether they had an observer in the trees and really knew what they were doing or whether it had just been a lucky hit. We had two dead and five or six wounded. Medics quickly came and took the dead and wounded away. Since we received no additional fire, we assumed that it was again just a lucky hit for them as it had been at the bridge.

The oberleutnant killed beside me was a reserve officer. One moment we were discussing our plans, and the next moment we lay side by side in the dirt, one dead and one unharmed. That I happened to land where I did and he landed where he did was just a throw of the dice. He remained where he dropped and I walked away. How much longer would fate keep me alive? I knew the next time I might very well be the unlucky one who would drop in the wrong spot.

I had to become fatalistic about it and assume that eventually it would happen to me and there was nothing I could do to prevent it. I did not wait for it to happen or stand up and present a big target—I tried to be as small a target as possible—but I knew that I was going to be killed or badly wounded sooner or later. The odds against my escaping unscathed were impossibly high, and I accepted my eventual death or maiming as part of my fate. Once I had forced myself to accept that, I could put it out of my mind and go on about my duties; I would not have been able to function had I not done so.

At Orsha, between Minsk and Smolensk, the Russians had a prepared defense line that we had to overcome before we could proceed to Smolensk. A prepared defense line always consisted of several consecutive lines of trenches or foxholes, and when we attacked we had to overrun them all. The standard procedure in all combat until now was that when attacking infantry passed over the first line of trenches or foxholes, the enemy soldiers who had been overrun and were still alive and not badly wounded would stand and raise their hands in surrender to the soldiers advancing behind the first line of attacking troops. The captured enemy soldiers, including the wounded, would then be collected and taken to the rear.

While advancing in a large wooded area near Orsha, we were spread out in a line. I was with the point company, in the center of the line. The Russian soldiers in the first line of defense were dug in so that only their heads were out of the foxholes, and they had branches over their heads, so they were very difficult to see. We received rifle fire from them, and we returned their fire and kept advancing. Then the fire became heavy. All around us were the crack of rifles, the boom of mortars, and the hollow chatter of machine guns.

We overran their first line and were attacking their second prepared line when we were suddenly aware that we were taking rifle fire from behind as well as from in front of us. Advancing German soldiers were being shot dead from behind. The Russian soldiers in the first line of trenches, who should have surrendered, had turned and were shooting us in the back, and some of our people were killed and wounded by this fire. Of course, their country was being invaded by the German Army and they were desperate. Still, this was at a personal level, and no German *or Russian* soldier could have that code of honor broken by the enemy without going almost mad, because it was the combat infantry soldier's only hope of survival in a hopeless situation. If that hope was taken away, death was certain—and nobody *wanted* to die! In a combat situation, the soldier is under inhuman stress to begin with, and when he sees a friend he has been sharing his life with suddenly drop because he was shot in the back, it is too much. Men who share combat become brothers, and this brotherhood is so important to them that they would give their lives for one another. It is not just friendship, and it is stronger than flag and country.

Our soldiers went berserk, and from that point on during the attack they took no prisoners and left no one alive in a trench or foxhole. I did not try to stop them, nor did any other officer, because they would have killed us too if we had. They were out of their minds with fury. If the Russian soldiers had put down their weapons and stood up with their hands raised, they would have been collected and marched to the rear as had always occurred in the past. Their cause was lost; they could only be taken prisoner or die. As it was, they were all killed, without mercy or remorse.

That evening was a turbulent one for me, because I had never before experienced such brutality in combat. It was a quiet evening after such savageness, with blue-gray smoke rising from our field kitchen as burning logs crackled under the coffee and tea. Dusk dimmed the birch and fir trees around us. Some of the infantrymen sat about, smoking and drinking coffee or tea from the field kitchen. Some ate their rations, some repaired their boots, some wrote to their wives or girlfriends or parents—at a time when it would seem impossible for them to think or to feel anything but horror and exhaustion. They had clearly adapted to this new type of combat better than I had.

Perhaps they felt avenged. We had buried our dead beside the trenches and foxholes where their surviving comrades were now writing letters, shaving, eating, and washing in improvised baths. These young soldiers were just glad to be alive one more day; in fact, they felt almost astonished each evening to have survived another day. I was learning to know them, and I knew that when a friend was killed it was as though some particle of life inside them had died, and yet amid the deafening roar and horrors of battle the next day, their dead comrade's voice still sometimes would make itself heard at strange moments.

I went to Kreuger's command tent to prepare for the next day's attack, as I did every evening when we expected to attack the next morning.

"Hello, Knappe," he said when I entered. He drew back from the map he had been studying and motioned toward a folding chair. He looked at me for a long moment. "You did not like what you saw today," he said finally. It was not a question.

"No," I admitted. "But I understood it."

He looked at me for a long moment again, as if to see if my actions and facial expressions matched my words. "Good," he said finally. "That is important. There is nothing you or I or anyone else can do about an incident like that. The Russians took control of the situation out of our hands."

"*Jawohl,* Herr Major," I agreed. "About tomorrow morning . . ."

The weather was dry and very hot. The days were long and the nights were short during the summer. June, July, and August gave us good weather in spite of the extreme heat, and we marched endlessly across this land of boundless expanses, this land with which none of our memories were linked. Every day of marching was just like every other day. It turned very hot in late summer, and the heat and insects did not go away at night. Nothing could have prepared us for the mental depression brought on by this realization of the utter physical vastness of Russia. Tiny little doubts began to creep into our minds. Was it even possible that such vast emptiness could be conquered by foot soldiers?

Occasionally some of the peasants would still be in the villages when we arrived, not having had time to flee. They would be women, children, and old men, because everyone else had been drafted. Only when we went forward very fast would we find these people. They would be either those who could not get away or those who did not want to get away. They were never mistreated in any way by the combat troops, and they showed no outward hostility toward us. They seemed to be neutral, and some actually greeted us. Of course, any Russian civilians who were communists probably had left with the Russian Army if they could, and those remaining were people who had been oppressed by the Communist Party. The only hostility I ever witnessed from Russian citizens came when some of our soldiers laughed as they watched two children scratching themselves because of lice. Their mother became angry.

"These are German lice. You brought them here," she said sternly.

We had picked up enough of the Russian language to understand her. It was not true, because we had got the lice from sleeping in Russian huts, but I apologized for the men as best I could with the language barrier and tried to appease her.

Sometimes during the fighting the Russians would shell their own villages if we were in them. When that happened, the Russian civilians were in the same boat we were in, and in situations like that, nationality is not a factor—survival is all that matters. We would all just try to protect ourselves, and we also protected the others if we could. They cooperated with us in extinguishing lights at night and keeping their windows covered. At times it became almost a conspiracy. I have a vivid recollection of lying on the ground near a peasant hut as Russian artillery shells exploded nearby. I slowly became aware of an elderly Russian peasant woman lying near me. When she saw me look at her, she smiled reassuringly. She reminded me of nothing so much as a mother reassuring her child.

Smolensk had been pretty much destroyed by the time we got to it. The railroad station had been obliterated because it had been defended so fiercely. Hundreds of thousands of Russian prisoners had been taken there. Although we did not stay in the city, we were in the Smolensk area for about a week, resting, repairing equipment, replenishing worn-out equipment, shoeing horses, and recuperating in general.

It was the first really extended opportunity that Obergefreiter Knecht and his assistant had had to make many badly needed permanent repairs to equipment and to change shoes on the horses except on an emergency basis. The cobblestone highway was very hard on both our equipment and our horses' feet. Knecht and his assistant put in some sixteen-hour days during this week. Theirs was no easy life.

I wrote to Lilo every day while we rested at Smolensk to try to make up for the days I had not written during the march. I did not tell her about the killing and dying, or about the heat and the dust. I just told her of the beauty of the country around us and of the more interesting people I had met. Lilo represented beauty, civilization, and the finer things of life to me. I did not want her to know about the dehumanizing things I had seen during this endless trek across a nation where people were forced to live almost as animals. Writing these letters also helped me keep a balanced perspective: there is beauty to be found in even the most gruesome of circumstances.

We launched a new offensive in early September. From Smolensk on, the Russian resistance grew stronger as we got closer to Moscow. Somewhere between Smolensk and Vyazma, our tanks and infantry had surrounded a huge number of Russian soldiers, although at the time we did not realize it. The infantry we were supporting encountered resistance, so my battery went into position to support them. I was up front with Major Kreuger when night came, so we stopped for the night with the intention of attacking at dawn. It was a typical situation, the type we studied at Kriegsschule Potsdam and practiced so much. We march, our forward scouts draw fire, and our point battalion deploys and tries to find out how strong the resistance is. I was with the infantry, so I called back to my battery officer, Leutnant Steinbach, to get the guns into position to fire the next morning.

About an hour after midnight, all but the sentries were wrapped in their blankets and sound asleep. Major Kreuger and I were still working on our plans for the assault at dawn when we were startled to hear rifle fire behind us, in the direction of my guns. We looked at each other with immediate concern. That could only mean that a battle was taking place in back of us instead of in front of us, where we thought the enemy to be—back at the approximate position of my battery. The telephone rang. It was Steinbach, my battery officer.

"Herr Oberleutnant, we are under attack from the south," he said with just a touch of fear in his voice. "But their main attack appears to be farther back, where our ammunition handlers and fahrers are with the limbers, wagons, carts, and the field kitchen."

"What weapons are they firing at you?" I asked.

"Only rifles. No machine guns or mortars."

"Good. Keep me informed, especially of any change in the situation."

"*Jawohl,* Herr Oberleutnant."

The surrounded Russians, of whom we had not been aware, apparently had decided to try to break out under cover of darkness. They were attacking my battery, which apparently lay directly in their path, and my men were defending themselves and our guns and horses, although they had only rifles with which to do so. They could not see the Russians they were shooting at, but they could hear them—and they could smell them! The Russian soldiers smelled of *makhorka* tobacco, which had a very strong unpleasant odor. It was made of the stems of the tobacco leaves instead of the leaves (only Russian officers were issued tobacco made of the leaves). This awful smell got into their thick uniforms and could be smelled for quite a distance.

I relayed the report I had received from Steinbach to Kreuger, who passed it on to regiment headquarters, and it went from there to division. Kreuger ordered his reserve infantry company into the attack. This stopped the Russians, but the battle continued until morning with heavy losses on both sides. My battery lost a few men, the infantry company lost over a hundred, and the Russians lost many more. They were very disorganized and confused, and they surrendered when daylight came because they did not have heavy weapons and did not stand a chance in the daylight.

We counted our losses, buried our dead, and took prisoners. Hundreds of dead Russians lay everywhere. There must have been more than a battalion of them; it may have been a corps staff or something like that. We organized a defense line against the same thing happening again the next night, and then we stayed there a day or two, licking our wounds. By then, the resistance we had encountered in front of us the day before had been fought down to small mopping-up actions, and when we started forward again, even the small actions had been cleaned out.

Because the division had taken a lot of casualties and needed to rest and replenish, we stayed here for three days. The mail caught up with us, and I received a letter from my parents with the news that my brother, Fritz, had been gravely wounded with Army Group North in September, about halfway to Leningrad. A bullet had entered his neck and lodged in his spine. He was paralyzed from the neck down, and the doctors could not remove the bullet without running the risk of killing him. He was in the hospital in Leipzig, where my parents and Inge visited him daily.

In late September, it began to rain, and mud started to become a problem for us. Wind whipped the rain into our faces and soaked our uniforms as we marched. Snow came in early October, but it was not cold enough for the ground to freeze and everything turned to mud. By October 8, the earth was simply a quagmire of mud. Great clumps of mud clung to our boots and every step produced a smacking suction noise. It played havoc with the horses. We were also unprepared for the snow, because we had not received winter clothing.

We reached Vyazma around mid-October. This was near Borodino, the scene of Napoleon's last big battle before he reached Moscow. Here our tanks were stopped by determined Russian resistance, and we caught up with them and fought the Russians in the same hills where Napoleon had fought them. The difference was that after Borodino, Napoleon had encountered no further resistance until he reached Moscow. Unfortunately, this was not true in our case.

Kreuger asked his company commanders and me to meet with him in his tent shortly after we reached Vyazma. This was a rare occurrence, so we knew it was important. When the four of us had seated ourselves on the folding camp stools, we learned what was on his mind.

"Gentlemen, from now on, our division will be a front-line unit," he said. "The panzer divisions are being pulled out for other deployments." (Later, we learned that they were used to attempt to throw a pincer movement around Moscow in order to prevent Moscow from receiving any further aid from the rest of Russia. General Hoth's panzers were going north, through Kalinin, and General Guderian's were going south, through Tula.) He paused, and we looked at each other uneasily. "From here on until we reach Moscow, it is just infantry and artillery. Until now, the panzers have had all the glory in this campaign. Let's show them what infantry and artillery can do without them!"

From Vyazma on, the 87th Infantry Division was never out of combat, and it was infantry and artillery only, fighting as a broad front toward Moscow. My battery marched, as always, with the infantry battalion we supported. We would occupy one village, and the Russians would be in the next village. During the night, the infantry would send out patrols to try to find out where the least resistance was. In the morning, my battery would open fire on targets in the next village, which would be seven or eight kilometers away. Then our infantry battalion would move forward. In most cases, we would take that village and the next one and stay overnight there before repeating it all again the next day, depending on how difficult the terrain was—how many creeks, hills, and so forth—and how much resistance we encountered.

The sound of combat was deafening. It was like combining every loud noise anyone ever heard into one colossal, deafening roar. It was a virtual hurricane of noise, but it did not pass by as a hurricane does; it remained as long as the fighting went on. The roar of combat was the combined sounds of heavy artillery, light artillery, mortars, machine guns, hand grenades, rifles—every weapon used on the battlefield. The roar of combat alone was enough to shatter a soldier's will. But combat was a great deal more than just noise. It was a whirlwind of iron and lead that howled about the soldier, slicing through anything it hit. Even inside the roar of battle, strangely, the soldier could detect the whistle of bullets and the hum of slivers of shrapnel, perceiving everything separately—a shell burst here, the rattle of machine-gun fire over there, an enemy soldier hiding behind cover in another place. In spite of the confusion swirling around the soldier in combat, he still retained a clear sense of his own strength and the strength of the men beside him; he felt an almost palpable sense of solidarity with his fellow soldiers. This was the brotherhood of the combat soldier.

Improbable as life in combat was, after a while it became the only reality, and the combat soldier soon found it difficult to remember anything else. He would try to remember the face of a loved one and he could not. The soldier on his left and on his right became the only reality and now, in truth, the only loved ones. To the combat soldier, life became an endless series of hard physical work, raw courage, occasional laughter, and a terrible sense of living out a merciless fate that would inevitably culminate in his death or mangling. It was a hard fate for young men. Strangely, the more stalwart and robust-looking men were more likely to lose their nerve in combat than the supposedly weak ones.

By late October, the mud was so bad that nothing

could move in it. All movement stopped except on railroads and paved roads, which gave the Russians time to build up their forces behind the line. Even infantry on foot could move only with the greatest of difficulty. Nothing on wheels or tracks could move at all except on the post road or railroads. The only way we could move vehicles was to corduroy the roads with small tree trunks laid side by side to provide a solid surface. We established corduroy roads between our gun positions and our source of ammunition and supplies at division headquarters. Such roads were difficult footing for the horses, and the vehicles jolted over them, but at least we could transport supplies and ammunition.

A hard freeze came on November 7, which proved both an advantage and a disadvantage. We could move again, but now we were freezing because we still did not have winter clothing. We had the same field uniforms we had worn during the summer, plus a light overcoat. It seemed inexplicable that they could not get winter clothing to us. The quartermaster people were doing a good job of getting everything else to us—but no winter uniforms. We tried to spend the nights in villages so we could get out of the weather. In November this far north, we had only seven hours of daylight. We would start well before daylight and keep going long after dark because of the short hours of daylight. As long as we marched, of course, our physical movement kept us from freezing.

The fahrers would keep the horses behind houses at night, and strap blankets on them as well, to try to shelter them from the wind. The horses had winter coats of fur, which helped them, although a few of them died at night from the cold. On November 12, the temperature dropped to 12 degrees below zero Fahrenheit. Even during the day now we looked forward to passing through villages so we could warm up in the local peasant huts. When we reached the village that was our objective for that day, I left the infantry and went back to my battery to see how they were taking the cold. I found Steinbach in a hut, trying to get warm.

"How are the men doing?" I asked him.

"They are freezing, Herr Oberleutnant," he said. "I am seriously concerned about the possibility of frostbitten toes if this continues."

I went outside and wandered among the men as they parked the guns for the night—in a position so we could fight if we had to—and fed, watered, and rubbed down the horses. I tried to inspire a little more confidence in them by my presence. I found Jaschke helping to strap blankets around horses.

"How are you doing, Jaschke?" I asked.

"We have to get all the men inside, Herr Oberleutnant," he said. "At least for part of the night. They will die in this cold if they have to stay out all night."

I called Jaschke and Steinbach together, and we arranged a schedule that rotated the men in and out of the available huts during the night. The Russians had a real advantage over us, because they had warm felt boots and quilted uniforms, and we had only our thin overcoats, which did not offer much protection from the cold. The only reason we were ever given for not receiving winter clothing was that we were moving too fast. The reasons given for failure always sound plausible. Some of our soldiers took felt boots from dead Russian soldiers, but we did not dare risk wearing their heavier quilted jackets for fear of being shot for a Russian. Fortunately, we could pull the flaps of our field caps down to keep our ears from freezing. The men wrapped their blankets about themselves, over their overcoats and caps, and cursed those responsible for not providing us with winter clothing.

The snow blew almost horizontally in blizzards that sometimes lasted all day long, with the wind piercing our faces with a thousand needles. The cold numbed and deadened the human body from the feet up until the whole body was an aching mass of misery. To keep warm, we had to wear every piece of clothing we owned to achieve a layered effect. Each man fought the cold alone, pitting his determination and will against the bitter winter. We reduced sentry duty to one hour, then to thirty minutes, and finally to fifteen minutes. The cold was, quite simply, a killer; we were all in danger of freezing to death.

We learned now that getting warm in a peasant hut could be dangerous. The combination of newspapers on the wall and dried-out wooden walls set the stage for disaster. I was in one of them with several other people trying to get warm and talking about our next operation when all of a sudden the room burst into flames. Although we all escaped through the doors and windows, we learned then that if a fire was kept going in those peasant stoves for weeks on end the whole hut became extremely flammable. The stove stayed hot and the walls stayed hot, and if the walls reached a flash point and someone struck a match to light a cigarette, the whole place would ignite.

We stopped in a village to rest and get warm and plan our attack for the next morning. My pferdehalter, Schmitt, had taken my horses to a nearby barn so they could get warm. It was almost dusk when we took Russian artillery fire. A familiar slow whine rose to a piercing howl, followed by a series of thunderous explosions that shook the earth. The hut I was in was not damaged. When I went outside to inspect the damage, I found that the barn had taken a direct hit and both my horses lay dead in the snow.

Although losing Schwabenprinz was a great emotional loss to me, it was not a practical loss, because we were in constant combat and in combat we marched on foot with the infantry rather than riding, partly to protect the horses and partly to keep warm. Horses were now used only to pull the guns, ammunition, and supplies.

The Russian resistance became more and more determined now as we neared Moscow, and our casualties were becoming much heavier. At first, we had had fairly light casualties, and we had taken a seemingly endless stream of prisoners. But now our progress was slowing considerably, resistance was stiffening, prisoners were fewer, and our casualties were higher. Stalin, who understood the Russians' great love of their country, had declared this war to be the Great Patriotic War and convinced his people that it was not communism they were fighting for, but Mother Russia. It worked for him.

By December, we were no more than twenty-five kilometers from Moscow, but the temperature was paralyzing. Heavy snow fell on December 1, and the pitiless cold became unbearable. Our world had become a huge frozen abyss in which the white snow glittered in the flashes of our gunfire and turned pink or green in the light of signal flares. Mortars were of little value because the explosion was muffled in the deep snow.

Although we were freezing, we still provided enough warmth for the lice that fed on us. We had become, quite simply, frozen and exhausted men who were being constantly tormented by vermin. We felt like livestock rather than human beings. The snow seemed to fill the air with a soft mist, bringing the earth and sky together into one meaningless blur. It drifted about over the level ground, swirling and forming strange and surrealistic patterns. Frostbite was beginning to account for many casualties, sending men home with amputated toes or fingers. I had not worn clean clothes for two weeks. I tried to imagine what it would be like to stand under a hot shower and scrub my back with a stiff-bristled brush. The image was maddening, and I quickly ejected it from my mind.

On December 4, we were in Rasskazovka, a village just outside Moscow. We had established a defensive line around the village the evening before. In the early hours of a freezing, disagreeable morning, just as my battery was about to lay down a barrage on the next village, we saw a group of thirty to forty Russian soldiers moving toward us across open ground. Our infantry opened fire on them with mortar and machine guns and drove them back. A while later, they attacked again, this time in company strength of 150 or so men. Again, the infantry drove them back. Then they attacked in battalion strength, with about five hundred men! We could see them moving out about three kilometers away. I got my guns ready and opened fire on them, but they kept coming. It was just suicide, because they were out in the open and they had no tanks or artillery or protection of any kind. They got as close as two hundred meters before they were totally decimated. Because I could not believe they would behave so irrationally, I went out to learn anything that might shed some light on their reason for such suicidal behavior. Hundreds of dead and wounded lay in the reddened snow, horribly mangled and splattered with blood, their eyes growing dim as their lives ran out. Our medics moved among them, tending to those who were still alive.

"They all appear Mongolian," a voice said behind me. It was Kreuger. He was also apparently looking for clues. "All the Russians I have seen until now have been Caucasian."

"You are right," I agreed. "What do you suppose that means? And why in God's name would they waste infantry against artillery? That is worse than stupid—it is criminal to waste lives that way."

"Maybe they thought we were so weakened by the cold that they could just walk in and take us because they had fresh troops," Kreuger speculated.

If they had waited until night they would have had a better chance, but they did not stand a chance in daylight when we could use artillery against them.

As we approached the outermost suburbs of Moscow a paralyzing blast of cold hit us, and the temperature dropped far below zero and stayed there. Our trucks and vehicles would not start, and our horses started to die from the cold in large numbers for the first time; they would just die in the bitter cold darkness of the night, and we would find them dead the next morning. The Russians knew how to cope with this weather, but we did not; their vehicles were built and conditioned for this kind of weather, but ours were not. We all now numbly wrapped ourselves in our blankets. Everyone felt brutalized and defeated by the cold. The sun would rise late in the morning, as harsh now in the winter winds as in the heat of August, and not one fresh footprint would be visible for as far as the human eye could see. Frostbite was taking a very heavy toll now as more and more men were sent back to the field hospitals with frozen fingers and toes. Many infantry companies were down to platoon size.

On December 5, the temperature plummeted to 30 degrees below zero. It was almost impossible for the human body to function in such numbing cold. We reached our objective, Peredelkino, by noon. Our feet felt like awkward blocks of ice as we struggled to put one foot in front of the other and keep walking. I found myself wondering if anything could possibly be worth such suffering. The flesh on our faces and ears would freeze if we left it exposed for very long, and we tried to wrap anything around our heads to prevent frostbite. I could not help thinking of Napoleon's army retreating from Moscow. Our fingers froze even in gloves and stuffed into our overcoat pockets; they were so stiff from the cold that they refused to perform any function. We could not have fired our rifles. I could not help wondering if our superiors in Berlin had any idea of what they had sent us into. Such thoughts constituted defeatism, I knew, but that threat seemed of little consequence at the moment.

Instead of moving on immediately after reaching Peredelkino, as we normally would have, some of us went into a peasant hut to get warm, because the cold was surely going to kill us if we did not. Oberleutnant Schumann, battery commander of Third Battery, and I, along with our forward observation officers and an infantry leutnant, went into the same hut to try to warm up. We should not have congregated the key officers from two artillery batteries in the same spot where we could all have been killed en masse, but the cold was beyond human endurance and we had to get warm if we were to survive.

We were sitting on the stone stove in the middle of the hut, just beginning to thaw out, when we heard the sharp cracks of tank cannons. We had received no warning from our infantry, and we had just got up to investigate when a tank shell crashed through a corner of the hut and exploded. Shrapnel blasted through the room, scattering broken and bleeding bodies, filling the room with smoke, the smell of burned powder, and the astonished cries of wounded soldiers.

Two people were killed instantly. Although he was alive, Schumann's face was covered with blood from a head wound that was obviously very serious, and blood was coming from his arm and neck as well. The blast had knocked me down, and when I tried to get up I fell again. I realized that I had a head wound also and had lost my sense of balance. Seeing blood on my sleeve, I inspected my arm and discovered that a chunk of flesh about the size of a large coin was missing from the fleshy part of my upper left arm. Further inspection revealed a piece of shrapnel sticking in the metal insignia of my collar, which had obviously spared me a very nasty neck wound.

Everyone in the room was dead or wounded. I called for a medic to come and tend to Schumann. Schumann could speak, but he was very seriously wounded. He was a big man, six foot five and well over two hundred pounds; perhaps he had just been too big a target. The medics applied rough bandages to our wounds.

Eight or ten Russian tanks had been able to slip past our weary infantry unnoticed. We had not seen Russian tanks for some time and were probably not as alert as we should have been. They had found an area of depression in the terrain that they could slip through undetected. Letting them catch us unawares was a poor performance on our part. If we had not all been so concerned about getting in out of the cold, it would not have happened. Their tanks did not have infantry with them, however, so they just came close enough to the village to shoot into the houses and then withdrew, because tanks without infantry were very vulnerable.

The first time I had been wounded, in France, I had been surprised, but when it happened the second time I just thought, "Okay, it has happened again and I am still alive, so I am lucky and I hope I am just as lucky next time."

17

AFTER I KNEW I had not been permanently maimed, I was glad to be wounded and out of the fighting—and especially to be out of the horrible Russian winter. We were not dressed for it, equipped for it, or ready for it in any way.

The medics administered first aid and applied bandages to the wounded. Schumann and I were put on sleds and pulled back to my battery by hand. I turned command of my battery over to my battery officer, Leutnant Steinbach, who reported our losses to battalion, including the fact that both battery commanders had been wounded. Leutnant Jaschke had been only slightly wounded.

Schumann and I were then loaded into the back of a truck to be taken to a field hospital in Vyazma. The truck had brought supplies in and was taking wounded out. We were on the outskirts of Moscow, only about twenty kilometers from the Kremlin, and the trip to Vyazma was approximately 120 kilometers. Nine of us were in the bed of the truck, with a driver and a guard up front. Over frozen ground, it was a cold, jolting, painful ride for wounded men, bouncing around in an empty truck bed, but there was no alternative.

I tried to make Schumann as comfortable as possible. His head and neck wounds were obviously serious, and the jolting of the truck was terribly uncomfortable for him. I folded my blanket and put it under his head for a pillow to keep his head from banging on the metal floor of the truck bed. As uncomfortable and painful as my own wounds were in the bouncing truck bed, Schumann's were much worse. After an interminable three or four hours, we finally arrived at the field hospital in Vyazma.

They redressed our wounds at the field hospital. My arm wound was a clean flesh wound, but my head wound had robbed me of my sense of balance and I was not able to stand. I was at the field hospital only one night, because the Russians had mounted a major offensive, many wounded were coming in, and the hospital staff was eager to move people on. By the time I was put aboard an ambulance train to Warsaw the next morning, I already had lice under my bandages—a terrible experience because I could not get to them.

Schumann was too seriously wounded to travel, so they kept him at the hospital in Vyazma, where he later died. I had known him since France, so we had been together over a year—a long time in combat. We were not close personal friends, but he had been a good comrade and fellow soldier. As battery commanders in the same battalion, we had shared the same combat in Russia, and we had also fought together in France. At thirty-one, he was old for his rank, because he had been promoted through the ranks instead of attending a military academy, a practice that had begun with the start of the war in 1939. Unfortunately, such people were looked down upon by many officers. Many of them were as good as or even better than the rest of us as officers, because they had more practical experience, but they were not as educated or as sophisticated. There was even a bad joke about them. They were called "vomags," a term composed of the first letters of the expression "folk officer with a laborer's face." It was a very degrading expression. Schumann had felt the insult keenly, but he had borne it manfully and showed no resentment or bitterness. He had been a good soldier and a good officer—and now he had given all he had to give for folk and Fatherland.

We did not know it then, but on December 5, the day I

was wounded, the Russians had thrown hundreds of thousands of fresh, motivated, well-trained, and well-equipped Siberian troops against us, and they were now pushing us back, away from Moscow. I was spared the experience of the retreat because I was wounded at the very beginning of it. It is terrible to be wounded during a retreat, because retreating soldiers can rarely take wounded with them; the wounded usually lie where they fall during a retreat, to die of their wounds, freeze to death, or be taken captive by the enemy.

I did not yet know that the German Army had begun a general retreat. I did not know that our tanks had not been able to capture Kalinin and Tula, north and south of Moscow. I knew only what had happened at my own little part of the front, and nothing had happened there to indicate a general retreat. The tanks that had attacked us did not have infantry, and if you stop a couple of tanks that are not accompanied by infantry, the other tanks retreat. I not only had no idea that anything catastrophic was in the making, but on the contrary I thought the same thing that had happened in the Sudetenland and again in Paris was about to happen the third time—I thought my division would soon be holding a victory parade in front of the Kremlin and I would miss it again because of being wounded, for the third time!

The ambulance train took two days to go from Vyazma to Warsaw, a distance of about eight hundred kilometers. By this time I was able to sit up; the more severely wounded who could not sit were in different cars under the care of medics. We were all utterly thankful to be out of the inferno of combat and the murderous Russian winter. We talked about our experience in Russia, about home, and about the food we were receiving aboard the train, which was considerably better than any we'd had in a long time. We all also could not seem to get enough sleep. It was a very pleasant feeling of tranquility.

Sitting in the warmth and comfort of the train and

watching the Russian landscape pass, we were impressed anew with the vastness of the area we had covered on foot. We now crossed in two days an area it had taken us over five painful months to cross on foot. But we had crossed most of it in the summer when it was fairly hospitable, and now it was under a cruel blanket of snow and life-taking cold. We marveled at the Russians' ability to keep producing new divisions, no matter how many we killed and captured.

At Warsaw, we were admitted to a former civilian hospital that was now being operated by the German Army. There they cleaned my wounds and redressed them, finally getting rid of the maddening lice that had infested my bandages. We were also finally deloused and would not have to worry about those degrading and devouring creatures again until we returned to the front. It was like a gift from heaven to have a bath and be able to soap ourselves down and get clean. The doctors checked me carefully to make sure that further travel would not be detrimental to my condition; the doctors were always especially concerned about head wounds.

I stayed in Warsaw only a few days. I called my parents and Lilo to let them know I had been wounded and would be coming home. The Army notified families when a soldier was killed, but not when a soldier was wounded; because of the constant losses, that was not possible.

While I was in the hospital at Warsaw, I learned that the Japanese had attacked the United States at a place called Pearl Harbor. So now it was another world war. I did not realize the significance of the event, however; even when Hitler declared war on the United States, I did not realize what it would mean for Germany. In school, I had not learned much about the economic and political significance of the United States in the modern world. I just felt that the United States had been helping England and Russia with material aid all along and that now we would finally be able to strike back at them. Thinking that the

United States would be fully occupied with Japan, I did not realize that its entry into the war, with its vast resources, virtually guaranteed that we would have to fight a two-front war—every German general's most dreaded nightmare because of Germany's experience in the first World War.

After Warsaw, I was sent briefly to hospitals in Olmütz and Brünn (Brno), Czechoslovakia, before being reassigned to the hospital in Leipzig. Although I had to be very careful because of my head wound, I could at least walk by now. I reported to the hospital and then went home that first day.

Being at home again after so much combat all across Russia was like being a frightened child in its mother's arms. My mother held me so tightly for so long I thought she would never let go. I knew it was because of what had happened to Fritz and now my being wounded again. My father was the same way. What was happening to their sons was a great tragedy in their lives.

The next day I went with my parents to see Fritz. Seeing him was terrible. He was suffering horribly from the pain, and the hospital staff gave him morphine to ease it. He could talk to us when he was not too drugged by the morphine, but then he was in terrible pain. He could not move, and his body was covered with seeping bedsores. He knew he was going to die, and he grimly accepted his fate. We tried to give him hope, but he was just getting worse and worse. It would have been more merciful if the bullet had killed him cleanly.

I went to Lilo's studio when I knew she would be quitting and surprised her there. She squealed with delight and threw her arms around my neck, hugging me in spite of my wounds. It was great to see her again and to know that she felt the same way about me. My memory of her had not failed. She was as fresh and delightful as I remembered. We fell into our old pattern of meeting at her studio when she got off work, going to dinner and then to a movie, concert, or party. For me, she was a real antidote for the war.

Christmas was sad for my family that year. We visited Fritz every day, and he was always happy to see us. Just before Christmas, he was awarded the Iron Cross Second Class and the wound badge. He received the wound badge in silver because of the severity of his wound (it was normally black for the first wound). Receiving his medals made him proud and happy, because they represented the only concrete achievements in his short life. At Christmas, we brought presents to the hospital and went through the motions, but under the circumstances we could not get into the spirit of the season.

I was glad every day that I had Lilo during this convalescent period. Fritz's condition was extremely depressing, and the news from Army Group Center was not good. I remembered the total confidence with which we had begun the Russian campaign and realized now how overconfident we had been. We'd had no concept of the vastness of the Soviet Union or the size of her population and resources. Being able to go out to dinner and to a movie or a concert with Lilo in the evenings helped me momentarily put Fritz and the things that I knew were happening with my battery at the front out of my mind. When I was not with her, it all came rushing back to fill the vacuum.

The morale of the German population did not seem bad. Until the invasion of France, most of the people felt that Hitler was just getting back what had been taken from Germany at the end of the World War. The campaign in France had been popular, because we'd had to pay heavy reparations to France after the war and because France had declared war on us in 1939. And, of course, the fact that we had won the campaign also made it popular. The German people seemed to be quite happy with the way things had gone early in the war. Even with the invasion of Russia, morale was good when things went well in the beginning. The German population in general saw communism as a social evil because of the reports coming out of Russia prior to the war—reports of mass starvation as government policy, of mass executions of political opponents, and of the brutal forced relocation of millions of peasants. All these things were known in Germany, and of course the Propaganda Ministry emphasized and magnified them. And, of course, the population, perhaps cynically, would not have objected to our acquiring the food-producing Ukraine and the oil-producing Caucasus.

Since our losses in Russia were becoming more and more severe, however, things were beginning to change. During the quick campaigns in Poland, France, Denmark, Norway, Yugoslavia, and Greece, we'd had heavy losses, but our losses ended quickly because the campaigns were short. On the Russian front, our per-day losses in the beginning were lighter, but they never stopped—they continued day after day, week after week, month after month. And as time passed, our casualties kept getting heavier. Our losses were never reported at home, but more and more families had sons who had been killed or badly wounded. Slowly, the people began to get the picture, not from the government, but indirectly from talking to one another. Strangers in a store or in a line waiting to buy bread or milk would talk to each other. What had happened to my family was not different from what had happened to many others, and now it was becoming apparent to everyone that things were not going well in Russia. Of course, everybody hoped that with a spring offensive things would go well again. We learned how to interpret the news, because the Propaganda Ministry always used the same language to describe the same situations. For example, the use of "heroes" or "heroic" always meant we had suffered heavy losses. When we read about "the heroes of Tula," we knew we were losing the battle for Tula.

But it was only at Moscow that things looked bleak. Army Group North still held Leningrad under siege, and Army Group South was doing fairly well against Russian counterattacks in the Ukraine and the Crimea. When the offensive began again next spring, however, I knew the losses would be much heavier, because then the Russians could put up a much stronger resistance. They were much better motivated now than they had been in the beginning.

I did not know yet that the momentum and the initiative had shifted to the Russians. In the beginning, the Russian troops we encountered just ran away for the most part. But the soldiers they sent against us in the vicinity of Moscow were of much better quality. They were determined to save Moscow, and they knew how to fight in the winter better than we did. They were fresh, and we were exhausted; they had new equipment, and ours was worn out; they were motivated, and we were becoming demoralized. I could not avoid the irony of the vaunted German Army, so admired by the rest of the world as masters of the battlefield until now, being fought to a standstill by a people whom our government described as "subhuman."

In January 1942, I was awarded the Sturmabzeichen, the medal for participating in hand-to-hand combat with the infantry. In the spring of 1942, the time had come for me to return to the front. Having been wounded twice already, and having seen hundreds of others killed and badly wounded, I had no illusions about what was in store for me eventually. I was weighted with a sense of impending doom. But there was no other way. I felt that we had to see the fight through to the finish.

My parents and Lilo accompanied me to the train station in Leipzig. I dressed for the front, in the winter field uniform I had received from my home unit. It was a sad leavetaking. I hugged Lilo longingly, knowing I might never see her again. How much luck could I have?

I had taken my leave of Fritz the day before. We both knew it was farewell forever. Although he tried to resist the morphine so he could talk to me, he finally had to ask for it because of the pain. For the few minutes before the morphine stole his mind away we tried to find something meaningful to say, but the anguish of the moment robbed us both of thought and speech. His eyes filled with tears, and so did mine. I took his hand and held it until his eyes closed in peaceful repose. Then, after one last look, I slipped quietly from the room. He had always been so proud of me and my accomplishments, and now he was going to die before he had any real chance to achieve any of his own.

I had left my battery in early December at the outermost suburbs of Moscow, but by spring it had been pushed back to a defense line just east of Smolensk. My battery was in log bunkers in a wooded area. Very little was happening on our front. The main thrust of German offensive operations now was being conducted by Army Group South to try to take the rest of the Ukraine and the Caucasus for food and oil. We would exchange artillery salvos with the Russians occasionally just to annoy each other, but there was no sustained combat at this time. It reminded me of the "sitzkrieg" period in 1939 in the Eifel Mountains. During the winter, Army Group Center was not ready to fight an offensive battle because our men and horses were exhausted and our equipment was worn out, and the Russians apparently did not have the resources to mount another offensive campaign after we had absorbed and blunted their December offensive. They had regrouped, as we had, and were just waiting to see where we would take the offensive.

It was spring and the snow was beginning to melt, ushering in the mud period. Only the Russian farm vehicle called a troika—pulled by three little "Panje" (peasant) horses—could move on those roads. Roads had been corduroyed between our battery and the division, so we could get ammunition and supplies to our position, but any major movement by wheeled vehicles was out of the question. Our bunkers had been built the previous fall from fresh-cut logs, and when the thaw started our area of the front became a virtual swamp. The logs of our bunkers even began to sprout new twigs!

I had been back with my battery only a few weeks and had just become readjusted to the routine when I received orders to report to Berlin to attend a special artillery school, something like a general staff school for artillery officers. I caught a ride in an ambulance to the train station in Smolensk, where I boarded a train to Berlin. I called home from Berlin to let my family and Lilo know I was out of the danger of serving at the front, and then I reported to the school.

The students in the school were all experienced combat battery commanders, oberleutnants and hauptmanns. The purpose of the school was to produce operations officers for artillery generals who commanded very large units of artillery.

I saw Lilo often during the artillery school. I went to Leipzig, only 175 kilometers away, some weekends, and Lilo came to Berlin on others. We were getting serious enough about each other to talk about marriage, but we did not want to get married while the war was going on. Of course, we had no idea at that time how long the war would last.

In May 1942, I received a telegram from my parents: FRITZ DIED THIS MORNING STOP FUNERAL DAY AFTER TOMORROW STOP CAN YOU COME STOP. Even though I had been expecting it and even though it was merciful, it was an emotional blow. I had seen many young men die and I knew this was the price we had to pay for all the victories, but the personal loss was very keen. It was hard to stand by Fritz's grave and bear the heavy pain of losing my only brother. It was even more difficult for my devastated parents.

Before I graduated from this school, the school commander offered to recommend me for another school that would lead to a career dealing with the weapons industry for the German armed forces—as a coordinator between the armed forces and the manufacturers' research and development people. It would have been a nice safe job—I would never have had to go back to the front. It would also have enabled me to get an engineering degree at a university in Berlin at government expense, so I would have been all set after the war. But I turned it down, because I hoped to eventually attend the Army's General Staff College, and I felt the only way to achieve that was to be at the front until I was selected. I felt almost certain that taking the safe, easy job I was offered would rule out my consideration for the General Staff College. Attending the General Staff College was extremely important to a career Army officer. Also, I was still young and idealistic: I felt that as a young soldier I should be at the front.

I never actually performed in the job this school trained me for. We did not have many such artillery units, and the training was really preparatory to forming them. They wanted to have people trained and ready, but most of us went back to our old units until such time as we were needed for the new units.

When I graduated from the advanced artillery school, Lilo and I took a short vacation to Lake Constance on the Swiss-German border. We stayed at a hotel that had previously been a monastery. We went swimming and took boat trips on Lake Constance and enjoyed the brief few days we had together. I wore civilian clothes and tried to forget about what was waiting for me when I returned to the front. We tried to live for a few days as though the war did not exist and the two of us were having a pleasant little vacation in a peacetime world.

All too soon, Lilo had to return to her job. After she had gone I visited my mother, who happened to be vacationing in the Alps at the time, and then I boarded the train to Smolensk and my battery at the front.

Although most of the fighting during the summer had been conducted by Army Group South in the Ukraine, the Caucasus, and the Crimea, there had been some fighting at our front near Smolensk. My battery was again in a prepared defense line, although not the same one I had left it in.

I arrived just in time to take over my battery for the counterattack to regain the lost territory. We laid down a barrage of artillery fire in preparation for the attack, and then the infantry moved out. I went with them, accompanying the point infantry company so that in case of a counterattack I could call in artillery fire on the counterattacking Russian infantry. The din and confusion of battle, as well as the racing adrenaline that accompanies it, were all too familiar. As we were moving forward on foot, the Russians opened up on us with mortar fire. When one of the mortars exploded near me, my legs went out from under me. I stayed down because of the continuing mortar fire, and Leutnant Jaschke took over directing our artillery fire. I hugged the earth and listened to the whistle and the hum of bullets, shrapnel, and slivers of metal splitting the air above me. It was a short fight, and when it was over a corpsman treated my wound. I had been hit in the knee by shrapnel from the mortar. Medics took me first to the regimental dressing station and then to the division's medical facility. I appeared to have shrapnel lodged under my kneecap. Once again, I had been lucky—I was going home with a wound that was apparently not disabling.

I went by ambulance to where I could catch a train, and then to Warsaw, where I stayed only a few days. From there I went to Bad Schandau near Dresden, from where I called home. It was only about 100 kilometers to Leipzig from Dresden, and both my father and Lilo came to visit me (my mother stayed home to take care of the business, because she knew I would be home soon). It was October 1942.

The doctors X-rayed my knee and verified the existence of shrapnel behind my left kneecap, but they did not want to operate to remove it, because the joint would never be the same again if it was operated on, and they felt the shrapnel would not do much harm. They just put my leg in a cast so I could not move it. After a week in Dresden, I was transferred once more to the hospital in Leipzig, where I stayed until November. Having been wounded the third time, I now received the wound badge in silver.

I felt at this point that I had been extremely lucky. Many German soldiers and officers had been in constant combat on the Russian front for a solid year, and even more, without getting to go home. I had been wounded and sent home for convalescent leave twice and had even been sent home once to go to school. I never had a really extended period of combat at the front the way so many unfortunate people did. Lady Luck had so far kept her eye on me.

I saw Lilo almost every day while I was home. As usual, I would meet her when she got off work and we would go to dinner and then to a movie, a play, the opera, or a concert. We felt that things were too uncertain to make definite plans for the future. We tried not to be too serious or think about anything really serious. Our concern now was just to get movie tickets and to meet friends and to enjoy ourselves. We concentrated on having a good time and tried to forget the war in Russia. Lilo was extremely good for me at this point, because she was always so light-hearted and gay, and I needed to laugh and have some pleasure now. I would have to deal with the war again soon enough, but until then we did not want to talk about it or let it spoil the time we had together.

Lilo, who was still managing the photographer's studio, made some portraits of me in my dress uniform as an oberleutnant, with my decorations: Iron Cross First and Second Class, Winter Medal (for the first winter in Russia), Sturmabzeichen (for having been in hand-to-hand combat), and Verwundeten-Abzeichen (wound badge) in silver (for being wounded three times).

Just as there were shortages of men and equipment at the front, there were shortages of everything at home, especially some food items (meat, coffee, tea, chocolate, and so forth), and things were starting to get worse. Earlier, when the war was going well for us, people had accepted the shortages without grumbling—but now that the war was not going as well, people resented the shortages more. The population seemed to be a little more cowed and dispirited.

The Russian campaign was just uncertain at this point. By looking at a map, we could see that the Russians still had a very big country behind the front lines. We had only a little of the western part of the whole country. It was the most important part, the part with most of the industry, but there was still a lot of industry around Moscow that we had not captured—and the Russians had taken much of the industry out and moved it back to the Ural Mountains, well beyond our reach. I knew we had not defeated Russia. I had experienced the fresh Siberian troops myself, and I knew now there was no longer any real hope for a quick end to the war. The situation was becoming depressing, especially with the death of Fritz, and I knew the odds were great that I would die in this war. But I still wanted to see the war through to a successful conclusion, as I think the German population in general did.

I visited Brunsbüttelkoog, my birthplace, with my mother in November 1942, before returning to my home unit for reassignment to active duty. She showed me where we had lived when I was born. My uncle now owned the business my father had started in Brunsbüttelkoog. I still had faint memories of ships passing through the canal and sounding their foghorns at night. It was good for my mother and me to spend a little time alone. After losing Fritz, she had almost clung to me, and I knew she had convinced herself that I would die at the front. Since I had reached the same conclusion, I could not really offer her comfort, but at least we could spend some time together and enjoy each other's company for now.

We went into a store one afternoon while we were there. She found a warm wool winter scarf and purchased it. When we were back outside on the sidewalk, she pressed it into my hands.

"This is for you," she said, as tears welled into her eyes and she threw her arms around my waist. We stood there clinging to each other until her tears subsided.

When I reported to my home unit after my convalescent leave, I learned that someone in the Supreme Command had decided that I should establish a school to train ski troops instead of returning to my old unit. My record from Kriegsschule Potsdam contained a comment that I was a good skier. The Army needed a ski school, so someone started combing the files and came up with my name. The winters in Russia required soldiers who could ski cross-country with full equipment, and that is what I was supposed to establish a school to teach. So my next assignment was to look for a good location to start a ski school for the Army.

I went to the Alps, where there was a good chance of having snow most of the time, and started searching for a site. I was told of a few locations that would be good. I went to each of them and looked things over, making sure there were sufficient places to house the soldiers. I spent a week or two in the Alps and then returned to make my report.

When I reported back to my home unit, however, I learned that my orders had been changed because Stalingrad was in desperate need of reinforcements. My new orders were to report to Generaloberst Paulus's Sixth Army at Stalingrad.

18

ON DECEMBER 17, 1942, I packed my things and caught a train for Rostov, near Stalingrad, where I was to receive my assignment to a specific unit at Stalingrad. It was basically a supply train with a few passenger cars attached. Such trains to and from the Stalingrad area were standard.

I had a layover of a day in Kiev, a beautiful old city that was the capital of the Ukraine. Although it had been damaged in the fighting, it was still functioning as a city and quite a few Russian civilians were still there. The opera was still active, and I went to a performance that evening. The cast was Russian, although the audience was mostly German.

In the train on the way from Kiev to Rostov, I passed the Sea of Azov at night on Christmas eve. I was in a passenger car attached to a slow supply train with a group of other officers going to Stalingrad. We all knew there was heavy fighting at Stalingrad and we were going into a dangerous situation, but we had no idea how bad it was, because the real situation was not being reported to the public. The temperature outside was extremely cold, far below zero. Under a bright moon, the frozen Sea of Azov presented the mirage of a desert in the frigid blue darkness of the night. It looked like a surrealistic painting rather than a real geographical place. In my mind's eye, I could imagine three wise men on camels being guided across the Sea of Azov by a bright white star in the dark night sky. I was jolted from my reverie by the realization that the seductive beauty of this frozen moonscape represented the same killing cold I had encountered on the frozen steppes outside Moscow. Both were beautiful but merciless killers. I left the window and retreated to the warmth of the passenger car, where I joined my fellow officers in singing Christmas carols.

I arrived in Rostov, a very old Russian city that was not quite as large as Kiev, on Christmas Day 1942. Although the city had been damaged by the fighting, it was still in fairly good shape. At the railroad station, I was advised to report to the headquarters of the Fortress Rostov Defense Force. There I reported to the chief of staff, Oberst i.G. Heisenberg, a tall and almost gaunt man in his forties.

"I am afraid you will have to stay here for a while," he said, almost sadly. "The Russians have surrounded Sixth Army, so vehicles are no longer running between here and there. The only way in now is by air, and weather has grounded all flights except those taking ammunition into Stalingrad and bringing wounded out."

"*Jawohl,* Herr Oberst," I responded.

"Until the weather lifts and you can get a flight into Stalingrad you will help me with some staff work. The commanding general of the Fortress Rostov Defense Force needs a daily summary of the reports transmitted by Sixth Army in Stalingrad to Army Group South headquarters. I do not have the time to do it, and I have no one else to assign to it. I hope you are good at writing reports."

Heisenberg assigned me quarters, and I went to work for him in the Operations Department of the Fortress Rostov Defense Force. Our offices were located in an administrative building that must have been Communist Party headquarters, because it was very elegant and beautifully furnished—something I had not seen in Russia until now.

We received all reports from Sixth Army to Army Group South, because it was important for the Fortress Rostov staff to know the situation in Stalingrad. The Don

River flows through Rostov on its way to the Sea of Azov, and the Volga River flows through Stalingrad. The original plan had been to hold the Don and Volga rivers, which were about 150 kilometers apart, and to create a fortified defense line between them that would protect the Caucasus area from counterattack. The oil from the Caucasus Mountains would then be secure. If we could not take Stalingrad, however, we would have to abandon this plan. Rostov, with its bridges over the Don River, was critical to our withdrawal from the Caucasus area if we could not take Stalingrad—and the situation in Stalingrad looked worse with each passing day. Rostov had been declared a fortress city (a term the government was now using to designate a city from which our forces would not withdraw under *any* circumstances) because it was the key to the only supply line to the Caucasus area and represented the only avenue of escape for our forces there.

Although I did not look forward to going into the hopeless situation at Stalingrad, my orders were to go there. I checked with the airport every day to see if I could get a flight, but the weather remained bad. Finally, on January 1, 1943, the sky was bright and clear—perfect flying weather. I went to the airport, certain that I would get a flight today, only to be told that a *Führerbefehl* (an order directly from Hitler) had just arrived from Berlin that no more troops were to be sent to Stalingrad. The government had finally recognized the situation as hopeless—and I had once again received a new lease on life.

Since I could not go to Stalingrad, I was added to the Fortress Rostov Defense Force staff on a permanent basis. Apparently I had worked myself into a job. I settled into my new quarters and new job.

Many Russian civilians in Rostov worked for the German Army, doing the same jobs for us they had done for the Russians—mostly cleaning and other menial tasks. Among those Russians who worked for us, I met an educated Russian woman who spoke German. I worked very late one evening and became so engrossed in the report I was preparing that I lost track of the time and did not realize how late it was until the cleaning lady appeared in the open doorway of my office.

"Excuse me," she said in German. "I did not know anyone was here."

"You speak German?" I asked, quite surprised.

"Yes," she replied. "I learned it at university." She appeared to be just over thirty, a bit on the heavy side, with braided blond hair, blue eyes, and a quick smile.

"Then I assume you were not always a cleaning lady," I said. Every place I went, I had always tried to make contact with the local people, and she seemed to present a good opportunity.

"I was a schoolteacher." She shrugged. "But the schools are no longer functioning. I have to live, so I take what is available."

Her name was Olga Malenkov, and I talked to her about what life was like in Russia. Apparently, the communist government involved itself in the most minute aspects of people's lives and employed so many spies that the Russian people dared not trust *anyone*—not even members of their own family. The slightest comment that could be interpreted as criticism of the government could get a Russian arrested and sent to a labor camp for years. She certainly had no love for her government, and yet she seemed to be indifferent about whether we or the Russians won the war, which seemed curious to me.

"At least the communists are Russians," she said when I asked about it. "I do not believe that German fascism would be better."

From several conversations I had with her, I gathered that life in the Soviet Union was terribly grim, even for those who were not rural peasants. Yet she steadfastly refused to believe that outside the Soviet Union people lived any better.

The daily reports from the Sixth Army to Army Group

South detailed the number of our people killed each day, the number wounded, ammunition supplies, food supplies, and weapon supplies. The reports also indicated the positions of our various military units and the type of action they were facing (artillery, tanks, small arms, and so forth). We could see the situation on our maps, and the reports created an extremely grim picture that grew worse with each passing day. It was painfully clear that I would have gone into Stalingrad only to be killed or captured. There was obviously no escape from there at this point. The reports indicated that the supplies of food and ammunition continued to diminish daily as the losses continued to mount. The Sixth Army finally reached a point where it could not even get its wounded out any longer. Hitler's order to stand and fight to the last man rather than retreat and regroup was obviously going to have very tragic consequences.

Since these reports went all the way up to Hitler, they had to be worded very carefully. They never said the situation was hopeless, because that would bring charges of defeatism against the responsible officer. An officer could not say that everything was lost and he was ready to surrender. He could only report the facts and let them speak for themselves. It had been sheer stupidity to keep our troops in Stalingrad with no way to relieve them instead of permitting them to retreat. But their orders were to stay, and they stayed. And my orders were to join them, and I would have joined them except for the intervention of providence in the form of bad weather. These remarkably stupid military errors were undoubtedly due to Hitler—a man with no military training or experience above the rank of gefreiter —taking over the day-to-day operation of the German Army. Yet we were supposed to be the "master race," according to Dr. Goebbels's propaganda, and the Russians— who had the wisdom to let their generals run their army— were the "subhumans." The irony of it all was becoming painfully obvious.

The Russians could have just bypassed the Sixth Army after surrounding it, leaving it to die on the vine, and then marched to Rostov to cut off our escape route from the Caucasus. Later in the war, they would have done that. Now they did not, perhaps because they did not have adequate resources to do it.

As part of the staff at Fortress Rostov, I helped plan the withdrawal of our forces from the Caucasus Mountains back into the Ukraine. Our job was to make it possible for the German Army to withdraw successfully from the Caucasus before the Russians could take Rostov and cut off the only avenues of retreat. In truth, however, the only reason all our people got out of the Caucasus area when the time came was that the Sea of Azov was firmly frozen and all but the heaviest tanks were able to cross it on the ice. With just two or three bridges across the Don River, which was about two hundred meters wide, it would otherwise have been impossible to get all our troops across the Don in an orderly withdrawal.

Helping to draw up all these plans for failure and defeat, in addition to reading the daily reports coming out of Stalingrad, was extremely depressing. We did not know for certain what was happening at the other fronts, because we knew the government did not report defeats, but we knew ours was the major front and we were being defeated. After all our military successes, from the occupation of the Rhineland in 1936 to the march almost to the suburbs of Moscow in 1941, it was a strange and foreboding feeling of helplessness to know that we were on the verge of suffering a defeat of catastrophic proportions. It hurt my pride to see such a fine professional army being wasted by the inept leadership of a man with no military training, knowledge, or experience. The front was still far from Germany, however, and we still hoped—perhaps rather forlornly at this point—for a change for the better. I was becoming bitter, however, about Hitler's cruel and stupid order to die rather than retreat and regroup—as were many others in the Army.

I would normally have been at Rostov until all our forces were out of the Caucasus and Rostov was attacked by the Russians, but providence intervened once more. One morning in early February 1943, when I went to work I was told that Oberst Heisenberg wanted to see me. When I reported to him, he returned my salute and smiled, a rare event for him.

"Good morning, Hauptmann Knappe," he said. "Congratulations. You have not only been promoted to hauptmann, but you have also been transferred to France to help form and train a new Sixth Army."

I could hardly believe my own ears. Once again, I was lucky: I was pulled out of harm's way at the last moment, before the Russians attacked and overran Rostov.

I took leave of Oberst Heisenberg and others I had worked with the next day and boarded the train to return to Germany. Regularly scheduled trains ran between Germany and Rostov, bringing supplies in and taking wounded, furloughed, and transferred soldiers out. I was first to report to my home unit at Altenburg.

When I reported there on February 17, 1943, I was given an automatic three-week "eastern front" furlough, even though I had been at Rostov only a few weeks. I went home to Leipzig, arriving just in time to hear the radio announcement—preceded by funeral marches—of the "heroic fight to the last cartridge" of our forces at Stalingrad. The government had been forced to announce our defeat at Stalingrad, because it was not possible to hide a disaster of that magnitude. We were all becoming bitter now about our government's constant attempt to mislead us and hide the truth from us.

Stalingrad was the turning point of the war for us. There had been little Stalingrads before, all of them brought about by Hitler's incredibly stupid orders to stand and fight to the last man, even though it meant the wholesale slaughter of young German men, instead of intelligently retreating to regroup and fight again. Such battles of desperation were becoming more and more frequent, our casualties were increasing, and the Russian Army was beginning to break through our defense lines more frequently. Not only were we suffering more battle casualties, but now many German prisoners were being taken in large numbers by the Russians. A whole German army corps had earlier been encircled and lost, for example, with all its equipment. It had been getting worse for some time, but it was the loss of the Sixth Army at Stalingrad and the withdrawal of Army Group South from the Caucasus Mountains that made it painfully clear to me that we were not going to defeat the Soviet Union. Goebbels's propaganda continued to try to put a good face on things, but after Stalingrad every thinking person knew we could not win this war against Russia. We had now had to give up capturing the rich food-producing Ukraine and the oil-producing Caucasus, without which we had no chance of defeating the Soviet Union. Even so, we did not even dream at this time that the Russians would ever be able to invade Germany. Our assumption of superiority was still intact—even after a defeat of the magnitude of Stalingrad!

My furlough was not as pleasant as it could have been because of our defeat at Stalingrad. A black mourning had fallen over Germany. Public dancing was not permitted, so Lilo and I had to limit ourselves to the theater and concerts. We took a skiing trip to the Austrian Alps, partly to get away from the depressing news and funeral marches that were constantly on the radio. We found the mountain air, the blue sky, and the clean white snow refreshing and invigorating after all the gloomy news of this bitterly bleak time.

Lilo and I now decided that we would get married on my next furlough. The war was obviously not going to be a short one, and we decided to wait no longer.

19

ON MY WAY to my new assignment in France, I stopped over for a day in Paris once more. I took in the sights of Paris again, but I took the elevator to the top of the Eiffel tower this time instead of climbing the stairs. The city did not have the same euphoric effect it had had on me in the past. I felt less enthusiastic, perhaps, because I felt older or perhaps because of our senseless defeat at Stalingrad. Had the experiences at Moscow and Stalingrad aged me that much? At twenty-six, I was certainly young in years. But having seen so much of death, and now of defeat, I no longer felt as young as my years, and I found it impossible to respond to Paris as I had in the past.

I was posted to a village near the French town of Quimper, in the province of Brittany, where we were to build our new Sixth Army. Quimper was near the Atlantic coast and the Atlantic Wall defense system that guarded against an invasion from England by the Allies.

I reported to my new battalion commander, Major Nickisch. He had been wounded at Stalingrad and sent home on convalescent leave before the Sixth Army surrendered. He was very serious about the training chore that was ahead of us, because he was sure we would be back in combat in Russia as soon as our new men were adequately trained.

My new battery was to be Ninth Battery, 3rd Battalion, 194th Regiment, 94th Infantry Division. My new hauptwachtmeister, Naumann, had already arrived, and he and I set about preparing for the arrival of men and horses. My battery officer, Leutnant Duestenberg, and my forward observation officer, Leutnant Euringer, arrived shortly, and the four of us had our hands full as the men, horses, and equipment began arriving. As I was putting this new battery together, thoughts of the old battery I had left in Russia flashed in my mind—Lammers, Boldt with his one eyebrow, our veterinarian, our blacksmith, probably all dead now. How long can anyone live in constant combat?

Approximately 10 percent of our new men were veterans from the old Sixth Army who had been recuperating from wounds or were on furlough when the surrender at Stalingrad occurred. The rest were recruits. Fortunately, Duestenberg, Euringer, and Naumann were all experienced combat veterans, which would make my job considerably easier. All four of us were familiar with and prepared for the job ahead of us.

We used the Sixth Army veterans to temper and help train the new recruits. Because we expected to return to combat as soon as the new troops were ready, we took our duties very seriously so we would be assured of leading well-trained troops when we returned to Russia. Our daily and weekly schedule was similar to what it had been at Plauen as we trained the kanoniers, the fahrers, and the communications people. Our day started at 5:00 A.M. for the horse people and 6:00 for the others as we covered all the things new recruits had to learn. Even the veterans had to repeat it, because they all had to learn how to work together and become a cohesive unit. We could only teach the recruits the mechanics and the skills and hope that the veterans among them could teach them what to expect of combat. In addition to the training, we were expected to man the Atlantic Wall if the Allies invaded from England, so we pushed the training to the limits of the endurance of the men.

The Quimper area had been untouched by the war so far. I do not think any military forces had ever been assigned to the area before, so a military presence was something new to the population. At the coast a short distance away were the Atlantic Wall fortifications and the German submarine bases at St. Nazaire and Lorient. These places had been bombed by the Allies, and the people of Quimper had seen the bombers fly over and heard the bombing, but they had not experienced the brutality of the war directly.

I visited the Atlantic Wall and the submarine base at Lorient one weekend. The submarines were housed in bunkerlike structures the Navy called pens, and huge balloons were anchored over them to protect them against low-flying aircraft (enemy aircraft could shoot the balloons down, but in doing so they would have to make themselves extremely vulnerable to ground fire). The Allies bombed the submarine pens many times from high altitude, but they did not do a lot of damage. It would obviously have been a different story if they had been able to bomb from low altitudes.

Brittany was a very pretty place, with nice villages. We did our job, training our troops, day after day. The local population did not want for anything as far as I could tell. They raised their own food, and they were glad to sell us anything we wanted.

Everything seemed quiet at the western front, so I asked for a furlough to go home and get married. My request was granted, and our families planned the wedding.

In Germany at that time, a celebration took place the evening before a wedding among the bride's and groom's families and closest friends. The guests, who had all arrived in Leipzig for the wedding, brought old dishes that they would break on the floor for good luck—and the prospective bride would have to clean up the fragments.

However, just as I was ready to leave, orders arrived canceling all furloughs because of an emergency somewhere. The worst of it was that I could not call or send a telegram to tell Lilo, because everything was secret. They went ahead with the wedding-eve party without me, correctly assuming that my furlough had been canceled for military reasons and I could not notify them.

Ten days later, the restriction against furloughs was lifted and we scheduled the wedding again. This time, I made it. Lilo was radiant when I arrived home. I had never seen her more beautiful, especially in her wedding gown. We were married first in a civil ceremony and then in a church ceremony. The church ceremony was conducted in the historic Thomas Church in Leipzig, where Martin Luther had preached his first sermon, where the famous composer Richard Wagner was baptized, and where Johann Sebastian Bach had been an organist for twenty-seven years and had written most of his music. Lilo wore a beautiful wedding gown and I wore my dress uniform, complete with sword. The infantry regiment quartered in Leipzig provided a horse-drawn carriage to take us to and from the church and to a reception in a hotel. We did not go anywhere for a honeymoon, because our time was too short. It did not matter, because we had what we wanted—each other.

All too soon, I had to return to my training duties in France. Leaving Lilo now that she was my wife was different from former leavetakings, but at least this time I was not returning immediately to combat.

In June 1943, after more than three months of intensive training, the larger units of the new Sixth Army held maneuvers in the field, practicing defending against an Allied landing on the beaches. Rommel came to observe these maneuvers. It was the first time I had seen him since he had been my commander at Kriegsschule Potsdam, and it was the last time I saw him.

In July 1943, after the field maneuvers had ended, I received a three-week furlough home. Lilo was pregnant with our first child, and I was very eager to see her. She was still radiantly beautiful and happy. Once more, we made the rounds of movies, plays, concerts, and parties—

just trying to have the best time we could in the little time we had together.

One night when Lilo and I were at a concert, my mother sent someone to me with a message to return home immediately because my father had had a heart attack. He was dead when I arrived home. He was fifty-eight years old, and he'd had a heart condition for some time. I think my brother Fritz's death hastened my father's. It had hurt him terribly to see Fritz suffer so much every day for seven endless months, and I think it damaged his health. The emotional scars left by that experience were permanent, and the knowledge that his only remaining son would almost certainly die in this war as well could only have been an additional emotional burden for him to carry. It all caught up with him in July 1943.

I had been at Quimper five months, from mid-March until mid-August of 1943, when we received orders to move out.

20

THE ALLIES HAD landed in Sicily on July 10, 1943, and by August the situation there did not look promising for us. My new division was detached from the Sixth Army and ordered to Italy as a precautionary measure. We loaded on trains at Quimper. The process of loading inexperienced, frightened, and balky horses aboard trains with mostly inexperienced soldiers was as difficult as ever. We managed to overcome all the problems, however, and traveled from Quimper to Modane, Savoy, on the French-Italian border. We unloaded from the train at Modane and marched to the foot of the Alps, where we camped for the night. I was ordered to report to the tent of my battalion commander, Major Nickisch, shortly after dusk. When I arrived, I found the other two battery commanders there as well.

"We are going to march over the Alps, gentlemen," Nickisch said. "The high command has decided the risk that Italian partisans might have mined the train tunnel through the Alps and could blow it up with one of our trains inside is too great. They think it more prudent to march over the Alps in the open, where we can protect ourselves if necessary."

This was going to be a tremendous feat! I returned to my command tent and called in my two officers, Leutnant Duestenberg and Leutnant Euringer. I briefed them on the situation. We were to follow the route Hannibal took across the Alps with his elephants. Our horses had to pull very heavy guns and loaded ammunition carts and wagons.

We were to march up to a pass at the crest of Mont Cenis and then down the other side into Italy. The Mont Cenis pass was approximately 2,100 meters high, and the road distance was about twenty-eight kilometers. It was obviously going to be a herculean task for our horses and for everyone concerned.

I was up at 5:00 A.M. the next day to oversee preparations for the march. We moved out at 6:00 and began the arduous climb to the pass. We did not ride the horses, of course, or ride on the carts and wagons, but walked and led the horses. We moved on a modern road, but at times we could see the old Roman road Hannibal had taken across the Alps, because it often ran parallel to the road we were on.

The horses strained in their harnesses to pull their heavy loads up the mountain. At least the road was paved and the wheels of the vehicles rolled easily; if it had been cross-country terrain, I do not think we would have had a realistic chance of making it. We stopped every thirty minutes for a break instead of every hour as we normally would. The weather was beautiful, with sunshine, clear air, and bright skies. The area was also beautiful, with high mountains all around us. But the climb up the steep mountain road pulling their heavy loads was an extremely arduous task for the horses. Nine hours after we started—in midafternoon—we finally reached the pass and the Italian border.

We stopped by a small lake with crystal-clear water, where we fed and watered the horses and gave them two hours of rest before we began the descent down the other side of the mountain. We considered it a moral victory just to get all our guns and equipment up to the pass. From the pass, we could see all the way down the other side of the mountain, with its winding road, hairpin turns, and rushing white-water creeks.

We knew that going down was not going to be an easy task either; it should certainly be easier and faster than the trip up had been, but it would be much more treacherous. For the horses, going down the mountain could be both difficult and dangerous. Although the guns and other vehicles all had brakes, they were primitive brakes that consisted only of blocks of wood that rubbed against the wheels. Not only were they not terribly effective on a steep downhill grade, but they could also wear out quickly. Although the last two horses in the six-horse team could help hold the vehicle back, they would not last long if the whole weight of the vehicle pushed into them and they had to try to hold it back all by themselves.

It was a tension-filled journey down the mountain for all of us, because we knew the danger only too well. By the time we reached the bottom, the trip over the Alps had become by far the most exhausting exercise any of us had ever experienced. We arrived at the bottom well after dark. We pitched our tents near the Italian town of Susa, in a meadow surrounded by woods. A creek ran through the meadow, and the fahrers watered and washed the horses in the creek. My battery had 180 very tired men and 165 exhausted horses that night. It was probably midnight before we were all able to collapse in our tents and virtually pass out.

We stayed at Susa all the next day to allow the aching bodies of the men and horses to rest. The men washed their clothes in the creek and wrote letters home. The weather was pleasant, and sleeping in tents was not a real hardship.

Meanwhile, trains had been scheduled for the division, and the next day we boarded our train at Susa and went toward Piacenza. We unloaded from the train at Alessandria and marched to Piacenza. The Po River ran through Piacenza, and the bridges across the Po were strategically important because we needed them to get supplies to our forces in southern Italy. Our mission was to ensure that these bridges were secure. Italian soldiers guarded the bridges; we were there as a precaution, in case the Italians deserted us and dropped out of the war. We could not allow them to do that, because it would expose all of southern Europe to attack by the Allies.

Our advance people had arrived ahead of us, and all units had been assigned housing. My battery was in a village outside Piacenza. For the first few days, we lived in tents, under field conditions. Our forces around Piacenza included one infantry regiment and our artillery battalion. The rest of our division was at other bridges over the Po River. After the first few days, we moved from our tents into permanent quarters. We were issued the khaki uniform worn by Rommel's Afrika Korps to replace our field-gray uniforms (North Africa had been lost to the Allies, and the uniforms were now to be used in Italy).

Piacenza was a picturesque city, a typical medieval Italian city with fortifications. It had been fortified for centuries because of the importance of the bridges. Like most old Italian cities, Piacenza had a lot of archways and a market square in the center of town where the local people congregated.

We had been in the Piacenza area only a couple of weeks when we received orders one evening that the new Italian government planned to make peace with the Allies and join the war against us and that we were therefore to disarm the Italian Army before it could be used against us. We had planned an artillery exercise for the next morning, and my artillery battalion had invited all the officers of the Italian artillery regiment stationed in Piacenza to join us in observing the exercise. We had attended some of their exercises, and this kind of reciprocation was a normal thing. Now, when they arrived to observe our exercises the next morning, we would have to disarm them and detain them as prisoners of war. It was an onerous duty that we did not look forward to. We'd had a very friendly relationship with them, and some of them even wore Iron Crosses they had won serving under German command in the African campaign. We felt personally that what we had been ordered to do would be an act of betrayal. But we had orders, and we had to carry them out.

When their bus arrived with about thirty of them aboard the next morning, we apologetically told them we had been ordered to disarm them and the rest of the Italian Army. So we now had most of the officers from their artillery regiment. Our infantry regiment was already in position around Piacenza, and my battery was about a couple of kilometers away.

In the meantime, however, the remaining Italian forces had been ordered not to allow us to disarm them, and when our infantry approached them, they opened fire. Our infantry withdrew and asked for artillery support. Then a few Italian armored cars approached us in a threatening manner, apparently mistaking the pullback of our infantry for a retreat. When our infantry fired on them, the armored cars turned and fled. It looked as if we would have to take Piacenza by force, in spite of the fact that all the civilian population was still in the city. Because we wanted to avoid civilian casualties if possible, the infantry battalion commander and I decided to fire one salvo of artillery into Piacenza's market square to let them see what the city was going to be subjected to if we had to take it by force. The market square was empty, because the civilians knew that combat was likely to occur at any moment and they were staying indoors. The Italian Army had no chance of stopping us if we attacked, because they could not use their artillery—it was not in place, and we held most of their artillery officers.

I prepared my guns and fired one salvo of four artillery shells into the market square. Then we waited. About twenty minutes later, a motorcycle with a senior officer in a sidecar came out, waving a white flag, to surrender the city to us. The artillery salvo had convinced them that it was useless to resist. We confined the Italian troops to their barracks, and our infantry took over security for the bridges over the Po River.

It did not go quite as smoothly everywhere as it did in Piacenza. At Genoa and Savona, the Italian Navy was in charge of military operations, and it refused to submit peaceably; those cities had to be taken by force, and there were losses on both sides. Our division took part in the fighting at Genoa, our infantry being moved quickly by trucks; the artillery was to follow, but it was mountainous country and by the time we got to Genoa with our artillery the fighting was over. The whole matter of disarming the Italian Army lasted only a few days.

In Italy it was not really possible to use horses with artillery because of the mountains and the heat, so I took over the vehicles of a mechanized Italian artillery battery at Piacenza and for the first time became mechanized. German forces in Italy were now 100 percent mechanized; in Russia, the figure was about 25 percent; in France, it was approximately 60 percent. Becoming mechanized after years as horse-drawn artillery was like assuming a completely different life-style. With horses, everyone, even the kanoniers, was affected by the constant attention to horses —feeding, watering, brushing, and otherwise caring for them—whereas we could just park mechanized equipment, turn the key off, and then forget about it until morning. We left our horses with local Italian farmers whom we paid to care for them until they could be returned to Germany. Finally my dreams of being in the mechanized artillery had come true after seven years in the Army!

After the fight at Genoa, we began occupation duty in Italy. Our division assigned individual sectors of occupation to different units. My battery was assigned an area of the Italian Riviera that was about seventy-five kilometers long. I was to share occupation responsibility for this area with a battalion of motorcycle-mounted cavalry that was commanded by Hauptmann Otto Beloff.

Our mission was to guard against a possible Allied landing on the Italian Riviera. The Italians had built artillery into the mountainsides, and I took over their guns in addition to my own. This gave me enough guns for a battalion instead of a battery, although I still had the same number of men to man them. In an artillery duel with Allied battleships, however, we would have been badly outgunned. If the Allies had landed there, we would not have been strong enough to stop them for very long, but the Alps behind us presented them with a natural barrier. All the bridges, passes, and tunnels in the Alps had been mined by the Italians, and it was part of our responsibility to blow them up in the event of an Allied landing we could not contain.

My area of the Italian Riviera ran from Ventimiglia on the French border to Savona (a naval port), with Imperia falling roughly in the middle. I was responsible for the artillery and Beloff was responsible for the infantry. I chose Imperia for my headquarters, and Beloff chose another village nearby. I found a beautiful abandoned villa that belonged to a friend of Mussolini's named Faravelli and moved into it. I was told that the owner was staying at another home he owned in the mountains.

The villa had about twenty-five rooms. The bathrooms had both fresh water and seawater, and I could choose which I wanted to bathe in. The villa overlooked the Mediterranean, across a highway and a set of railroad tracks. I lived in the villa with my orderly and a motorcycle runner and had an office nearby.

Our stay in Imperia was my most pleasant military duty of the war. Except for becoming familiar with the Italian guns and ammunition, we did not have a lot to do, since we were guarding against a possible but unlikely invasion. The biggest bother would normally have been the horses, and since we did not have to care for them any longer, life was relatively easy. Hauptmann Beloff and I even changed into civilian clothes once (because Monte Carlo was neutral in the war) and drove to the gambling casino at Monte Carlo. From Monaco, we went on to Nice, and then returned to Imperia.

Our pleasant duty at Imperia was all too short. Allied forces landed at Salerno in September 1943, and Generalfeldmarschall Kesselring, commanding all German armed forces in the Mediterranean area, decided to use our division as part of an in-depth defense line across the boot of Italy, south of Rome, apparently on the assumption that the Allies could not invade Salerno and northern Italy at the same time. We received orders to board trains at six-thirty one morning, and we quickly learned that boarding trains is much easier with mechanized equipment than with horses. We went back through Piacenza and through the suburbs of Rome.

The portion of the defense line, called the Gustav Line, assigned to us was north of Naples. Two other divisions manned the other portion of the defense line. We unloaded from the train at Vallerti and marched the last several kilometers, as usual. We went into the prepared line, which was still about ninety-five kilometers behind the front lines. Our defense line went through the town of Castelforte, but we avoided the town because it would have been such an inviting target and went to the hills south of the town instead.

Our first job was to familiarize ourselves with the terrain and the area. We were to be ready and prepared so that if our infantry in the present front line near Naples could no longer hold, it could pull back behind our prepared line. When the Allies came they would face fresh and rested infantry that was defending an in-depth prepared defense line, supported by artillery familiar with the terrain and all the possible targets in the area. While we held the line, the troops who had withdrawn behind the line would have a chance to rest and become reserve. It is very difficult for retreating troops to stop and turn around and fight again, especially if the opposing troops are pressing hard, as they should always do. So our function was to let our retreating troops through our line and then to close the line and stop the pursuing enemy there. We were an army corps, with three divisions in the defense line and one in reserve. Our division had the section of the line that bordered the Tyrrhenian part of the Mediterranean. The division in the middle had the Monte Cassino area, and the third division had the section that bordered on the Adriatic Sea.

We were busy every day inspecting the area. The infantry had to look over every little creek and ravine in the area and put down a forward line, complete with trenches and foxholes. I had to establish the possible target areas for artillery support. I went through the area with the infantry and determined how they intended to defend, and then I set up my targets accordingly. We had time to do all this because the fighting was still well south of us. We were in mountainous country, which made it easy to defend, because enemy tanks were almost out of the question. Basically, the only way to attack us was on foot.

When we had learned the area and settled into the new defense line, we just waited for the fighting to reach us. The infantry was dug in. Our guns were in an orange grove behind a little ridge, and everything was in place. We could see Mount Vesuvius from our position. The place and the weather were beautiful, and we had all the oranges from the trees in the orange grove we wanted as we waited. The women from the local villages would come to wash clothes in the streams near our position. We thought it would probably be two or three weeks before the fighting reached us.

On November 19, 1943, I received a telegram that Lilo had given birth on November 12 to our son, Klaus-Jürgen. The telegram also said that Lilo and the baby had had to flee from Leipzig after a terrible air raid and that the baby was in a children's hospital in Braunschweig in poor condition. Since things at the front were quiet at the time, I was given a furlough to visit Lilo and the baby. When I left to go home, I took a whole trunk of oranges and a turkey with me, things that were very rare in Germany.

When I arrived in Leipzig, I was stunned by the devastation that had been done to the city by an Allied air raid. What a contrast Leipzig presented to undamaged Rome, which I had just left. Since I had to change trains in Leipzig in order to get to Blankenburg, where Lilo was at her uncle's house, I went to my mother's home, changed into civilian clothes, left some of the oranges for her, and went on to Blankenburg, still carrying the remaining oranges and the turkey.

When Lilo saw me, she threw herself into my arms and began to sob uncontrollably. Then she told me the whole story of Klaus-Jürgen's birth. A few days after Klaus was born at a small private hospital, Leipzig was subjected to the most severe bombing raid it had experienced during the war because of its importance as a rail center. The Allies dropped incendiary bombs, and large areas of Leipzig were burned. The hospital where Lilo and Klaus were was hit by incendiary bombs and set on fire. Lilo and Klaus stayed in the basement while people tried to put the fire out above them. They succeeded, but there was no longer any water or electricity—not just in the hospital, but in most of Leipzig. With neither water nor electricity, there was no way to sustain life. Lilo could not feed Klaus, because there was no milk to be had, and she had an infection that made breast-feeding impossible. It was obvious that she would have to get out of the city immediately or Klaus would surely die. Her mother suggested that they go to the home of her brother, Lilo's uncle, at Blankenburg, in the Harz Mountains.

The trip to Blankenburg by train normally took four hours, but this trip took more than twenty-four hours, not only because the bombing raid had disrupted the train service and damaged the tracks, but also because much of the population of Leipzig was evacuating the city. During the whole time, there was no food for Klaus and no heat in the train. When Lilo arrived in Blankenburg, Klaus was an extremely sick baby, and she knew she could not keep him in Blankenburg. He had to go to the nearest hospital, in Braunschweig, which was about sixty kilometers away. She got an ambulance and took him to a children's hospital over very dangerous icy roads.

When they arrived at the hospital, a woman doctor examined Klaus. He was almost dead, and the doctor gave him no real chance to survive. He weighed less than he had at birth. Although he did not die, he clung to life for weeks with very little chance of survival. Lilo eventually had to leave Klaus at the hospital and return to Blankenburg. The ordeal she'd had to endure by herself was terrible, and only now did I learn the story. I comforted her and found myself silently cursing the war that had done this to her and Klaus.

We caught a train from Blankenburg to Braunschweig, where Klaus was hospitalized, and there, on January 8, 1944, I first saw my son. He was about eight weeks old now, but he was still badly underweight and looked terrible. I had never seen a newborn baby before, but all the pictures of babies I had seen were of healthy, fat babies, and he looked incredibly small and sickly.

Before I returned to Italy, we were lucky to find Lilo a place to stay. Her uncle in Blankenburg had three children, and she did not want to impose upon him any longer than necessary. We found a room for her in a doctor's home (the government required those who had extra rooms to rent them to those who had been bombed out of their homes). Klaus had to stay in the hospital several more weeks after I left, but his life was no longer in danger. He started to recover before I left, although it was quite some time before he looked fat and healthy.

I left to return to Italy on January 24, 1944. As I returned through Leipzig and saw the burned-out and destroyed areas of the city, I knew the bombing was beginning to demoralize the population. The propaganda line that the bombing was just drawing people together and hardening their resolve was true, because you hate the people who are doing this to you, but the bombing was also having a demoralizing effect—especially on workers, who could not get enough sleep or rest because they had to keep going to air raid shelters during the night. They were beginning to just wish this was all over.

When my train pulled into the station in Florence and I disembarked, German Army officers were in the station directing everyone in a German uniform into a special area of the railroad station. The American Army had landed at Anzio (we called this operation the Nettuno bridgehead, because Nettuno was the main community in the landing zone), and with all our regular infantry divisions tied up at the front against the Allied forces moving north from the Salerno landing area, no troops were readily available to oppose them. So all military returning from furlough or convalescent leave were being collected at the major railroad stations to form makeshift units to try to contain the American forces at Anzio/Nettuno until a regular infantry division could be brought in. As an officer, I was directed to go to a nearby hotel for further directions. All officers were interviewed to determine their experience, and I was placed in command of a battalion of three companies of makeshift infantry, including Navy and Air Force people who had infantry training.

Florence was approximately 370 kilometers from Anzio. We went to Rome by bus and then loaded aboard trucks for the rest of the trip. Army officers were waiting at Anzio to direct us into a defense line that was already being established. My battalion was assigned a section of the southeast side of the defense line around the landing area. I assigned a sector to each of my company commanders, held some troops in reserve, and waited to see what was going to happen. The defense line we were establishing was about forty-five kilometers long, in a half-circle around the American bridgehead. We had small arms, but we did not have tanks, artillery, or even machine guns. With inexperienced troops who had never worked together before and who were under strange officers, we would not have been a very effective fighting force at best, and without machine guns, mortars, tanks, or artillery, we would not have much of a chance if the Americans had attacked. But they did not attack. They just dug in. We waited for them to attack, and they apparently waited for reinforcements. It was the quietest battle scene I ever experienced. We saw their ships out at sea, with balloons tethered to the ships to protect them from attack by low-flying aircraft.

The two enemy forces just sat and watched each other. A few days later, regular infantry arrived to replace us and we returned to our own units. I am glad the American commanding general was not Patton, because an aggressive general could have taken Rome with very little effort at that time. Once they allowed us time to get real infantry into position opposite them, however, they had to fight fiercely for every foot of ground.

As I approached the Gustav Line on my way back to my battery, the fighting was raging near Cassino. About thirty-five kilometers away I began to hear the heavy artillery, which sounded like a thunderstorm somewhere in the distance. Then as I got closer I began to hear the light artillery as well. Finally, as I got closer still, the sound of battle became the old familiar constant roar, with the sounds of mortars and machine guns and rifles in addition to the artillery. Always before, in France and in Russia, this constant roar of battle had been a natural part of my life at the front and I had thought nothing of it, but this time was strangely different, and I found myself thinking, "Oh, God, here we go again, with this constant day-to-day combat." I had never thought or felt that way before, and it never happened again. I had always controlled fear in the past. It may have been because I had just seen Klaus for the first time, had more to live for now than ever before, and was more keenly conscious of my own mortality than ever before. Perhaps it was because I had been out of combat for some time. Or perhaps it was because we were obviously going to lose the war. For whatever reason, returning to the front was extremely unnerving for me this time.

When I reported to my battalion commander, Major Nickisch, he greeted me with a huge smile.

"What would be your greatest desire, Knappe?" he asked.

"That this war would be over," I said wearily.

"After that," he prompted.

I looked at him. He obviously had news for me.

"You have been selected for general staff training," he said. "Congratulations!"

I was tremendously pleased and proud, because being selected for general staff training was the greatest honor a junior officer in the German Army could receive. You could not ask for it; you could only be selected for it. Probably one of the reasons I had been selected was my ranking of twenty-fourth in my 1938 graduating class of four thousand at the four military academies. By then my number had changed from twenty-four to twelve, which meant that half of those above me were either dead or very badly wounded. A chilling statistic! Probably most of them were dead, having been killed in Poland, France, Russia, North Africa, or Italy.

A replacement had already been selected to take over my battery, and I was assigned to the staff of the neighboring 71st Infantry Division to begin on-the-job general staff training. General staff training was in three stages. The first stage was on-the-job work, during which the trainee was progressively assigned to a division, corps, army, and army group to learn by direct observation what general staff work was all about. The second stage was a series of short specialized schools on tank warfare, artillery, engineering, and so forth, to provide the trainee with the broad knowledge of all types of military operations necessary for good staff work. The third stage was the General Staff

College, which was designed to teach the trainee to lead a division in combat.

During the on-the-job training, one of the first things I learned was that as part of a staff one of my responsibilities was to know all the key people in the division. As a battery commander, I needed to know only my own battalion commander and the other battery commanders in my battalion in addition to the infantry commanders we had to support. But now I learned that a division staff must know all the regiment commanders, the ranking artillery commanders, and so forth. I spent the first day getting to know people, studying our positions on the maps, and going over the division's plans for the defense of its section of the Gustav Line. Some fighting was going on, and the division's operations officer briefed me on what was happening, where our positions were, and who the commanders were. I was assigned to spend a few days with the operations officer, just observing his duties and functions. I could take some phone calls, but mostly I was just observing. Then I spent a few days with the intelligence officer, and then with the quartermaster, just observing the functions and duties of each. Then I spent a few days with the operations officer, dealing directly with the division's regiment commanders. I observed what the different people were doing, how they received reports from the regiments, and how they put them together and sent a report to the corps. I could occasionally relieve people, but it was mostly learning by observing. Although I had been a battalion adjutant and worked briefly on a higher staff at Rostov, I had basically always been a frontline officer and did not know a great deal about staff work.

While I was with the division staff, the battle for Cassino was taking place. The Allies were trying to break through there for a drive on Rome, and the battle went on for days. My division headquarters had a panoramic view over the whole valley, and watching the American bombing of the monastery at Monte Cassino was almost like watching a movie on a screen. The monastery was on a ridge that ran down the center of a valley. The ridge was like a fortress overlooking the valley, which was what made it important. Because it was in the middle of everything, the ridge was an ideal place from which to defend the valley, and the Allies assumed we were using it for that purpose. The planes came over in waves, dropping bombs on the monastery and the ridge. No German soldiers were in the monastery, only on the ridge below it. After two days of bombing, the entire ridge was covered with smoke, and the monastery had been effectively destroyed.

After about three weeks with the division staff I was assigned to the staff of the 14th Panzer Korps, where I repeated the experience, getting to know the division commanders and so forth. As part of a corps staff, I met all the key officers of each division, and I met the neighboring corps' staff people as well. I learned that corps staff people should always know their neighbors personally, because they have to deal with them frequently. I learned that if I knew someone personally, it was different from having only talked to him on the phone—and that knowing personally the people I had to deal with was very important in general staff work. I learned that it was also important to notice what military decorations those people wore, because that told me a great deal about their character and their general capability: a division commander who wore the Knight's Cross with Swords was a very experienced and proven frontline commander compared to one who wore only the Iron Cross. I visited the division staff people with the corps staff officers when they inspected their positions to make sure everything was ready for when the fighting hit us.

In April 1944, I joined the staff of Generalfeldmarschall Kesselring, who commanded all German forces (Army, Navy, and Air Force) in the Mediterranean area. His headquarters was located in tunnels inside a mountain chain north of Rome. At the appointed time, I reported to

Kesselring's chief of staff, General Westphal, who congratulated me on my selection for general staff training and wished me good luck. Kesselring's operations officer found quarters for me in the tunnel and assigned me to a job. Somebody was on furlough, so they put me in his job (under another officer's supervision, since I did not know the job). So here, I had work to do instead of just observing. My job was to receive the reports from the various armies and put them together into one report for the operations officer and the chief of staff. In the higher staff, this is night work, because the higher the staff, the later you get these reports. At the end of the day, the battalion reports to the regiment, which then reports to the division, which reports to the corps, which reports to the army, which finally reports to the army group—and all this consolidating and summarizing and passing on of reports takes time.

Several different tunnels connected inside the main tunnel, and in these connecting tunnels were wooden barracks that were divided into offices and living quarters. The barracks actually had roofs and windows, just as if they were outside, because they were prefabricated. I could sometimes see rats scurrying outside the windows on the side that was against the wall of the tunnel. Outside the wooden barracks on the opposite side was a hallway, and beyond it was the opposite wall of the tunnel. I had a small room to sleep in, and I shared an office with several other officers. Approximately 250 people were living and working in the tunnel. It was a very interesting time for me. For the first time, I knew what was going on not just at my own front, or part of it, but at all fronts.

I also spent some time with the quartermaster of our army group. We would occasionally go to Rome on business, which gave me a chance to see a little of that city. Until then I had only been through the train station in Rome. I was able to see some of the tourist sights, like the Colosseum and the Forum, on these trips.

During the night I would work to help summarize all

the reports so that new orders could be issued very early the next morning. Then, after daylight, I would often go outside, climb up above the tunnel entrance a few dozen meters, and sunbathe and get a little fresh air. A number of other people would do the same thing.

One morning after I had been with Kesselring's staff about three weeks, I finished my work at 6:00 A.M. I had some breakfast and went outside for some fresh air and sun, climbing up the mountainside above the mouth of the tunnel. I planned to stay out for an hour or two, sleeping and getting a tan at the same time. The terrain was rocky, with a few scrub bushes. It was a beautiful day, with clear blue skies and lots of sunshine, and a half-dozen or so other people were scattered about the area, getting sun and fresh air.

About half an hour later, the air raid siren began to wail. This happened frequently, because there was fairly constant Allied air traffic overhead, and since the Allied bombers had always before been on their way somewhere else I paid little attention to the sirens. Then I realized that the sirens had become constant, which was an indication that this was serious. I rolled over onto my back and searched the skies for the airplanes. They were very high, which indicated to me that they were again on their way somewhere else—until I saw something glittering beneath them. Then I realized they were dropping bombs! I jumped up and tried to run for the tunnel, but it was too late. The bombs were already exploding about me. I threw myself to the ground and tried to hug the earth, which began to boil violently all around me with the explosions, and I could feel the heat of the blasts wash over me with each ear-shattering explosion. I dug my face deeper into the earth, trying to burrow into it, squeezing my eyes shut and clenching my teeth. I thought my luck had finally run out.

Suddenly it was very quiet. When I opened my eyes the world was completely dark—smoke and powder and dust obscured the sky and the sun. I knew I was still alive, because I could smell the smoke and burned powder and I was conscious of thinking, but I could see nothing. Then the sky began to hail rocks that had been blasted into the air by the bombs, and I covered the back of my head with my hands and endured the avalanche. Slowly, a little light began to seep through the darkness, and suddenly it occurred to me that bombers always came in two waves (the second wave can see the results of the first and make corrections). I knew I had to get out of there fast or risk enduring the same horror again. Although I could not see more than three meters in the darkness, I knew the tunnel was downhill somewhere, and I jumped to my feet and made a dash down the hill. When I hit the road leading to the tunnel, I knew I had to turn left; then I saw the entrance to the tunnel and leaped for it, but my legs suddenly failed me and I fell into the tunnel entrance.

Some people there picked me up and carried me to a first-aid station. Then the second wave of bombers came, and the tunnel shook and vibrated from the impact of the bombs. I did not feel any pain, although I was covered with blood. I knew I had been hit by all those falling rocks, and I knew I had felt the heat blast of the bombs and was probably burned, but I was not aware of much else. In such a situation, a soldier just wants to be safe, and he does not care about anything else. He reacts first, and the pain comes later. He feels that something is wrong, but it is not a localized pain. Only when he is out of danger does he begin to feel pain.

The medics began to clean and treat my back for the relatively minor rock and burn wounds, and then they discovered that a piece of shrapnel from a bomb had taken a huge chunk out of the calf of my left leg. It was a very deep flesh wound, almost to the bone, but I was fortunate because the bone had not been broken, no artery had been severed, and no nerve had been cut. When I saw that the blood was dark red and not coming out in spurts, I knew that was a good sign.

Of the half-dozen or so of us who were up there, two were never found. Evidently they had both taken direct hits. The rest of us were all wounded. The medics patched us up the best they could and arranged for us to be taken to a field hospital about three kilometers away.

When I arrived at the field hospital, I was immediately given a tetanus shot, which was standard procedure for anyone who had been wounded by shrapnel or bullets. I had been given tetanus shots before with no ill effects—*but not this time*! I was allergic to the type of tetanus serum they gave me, and I started breaking out in wet running sores. They itched, they burned, they hurt—and they were all over my body. I could not sleep because of the pain and the itching; I could not get comfortable in any position. I could hardly eat or drink for four days, because I had sores in my mouth. They were even inside my nose! This was the worst medical experience of my life, and the doctors became very concerned. They gave me calcium shots as an antidote, and after another day or two the rash started to clear up.

The Allies had begun their offensive in the meantime and were threatening to break through our defense lines. The bombing and strafing around us at the field hospital were becoming intense. Of course, some of the local population was spying on us, and the location of Kesselring's headquarters was no secret to the Allies. They knew that any German military vehicle could contain staff officers or supplies, so fighter planes chased and strafed every vehicle. From the window of my hospital room, I could see the roads and the tunnel entrance, and I could see this action taking place. Although the Allied fighter pilots honored the big red cross on the roof of the hospital, they attacked everything that moved on the road. They now bombed the tunnel entrance regularly, apparently trying to seal it shut.

The Army decided to start evacuating patients from the field hospital, since the fighting was getting close, so they put four of us in an ambulance and we started toward

Florence with a driver and a medical corpsman. Of the four of us, two were severely wounded and bedfast, and one was out of his mind from too much combat or from a shell exploding too close to him. I was in the best shape with my leg wound.

When we were about halfway to Florence, we were attacked by two American fighter planes. The ambulance was clearly marked with a red cross on the roof, but the pilots either did not believe it was really an ambulance or they were just having fun by trying to scare us. When they made the first strafing run, the ambulance driver stopped the ambulance and he and the corpsman ran for cover. The four of us who were wounded were left in the ambulance, just sitting there helplessly. The two who were severely wounded could not stand, and I could barely hobble. The crazy man went berserk, and I had to hold him down to keep him from hurting the others. I tried to talk to him and calm him down as I held him. He was just a boy, and he was very frightened. The planes made several passes. We could see the splashes in the road where the .50-caliber bullets hit all around us, but they never hit us. Either the pilots were very poor marksmen or they were just playing cat and mouse with us and never intended to hit us. Although they may just have been having fun, it was a terrifying experience for us.

The hospital at Florence had been converted from the Italian Air Force's military academy. It was a beautiful place, with magnificent buildings and a pool. Now it was a normal military hospital, with many wounded from the fighting. Young Italian girls visited us—although the Italian government had joined the Allies in the war against us, a part of the Italian population still sympathized with us and did not like what their government had done. I practiced my Italian with them. I was in a room with ten or twelve others.

We learned while I was there that the Allies had landed at Normandy on June 6, 1944. This was the third front for us, but of course the news given us was that the Allies had been "beaten back" with terrible losses. After the first few days, we could sense that things were not going well for us there. We were given no details except that Cherbourg was holding out, and this was deceptive, because Cherbourg was on the coast. But then we began to hear about "heroic resistance," and we knew that things were going badly for us in France. In addition, we were being pushed up the Italian peninsula and the Russians were advancing on us from the east. It was evident that the end was approaching.

After I had been there almost four weeks, even Florence was being threatened as the front came closer, and the Army decided to evacuate this hospital also. By then I could walk, although I still had a cast on my leg, and I got permission to go by train to the hospital in Leipzig.

Lilo was back in Leipzig with her mother now. I arrived there in late June 1944. Klaus was finally beginning to look fat and healthy, like a normal baby, and I was very glad to see that. Lilo, of course, was happy to have me home again. She had learned almost to look forward to my being wounded, as long as it was not too serious, so I would get to come home. I reported to the hospital regularly, as usual, to have my leg inspected and treated and for physical therapy. My wound was healing on the outside, but not on the inside. Consequently, it appeared to be healing quite nicely for a while, but then it broke open again. Apparently a big flesh wound like that should be kept open so it heals from the inside out instead of from the outside in.

The first of my specialized weapons schools (the second part of general staff training) was scheduled to begin in early July but was delayed for a few days. I should not have gone back to active duty that quickly, but general staff training was too great an honor and opportunity to miss, so I convinced the doctors that my leg would heal just as well in a classroom as it would at home. The fact that it looked as if we had already lost the war and I would not be able to pursue my career for very long did not detract from the honor of being selected to attend the General Staff College. It never occurred to me, right up to the bitter end, to do anything differently because we were losing the war. My whole career as a professional Army officer had been aimed at attending the General Staff College if possible. Because of my eagerness for the general staff training, however, my leg did not heal properly. I should have stayed at home and given my leg time to heal, but I did not. So, although walking with a cane, I started the specialized weapons schools.

21

THE FIRST OF the specialized schools started in mid-July 1944. There were a number of them we had to attend: Panzer School, Communication School, Artillery School, Engineering School, and so forth. We did not have to attend the school in our own specialty, so when it came time to attend Artillery School, I would get to go home instead.

Between schools, I would have to report back to the hospital in Leipzig to have my wound inspected, although at the schools I could have the bandages changed at the dispensary.

We had two months to complete the various specialized schools, because the main General Staff College started in September. Although we were all experienced officers with much time in combat by then, we needed more exposure to the things in which we did not have direct experience. Lilo was able to go with me to some of these schools, including the first one, the Panzer School in Bergen, near Celle.

We were at the Panzer School on July 20, 1944, when Oberst i.G. Klaus von Stauffenberg attempted to assassinate Hitler, and the Nazi Party leaders went berserk. The next several days were total chaos throughout Germany. Nobody knew what would happen next or who would be arrested next. The government and the Army were both in a constant state of uproar; there were endless rumors, whispered names, and some announcements on the radio.

It was at least a week before the situation showed any signs of abating.

Von Stauffenberg, who had planted a bomb under Hitler's table at a situation meeting at Hitler's headquarters in East Prussia and then immediately left for Berlin to help take over the government, was a general staff officer, and many of the group of conspirators involved in the plot to kill Hitler were general staff officers. Unfortunately for him and the other conspirators, the bomb did not kill Hitler, and Stauffenberg was arrested and executed in Berlin.

Immediately, everybody in the general staff was under suspicion. The Nazi Party leaders were particularly vocal and vicious in accusing general staff officers. They did not like Army officers in general, and they particularly hated general staff officers. The Minister of Labor, Robert Ley, was especially nasty. He ranted and raved and spewed hate in tirades on the radio, in newspapers, and in speeches in factories. He had an almost pathological hatred of general staff officers who came from the nobility, and when we heard him on the radio ranting and raving about general staff officers ("blue-blooded and inbred to idiocy"), we thought there was not much hope of our training continuing and we would probably be lucky if we were not arrested because we were in general staff training. We thought that at best the General Staff College would be abandoned, we would all be reassigned to the front, and there would be no more general staff.

Many of our instructors at the General Staff College were concerned for their lives, because they knew some of the convicted general staff officers. It was a very critical time for general staff officers, especially those who had been in general staff work for some time. An officer could be arrested because a friend or relative had been arrested. I was safe, because I had always been a frontline officer and was new to the general staff, but even some junior officers were arrested because they had been on an implicated general's staff for some time and had become confidants of the general.

Because I had spent three weeks on Kesselring's staff, some of the names being mentioned were familiar to me. Everybody knew someone who had been arrested. And with the Nazis' system of holding a man's family responsible if he did something wrong, even families were arrested and sent to concentration camps. Von Stauffenberg and the others who had been caught had been shot immediately. Now came the trials of all the others, and that news was constantly in the newspapers and on the radio. Rommel's death was announced, but it was attributed to injuries he had received during a strafing attack in France; because he was so popular with the German people, his death was not connected with the assassination attempt in the news.

After a week or so, the situation began to calm down a little. The rest of the Panzer School course was canceled and could not be rescheduled, but we were told that our next school would take place. Personally, I felt that it would have been good if the assassination attempt had succeeded, because it could possibly have ended the war under better terms than the "unconditional surrender" the Allies were insisting upon. It was an opinion I shared with only one other person—Hauptmann Heiner Engel, a fellow student whom I had just met but who had quickly become a close and trusted friend.

After the assassination attempt, the Army was forced to adopt the Nazi salute. The Nazi salute had been used indoors, when we were not wearing a hat, since I had joined the Army in 1936. Now, however, we were forced to abandon the normal military salute and adopt the Nazi salute exclusively. It was arranged by the Nazi Party, who wanted to show the Army that they were in charge, and Hitler agreed to it.

Political officers were also forced on the Army after the assassination attempt. The Nazi Party leaders wanted to know what was going on everywhere in the Army now, and this was their way of achieving that objective. They recruited reserve officers for this position (regular Army officers were prohibited from political activity). All political officers had been Nazi Party members before entering the Army. They were officially called National Socialist Guidance Officers. They would be placed in a position to watch commanding officers. If a commander failed to follow orders to fight to the last man, his political officer would report this to the Nazi Party, who would take action to have the commander relieved of his command. Their official responsibility was keeping up the ideological spirit of the soldiers. They used the patriotic approach rather than a political approach, although when conditions permitted they would give lessons on political subjects and an occasional pep talk.

The General Staff College was scheduled to begin September 20, 1944, after the specialized schools had all been completed. It had been moved from Berlin to Hirschberg, in the Sudeten Mountains of Silesia. We were invited to bring our families. Married officers were provided two rooms, with one kitchen for every four families; since we all ate in the Officers Club, that was not a great inconvenience. On most evenings, I had homework, but there were occasional parties with most or all of the married officers. Of course, the times were terrible, but Hirschberg was almost an oasis in the war; there were no air raids, and it was a nice town in a beautiful area.

The General Staff College was much like Kriegsschule Potsdam had been, except at a senior level. At Hirschberg the commander of the General Staff College was a generalleutnant, whereas the commander of the military academy at Potsdam had been an oberst. At Hirschberg the working group was about twenty hauptmanns and majors and was headed by an oberst i.G., whereas the working group at Potsdam had been about twenty-four fähnrichs and was headed by a major. At Hirschberg we learned to lead a division in combat, whereas we had learned at Potsdam to lead a battalion in combat. The oberst i.G. in charge of my group at Hirschberg was named Klostermann.

We learned how to lead a division in different kinds of combat situations: attacking, retreating, conducting a rearguard action, attacking across a river, attacking in mountainous terrain, establishing a bridgehead, attacking a bridgehead, and so forth. All these different situations were played out with maps or in a sandbox, with tests in between. The purpose was to make us capable of assisting a general in leading a division. We learned how to write orders, how to plan an attack, how to figure out the length of a column on a road, how long it would take the column to cross a bridge, how to group troops, how to arrange for reserves, how to defend against a massive attack by an enemy, how to conduct a massive attack against a defense line, how to position infantry, how to position artillery, where to put the engineers if there is a river in the attack line and when to move them forward. We also learned intelligence and counterintelligence work: how to find out what kind of units were opposite us and what to do with that information—how to handle all these details for the general commanding the division.

In war games, we would be given the situation we were in and what was happening. Then all of a sudden something unexpected would happen, which we would learn about in a report, a radio message, or a phone call. Then we would have to react to the new situation. In regular training, we would get the information and have to work out the solution overnight or over the weekend. In all situations, pressure was applied, because in combat you are always under extreme pressure. It was very much like Potsdam, but on a larger scale, and it was highly interesting.

In peacetime, general staff training—including on-the-job training, the specialized schools, and the General

Staff College—was a two-year program. In our case it was condensed. I spent about three and a half months in on-the-job training, two months in the specialized schools, and four months in the General Staff College, for a total of less than a year. Life is completely different in wartime than in peacetime. For one thing, we all had a great deal of combat experience, which peacetime officers would not have. For another, there was no significant social aspect to the training now, and social graces had been an important part of the peacetime general staff training. Our only social activity was a once-a-month event during which the whole school would have an evening in the ballroom, consisting of a cocktail hour and dinner.

The eastern front was not far from Hirschberg, and as the school continued it came even closer. It was very clear now that none of us could possibly have a prolonged career as a professional Army officer. We knew the war could not last much longer and we could not win it, but until the government decided to end the war—or until we were totally defeated—the Army could only continue to function normally, which included training general staff officers. We also thought there was a possibility that the western powers would join us to defeat Russia. It did not make sense to us that they would not want to stop Russia as much as we did in order to prevent them from dominating Europe after the war.

At Christmas, Lilo's parents came to visit us. Her father was home on furlough from Italy, where he served in a quartermaster unit, and they stayed in a nearby hotel for a few days. It was not a joyous Christmas under the circumstances. There was not much available in the stores in the way of gifts, but at least the Army provided us with good food, so we had it better than most people in Germany at the time.

The war was lost, and now we had to think of what would come next. To us, the western democracies were not as threatening as the Soviet Union. Part of the reason was that most of the government propaganda was directed against the Soviet Union, with hardly any against the western democracies. Part of it was because we had invaded Russia, and we knew the Russians would be terrible in their revenge—even though we did not know yet of the brutality of the Nazi Party people in Russia after the front lines had passed through. Part of it was also the things we discovered the Russians had done whenever we recaptured territory they had taken from us. In the west, things were terrible during the fighting, but the fighting lasted only a few days and then it was over. There were, of course, casualties among civilians, but they ended when the fighting ended. That was not true in the war against the Russians. There, when the fighting ended, the brutalization of German civilians began, especially the women. The raping and the killing were wanton. The famous and influential Russian writer Ilya Ehrenburg encouraged the widespread raping of German women by writing, "Soldiers of the Red Army, the German women are yours!" Since Ilya Ehrenburg was officially sanctioned by the Soviet government, the Russian soldiers took his announcement as coming from the Kremlin.

As 1945 began, the menacing shadow of Russian domination lay over Germany like an ugly, poisonous cloud, seeping into our minds and clinging there as stubbornly as a wet fog on a gloomy winter morning. The irony of our certainty that Russia would never be able to invade Germany came home now with appalling force. The Russians had reached the Vistula and were preparing their great final offensive into the heart of Germany. East Prussia had already been overrun by Russian troops, and the Battle of the Bulge had failed in the west. The end of the war was very near. It seemed to me that the government should be suing for peace—that even unconditional surrender would be better than having Germany destroyed. But I knew that the same man who had ordered masses of German soldiers to stand and die rather than retreat would not now negotiate a peaceful end to the war.

Even being at the General Staff College and able to live with Lilo and Klaus in Hirschberg, relatively secure even from air raids, could not lift my drooping spirits. We were preparing for our final exam, part of which was supposed to be a field trip to Mecklenburg, but we were sure that by then the Russians would in fact be where the war games would fictionally place the enemy for tactical purposes. My exam topic was to be "Establishing a Bridgehead from Forward Motion." Classroom routine was influenced more and more by the real events at the fronts, however, and the real battles taking place at the fronts were of much greater interest to us than the war games being staged in the classroom.

Those of us at the General Staff College became more and more irritable as we tried to find ways to cope with what was happening to Germany. From time to time I would go to hear a pianist or singer or to see a movie.

As January wore on and the Soviets drove from the Vistula River toward the Oder River, classroom activity became more and more irregular. On January 20, Generalfeldmarschall Schörner took over the Army Group Center from Generaloberst Harpe. As the end of the month approached, regular classroom activity ceased except for a class in Nazi ideology; instead, the class periods were spent listening to the news on the radio and discussing the situation at the various fronts. The Russians were pouring into West Prussia, Upper Silesia, and Pomerania. They soon were at Breslau and the Moravian Gate. At Steinau, they achieved their first thrust over the Oder River, almost causing a panic at the General Staff College.

On January 23, because the Army desperately needed manpower of all kinds, some of us were selected by the Personnel Department of the Army in Berlin to fill assignments even before our training ended. I was among that group, assigned to report to the 6th Mountain Division in

Norway as quartermaster. I was informed shortly before noon that I was to leave the next morning.

I dreaded telling Lilo, who was three months pregnant with our second child. This meant not only that I had to leave suddenly but that she would have to be responsible for moving all our household, in addition to herself and Klaus, back to Leipzig. When I told her, she tried to be brave but began to cry. She could not control her tears, and soon she was sobbing uncontrollably. It broke my heart to see her this way. I tried to console her, but nothing seemed to help; her body was racked with sobs. We were both helpless to do anything, and our personal problems were tiny compared to what was happening in the world.

In the late afternoon, Lilo began to hemorrhage. Fearing a miscarriage, I put in a panic call for a physician. When he arrived, he confirmed my fears that a miscarriage was a very real possibility. He tried to get her admitted to the hospital, but it was filled with wounded from the fighting.

I explained the situation to Oberst Klostermann, who was in charge of my group at the General Staff College. For me to leave Lilo while she was ill and in need of unavailable hospitalization, with a one-year-old child to care for in addition to moving all our belongings back to Leipzig, would have been extremely cruel. Oberst Klostermann agreed and called Berlin to ask them to assign one of my classmates to Norway in my place. They selected a bachelor, Hauptmann Weisser, to go to Norway, which allowed me to spend several additional days with Lilo. Her condition began to improve immediately, and I prepared the dissolution of our household. On January 26, I put all our belongings into boxes and suitcases and sent them to Leipzig by train.

The official termination of our training at the General Staff College was on Friday, January 26, 1945, in the form of a short farewell roll call. Our training was terminated early, because the Russians were only ninety-five kilometers away and we were needed at the front. The General Staff College was supposed to be moved farther west, away from the Russian threat, and continued there; in fact, it was never organized again, even though the new class was arriving as we left.

On Saturday, January 27, a group of us received orders to report to Army Group Center, commanded by Generalfeldmarschall Schörner, who was in need of general staff officers. *So I was to fight the Russians again, for the fourth time in as many years!* Oberst Klostermann denied my request for a three-day furlough to take Lilo and Klaus to Leipzig. His only concession was to send a medical corpsman along to help Lilo on the train trip back to Leipzig. Klostermann was a compassionate man, but he was a responsible officer and he felt that I should not leave now.

On Monday, January 29, I took Lilo and Klaus to the railroad station to board a special train for military dependents. The weather was very cold, 5 degrees Fahrenheit, and it was snowing. The station was crowded with refugees from the east who were fleeing the Russians. Fortunately, the train was ready to be boarded when we arrived and we did not have to wait. Lilo's compartment was too small for her and Klaus and all the luggage, so I fastened the baby carriage to the ceiling of the compartment. We wanted her to take as many of our belongings as possible, because anything that was left would be lost, and she had to make a life for herself and the children after the war, whether I survived it or not. We could not just drop everything and say it was of no use because we were losing the war. We had to go on, just as if there would be a future for us.

The train was very crowded. Hundreds of civilians were trying to get out of Hirschberg before the Russians arrived. They knew that advance Russian troops had already interrupted the railroad line once and that they could do it again. Trains were the only mode of transportation, because the government had banned the personal use of automobiles. This one was a special military train. The civilians had been warned to leave earlier, and they should have gone. Military police tried to keep civilians away from the train, but they were not entirely successful.

Then it was goodbye. I was sure I would never see Lilo or Klaus again. We had separated many times before, but never before with such likelihood that we would never meet again. I had no illusions; the end was very near, and the odds of my survival were extremely poor. Then the train started to move, and the parting could be delayed no longer. A last squeeze of her hand, a few silent tears, and then I was alone in the milling crowd of civilians on the platform. I returned to our empty apartment at the General Staff College, which now contained only the field luggage I would take back to the front with me. I was overwhelmed by the most lonesome feeling I have ever experienced in my life.

22

AFTER I PUT Lilo and Klaus on the train, I went to the officers' mess, as much to try to break the spell of loneliness as anything else, but I could not taste the food. I tried to join a conversation about the possibility of the Western Allies helping us keep the Russians out of Germany, but I could not really work up any interest, perhaps because I no longer believed it would happen. I could think of nothing to do to pass the time. I finally went to bed early and tried to go to sleep, but I spent an endless lonely night thinking of the train Lilo and Klaus were on and hoping it would get through without being intercepted by the Russians. The uncertainty of not knowing and of being helpless to do anything was difficult to endure. Even if Lilo and Klaus reached Leipzig safely, they still had to survive the endless air raids. I put that out of my mind—I could not allow myself to worry about things that *might* happen. Things had gone well for us until now, and I had to just hope our luck would not run out.

The next morning, the General Staff College held a short graduation ceremony in the assembly hall. Some bottles of champagne were distributed from the college canteen supplies—under normal circumstances, graduation would have been cause for celebration—and those of us who had been assigned to Schörner's staff headed for the train station. Although we had two hours to wait on the station platform in 5-degree-Fahrenheit weather, it was still not as bad as it had been when I saw Lilo off. We opened the first bottles of champagne from the college canteen, which helped to shorten the wait. We toasted each other and tried to be lighthearted and cheerful, but the snow and the cold kept reminding me of that first winter in Russia in 1941.

It was a brief train trip to Schörner's headquarters at Waldenburg, since the front was not far away. We arrived in the early evening and checked into the Hotel Waldenburgerhof. This had been the most depressing day of my life. I knew I had to shake off this depression if I was to function effectively.

After breakfast the next morning, an officer from Schörner's staff came and interviewed each of us. Then we took a walk through town until lunch. In the afternoon, we reported to Schörner's chief of staff, General Xylander, as we had been instructed to do. Xylander selected six of us for Schörner's personal disposal and dispatched the others to the various armies of Schörner's army group by courier vehicles.

The remaining six of us were instructed to report back that afternoon to meet Generalfeldmarschall Schörner. After lunch, I got permission from General Xylander to call Lilo in Leipzig. She had arrived safely after a terrible twenty-four hours on the train, with frightened civilians trying to force their way on at every stop. Being able to talk to her helped me dispel some of the gloom from my mind.

We reported to Generalfeldmarschall Schörner at 3:00 P.M. on January 30, 1945. Schörner was a capable and successful commander, but it was common knowledge that he had been promoted rapidly because he was a political general and a "yes man" to Hitler. He was a rarity: a high-ranking German officer who was also a Nazi. He was known as being both articulate and loud (most Nazis tended to be uncouth). He shook hands and exchanged a little small talk with each of us. Then a severe scowl clouded his face as he took a position in front of us.

"I have just returned from Breslau," he virtually growled. "It is a military pigsty! It is so bad that I considered having the commanding general of the fortress corps staff court-martialed. The Russians are practically there, and the city cannot hope to defend itself in its present state. I need two energetic young general staff officers with extensive combat experience to go there and help get the city in shape to defend itself." He paused and seemed to glare at us. "I need an operations officer and a quartermaster for the Army Korps Area VIII General Command in Breslau. You all have a lot of combat experience"—which apparently explained why the six of us had been singled out —"so I will send the oldest and the youngest of you to Breslau. You are to fly there immediately." He turned and disappeared abruptly through a doorway.

After he was gone, General Xylander determined that a major was the oldest and I was the youngest. Schörner had his personal kübelwagen and two Fieseler-Storch airplanes waiting to take the two of us to Breslau. The Fieseler-Storch was a small open-cockpit airplane large enough only for a pilot and one other person. It could take off and land on a very short runway, or even a meadow. We were driven to the airplanes. The major got into one of them and I got into the other, and we took off. We flew low over the picturesque snow-covered landscape of Silesia, one airplane following the other.

We landed at Gandau Airport near Breslau at 4:00 P.M. A short while later an aide to the commanding general of the Army Korps Area VIII General Command arrived to get us. He was Hauptmann von Wallenberg, a young officer in his middle twenties. I got to know him well during the next weeks. He was from a wealthy noble family that had a large estate just outside of Breslau.

We reported to the chief of staff in Breslau, Generalmajor von Lossberg. The thirty-nine-year-old von Lossberg was a big man, about six foot two and two hundred pounds, with short-cropped brown hair and brown eyes that were bracketed by crow's-feet at the outside corners. After a short conversation with the two of us, von Lossberg appointed me as operations officer and the major as quartermaster—a surprise, because operations officer was the more responsible job, and the major was both older and higher-ranking.

Then we met the commanding general, General Koch-Erpach. He was about sixty-two years old, portly and gray, with a fleshy face and pale blue eyes. He had no World War II combat experience, although he had seen combat as a young officer during World War I. Fortunately, Generalmajor von Lossberg was both experienced and capable, and he could compensate for Koch-Erpach's weaknesses.

The operations officer I was replacing had been killed somewhere east of the city, although the front was still perhaps eighty-five kilometers away (with mobile combat, we never knew where or when we might run into fast-moving forward Russian troops). He had taken two motorcycle riders with him to wherever he was going, which was standard operating procedure, and one of them had survived the incident and returned to report the death of the major and the other motorcycle rider. There was really little here that could be called a front. There was just a lot of movement in a very broad area.

Hitler had declared Breslau a fortress city, which meant that it was to be defended to the last man, even if it was surrounded and totally isolated. The army corps staff in Breslau was the home unit staff for the area, which meant that it was a peacetime staff, and that was why Schörner had wanted officers with extensive combat experience to get the place ready for siege.

The fortress corps staff in Breslau was about seventy people. Because Breslau was the capital of Silesia and had been declared a fortress, the responsibility of the Army Korps Area VIII General Command staff was broader than that of a normal military staff. In addition to purely military matters, it was responsible for the supply of food for the city, for the flow of refugees through the city as they fled from the Russians, and for everything necessary to keep a large city operating. Although the gauleiter of Silesia, whose name was Hanke, had all responsibility for the city in theory, the military staff in Breslau actually handled everything.

We were fortunate because we had a fortress commander—equivalent to a division commander—reporting to our staff whom Schörner had also sent to Breslau. Generalmajor von Ahlfen was a very experienced man who had lost an arm in combat, and his operations officer was also an experienced general staff officer. Generalmajor von Ahlfen and his operations officer organized the actual fighting units, so we had only to concern ourselves with things that went beyond the immediate defense of Breslau, such as transportation, communications, and supplies.

I took over the duties of operations officer on January 31. Most of the corps staff consisted of people who had never been in combat and did not know what to expect or how to prepare for it. My first job was to form the operations staff I had inherited into one that was capable of functioning in a combat situation. At first, I personally had to write every report, draw every sketch (of defense lines, troop positions, boundaries between units, headquarters positions, locations of supply depots, and so forth), make every entry in a map, make every telephone call, and write every order to our units for the general's signature. I found it impossible to sleep more than two hours without interruption or more than four to five hours in any twenty-four-hour period.

I was assigned an aide, Hauptmann Kafurke, to help me with my duties. He had been assigned to the staff at Breslau after being seriously wounded at the front. He had good knowledge of the staff and the situation at Breslau, which I found very useful. He was capable, and I learned that I could rely on him.

Schörner had been right: the place was a military mess. All the staff people were handicapped or old, and they had no idea how to fight or how to defend a big city. Defense lines had to be designated, ditches had to be dug, preparations of all kinds had to be made. Wounded coming in from the front had to be accommodated. A factory for making heavy water for atomic experiments had been abandoned east of Breslau, and we had to plan and conduct a counterattack to destroy it and keep its secrets from falling into the hands of the Russians. We were constantly occupied with issuing instructions to civil defense units, decreasing staff personnel, issuing ammunition and supplies, providing weapons, enforcing Schörner's order that no man able to fight was to leave Breslau, keeping refugees supplied and moving, finding engines for hospital trains, keeping utilities operating, preventing looting, preparing landing strips in the city in preparation for the siege—all in addition to normal staff functions like the daily military report to Schörner.

The hospitals were overflowing with wounded who had to be evacuated, and we had to get trains for them and ambulances to move them from the hospitals to the trains. We evacuated the civilian population as long as possible. Probably more than half of the city's population left the city.

In addition to the military, we also supplied the refugees, who needed fuel, food, hay for their horses, and just about everything else. All the refugees coming from the east had to pass through Breslau, whether they were coming from the northeast, east, or southeast. We had to try to help them, to feed them and their horses and cows (which they often brought along), to provide them with the necessities, and to keep them moving. They were practically all on foot, with horse-drawn vehicles and whatever they could carry with them. Thousands of women, children, and old men came through Breslau every day. The area they were going into west of Breslau was hilly, which would be difficult for them, and it was winter and very cold. It was a terrible feeling to see them come through and know there was very little hope for them wherever they went. Even though they were leaving everything behind, they did not want to fall into the hands of the Russians. They had all heard too much propaganda, and many had experienced too much firsthand.

I quickly went from civilian telephone service to a combat telephone network, which both simplified telephone communication and made it more secure. Slowly, with time, everything began to function better. I worked closely with Generalmajor von Lossberg and had an excellent relationship with him. A general staff officer with a good combat record, he was ready for the command of a division. He was a combat soldier at heart, and he wanted to return to the front as a division commander. He thought the government was stupid not to end the war—on *any* terms—because the only possible result of continuing to fight was the destruction of Germany. He loved to escape from present realities, when the situation allowed sufficient time, by playing bridge or skat.

Von Lossberg looked after overall strategy and left the details to me. He spoke very openly to me about the hopelessness of the military situation. In spite of everything, however, he thought we had to hold out in the east simply to keep the Russians out of Germany as long as possible.

We had just a short time to get Breslau ready for combat before it would be surrounded by the Russians. Days went by. I could hardly leave my desk and telephone. Our only relaxation was the occasional game of cards. On February 8, a classmate of mine at the General Staff College, Hauptmann Dagel, arrived as an observer from the supreme command of the Seventeenth Army. Disguised as an intelligence officer, he was actually a "spy" for Schörner (a favorite trick of Schörner's). But Dagel was sensible and I could really use him for productive work. He was likable and unassuming, a very capable officer with a good service record and combat experience.

One chore that Koch-Erpach and von Lossberg

thought to be of utmost importance was a report to the Army command that would prove that Fortress Breslau could not be defended with the present ammunition supplies for more than a few weeks after Russian encirclement. Also, the number of men who were in fighting trim would not be sufficient for a sustained defense. The purpose of this report was to obtain permission to evacuate Breslau in the event that it was in danger of being encircled. Of course, it was in vain, and our orders were to the contrary: the bridges were to be kept open for a "possible" German offensive across the Oder River. Somebody was living in a dream world! Only in case of extreme danger could the bridges be blown up. The only positive result of the report was a slight increase in weapons and ammunition—and perhaps also our departure by air out of the fortress later on.

Together with Generalmajor von Ahlfen and his staff, we got things into shape so that Schörner was finally satisfied. On about February 10, the Russian offensive across the Oder River began south of Breslau, near Grottkau, and in the northwest near Steinau. In front of the fortress itself, fairly insignificant combat activity continued at first, but our 609th Division soon became involved in heavy fighting and was pushed back almost to the southern suburbs of Breslau.

On February 11, the 7th Infantry Division, which had successfully completed the operation to retake and destroy the heavy-water plant at Dyhernfurth across the Oder River, sent their vehicles and baggage train into Breslau and pushed south through an enemy that was advancing toward Breslau from the west to form a new front in the area south of Kant. On February 12, two Soviet forces closed the ring around Breslau at Domslau. With that, Breslau had become a fortress under siege. Communication to the Army command was possible now only by radio or via an underground long-distance cable, which was not safe from wiretapping by the enemy. For important communications, therefore, we used only teletype messages from operations officer to operations officer.

The Russian Air Force became more and more active. At noon one day the first bomb burst in the center of the courtyard of our headquarters, blowing all my windows inward. I had some cardboard put up for protection, but from then on my staff and I had to wear our overcoats constantly. I ordered the signals officer to prepare a contingency command post in the basement, because it was apparent that it would soon be too dangerous on the ground floor. In fact, I had to dive several times during the afternoon when bombs fell in the immediate neighborhood.

We prepared an offensive out of Breslau, to be coordinated with an attack by the 24th Panzer Korps from the south, to open the road and the railroad near Domslau so we could get an ambulance train of wounded soldiers out of Breslau. The offensive was to begin on February 13. On the evening of February 12, I had to go to the 609th Division, whose headquarters was at a mansion south of the city. This was the first opportunity I'd had to get some real impression of the city of Breslau. Cattle and sheep wandered in the main thoroughfares, and refugees with carts and horse-drawn vehicles were camping everywhere. The military police were having trouble keeping the streets open for military traffic. I was stopped and asked for identification by civil defense men at every barricade in spite of the Army Korps flag on my car. After getting through all these difficulties, my driver and motorcycle escort and I finally had the city behind us and the front ahead. It was relatively calm, with only occasionally a few rounds of artillery shells or some machine-gun fire. Without lights, we proceeded very carefully. Any error in reading the map could have meant that I would suffer the fate of my predecessor. Finally, we reached the headquarters of the 609th Division.

I gave the division staff the overall situation, and they

filled me in on their situation. I then gave them the orders for the attack and departed with best wishes for the operation. The 609th would either break through tomorrow and escape the fortress or be thrown back in heavy fighting to its initial position. But the general who commanded the division and his staff were optimistic, and each of the men would do everything possible to get through, because they had all heard too much about the "heroically fighting" fortresses at Königsberg, Elbing, Thorn, Posen, Graudenz, and so on. They did not want to become the "heroic defenders of Breslau" if they could help it.

On my way back, I met columns of vehicles in all the streets. Vehicles of the armed forces and of civilians mingled in long columns. The 7th Infantry Division had received the order to get ready and stand by to leave the fortress after the road had been opened. The civilians learned this, and now everybody wanted to take advantage of this opportunity to get out. Even without enemy fire, it would take more than thirty-six hours to get these columns through on one road. If the columns were burdened with horse-drawn vehicles, it would be impossible; within a very short time, everything would be blocked. Because of this, I made sure after my return that all military police posts got a strict order to remove horse-drawn vehicles from the columns.

After reporting to the chief of staff, reading the messages that had arrived while I had been gone, and making the necessary telephone calls, I finally could get some sleep. At 5:00 A.M., it started getting busy again: the offensive had started, and the first reports of success were coming in. The attack of the 24th Panzer Korps, too, was progressing well. The Russians now bombed even more frequently around our headquarters building (fortunately, they were small bombs). We moved into the rooms prepared for our staff in the basement.

During the morning hours, the offensive had progressed so far that a narrow corridor had been opened up at Domslau. Vehicles were now starting to flow out of the city to the south, but with heavy losses under fierce Russian fire from both flanks. The railroad track, however, was blocked by a heavy tank that had been disabled and stood on the track at Domslau. All efforts to remove it failed, and it was impossible to get the two loaded hospital trains out of Breslau because of it. The heavy attacks that were soon launched by the Russians against the tubelike opening stopped the movement of traffic again in the afternoon, and by evening Breslau was a fortress again. Now the "brave," and later "heroic," resistance would begin.

As the Russians got closer, they bombed us more heavily; then they started shelling us with artillery as well. To defend Breslau, we had two combat divisions, plus the Volkssturm and the Hitler Youth. Although the Volkssturm and Hitler Youth were not trained troops, they could help. We could not use such people for offensive operations, but we could defend with them after a fashion, and because most of them were defending their homes, they would fight more fiercely than they might in another place.

In Breslau, I got all the reports from the front, and I learned then what was likely to happen when the Russians took a town or a city. When we recaptured a city or town from the Russians, we usually discovered that wanton murder and rape had been the norm while they had been there. German officers were often simply shot, and even enlisted men were sometimes shot just to get them out of the way. The rules of civilized warfare did not exist on the eastern front, and the Russians were made even more savage by the exhortations of the Russian journalist Ilya Ehrenburg to exact from the Germans "two eyes for an eye" and "a pool of blood for every drop of blood."

One great advantage of being on the staff at Breslau was that I could talk to Lilo often. As corps operations officer, I had unlimited access to the telephone. The Russians were probably not interested in cutting our telephone lines, as they were in cutting rail traffic, because they considered it a potential source of information.

After I had been in Breslau about two weeks, Schörner decided that he needed a corps staff at the current front, which was now about eighty-five kilometers west of Breslau. Our purpose in being at Breslau had been fulfilled, and Generalmajor von Ahlfen and his staff were charged with conducting the defense of Breslau, so our corps staff was ordered to leave Breslau and replace a corps staff that had been lost or decimated at the front. In the evening, von Lossberg, Kafurke, and I celebrated the termination of our fortress existence with champagne and a game of skat. General Koch-Erpach apparently celebrated his departure from the fortress alone in his apartment, since we did not see him at all during the evening.

The next morning, February 14, we drove to General von Ahlfen's underground bunker. The city was an eerie sight. Streetcars were running in streets that were empty of people. Bursts of artillery fire exploded here and there. Herds of cattle lowed as heavy artillery shells from big railroad guns exploded every five minutes or so. At von Ahlfen's headquarters, I exchanged telegrams with Army headquarters and learned that we were to fly out of Breslau that evening in two JU-52s and immediately take over an army corps at the front.

Von Lossberg delegated to me the unpleasant duty of selecting those of our staff who would fly out with us and those who would stay. Each airplane could carry only about twenty-five people. Those who stayed, of course, would be either killed or captured by the Russians. In most cases it was obvious who would be most needed, but there was always a way to rationalize and say, "We need him." It was not easy to sentence people to stay and be killed or captured, and I agonized over some of the choices. Some people came to me with all kinds of reasons why they should come along at all costs. The only one who actually volunteered to stay was the political officer in charge of

Nazi indoctrination. He was a hauptmann, about thirty-five years old, and he asked me to leave him in the fortress because his job was to be where the situation was most difficult. I had not planned to take him anyway, but I thanked him for his attitude. Those others who had to stay accepted their sentences gracefully.

I drove to Gandau Airport at about 7:00 P.M. Hauptmann Dagel (the "spy" planted by Schörner) succeeded in getting four pairs of epaulettes for the rank of major in the general staff, as well as red cloth for our trousers, since our promotions were imminent. In the officers' mess at the airport, we waited in vain for the airplanes. The airport landing strip already had considerably more bomb and shell craters than it had had when I had landed here two weeks earlier, and we could hear infantry fighting to the west.

After waiting in vain for the airplanes until midnight, I stretched out on a bench. Early the next morning, someone woke me and offered me a room in one of the airport barracks. There I stretched out on a real bed and fell into a deep sleep, in spite of the shell bursts nearby, after two weeks with so little sleep. The airplanes could land only during the evening hours, so I had at least until 7:00 P.M. In the afternoon the airport commander offered us a good meal and something to drink. Finally the announcement came through that the two planes were on their way to Breslau.

The first JU-52 landed at 7:15 P.M., and the second one followed shortly thereafter. The airport landing lights were switched on the absolute minimum necessary, and as soon as the airplanes touched down, enemy artillery opened up on the landing strip. The field was large, however, and the shelling did not come very close. The pilots were understandably in a hurry. The ammunition they had brought in was quickly unloaded and our staff was loaded aboard. General Koch-Erpach's orderly began to load a number of boxes and suitcases, but when he tried to put cases of chocolate aboard, the pilots objected angrily. Fortunately, Koch-Erpach was not there, so I allowed each member of our staff to take as much chocolate as he wanted.

Then we were ready. The engines roared, the landing lights went on, we raced down the runway, and our airplane lifted off the ground. The pilot immediately put the airplane into a sharp turn and then tried to gain altitude while staying within a tight circle above Breslau to avoid Russian flak. We had a spectacular view of a large city surrounded by a pearllike string of burning villages. The front was easy to identify by the flashes from firing guns. Von Wallenberg was even able to recognize his village and his mansion—all in flames!

Finally, we were high enough to be safe from the light flak, and we turned southwest over enemy territory. The heavy flak guns now began to fire at us as we passed over them. We could see their flashes on the ground as they fired and then the resulting red shell bursts nearby in the sky. Soon we could see the dark hills of the Zobten, a small mountain range to the south, and then we saw the landing lights at the airport. We touched down at Schweidnitz at about 8:00 P.M., with the second plane close behind us. We had made it! The tension, which I had hardly been aware of during the excitement of the flight, began to drain from me. I also felt an enormous sense of relief at being out of a city under siege.

23

AT THE AIRPORT at Schweidnitz, we reported our successful escape from Breslau to our army command. Then we made ourselves comfortable and started playing skat again to pass the time until von Lossberg could get the Personnel Department of the Army in Berlin on the telephone. He wanted to find out about his next position and about the promotions for Dagel and me, which were due that day.

At about 10:00 P.M. the call finally came for von Lossberg. When he hung up, he congratulated Dagel and me on our promotion to major in the general staff. We located a bottle of Martel in the airport and duly celebrated the event. My competence in the card game diminished considerably after that. Finally, after midnight, we fell into our beds in the Schweidnitzerhof Hotel—but not before Dagel and I had given orders to our orderlies to have the new epaulettes on our jackets by the next morning.

The next day, I had a lot of work to do to finish the war diary of Army Korps Area VIII General Command, which had to be submitted to our army command. At about eleven o'clock that night, we drove to Salzbrunn, where the Army had reserved a nice guesthouse for us, on roads that were crowded with refugees. Many of them had tired cows with them, which they were having to abandon. Fortunately for them, the weather was not as cold as it had been. It occurred to me as I watched them that I had seen the same scenes in Belgium and France and Russia, and that what was happening to Germany now was really no different from what we had done to those countries earlier. It had all seemed so detached then, when it was happening to others, but now that it was happening to my own people it seemed very personal.

Dagel, meanwhile, had sent our trousers to a tailor to have the red general staff stripes sewn on the sides of the legs. The tailor, who had never done such work before, demanded a pattern, and Koch-Erpach was kind enough to lend us a pair of his pants for that purpose. The next morning, when my orderly returned from the tailor, we learned that the tailor had managed to do only one pair of pants during the night, and they belonged to me. Poor Dagel had to go another day without them, while I strutted about with the red stripes of a general staff officer for the first time.

General Koch-Erpach and Generalmajor von Lossberg reported to Generalfeldmarschall Schörner and were invited to dinner. Later in the evening, we got together again for von Lossberg's favorite activity if he could not play bridge—skat. I went to bed early—I had to store up sleep in advance for what might be in store for us when we took over a corps at the front. Here, there was only one telephone in the house, and it was *not* near my bed!

The next morning, February 17, von Lossberg talked on the telephone with Schörner's chief of staff, General Xylander. Instead of taking over a corps at the front, Koch-Erpach and his personal staff were to take over the Army Korps Area General Command at Zwittau in the Sudetenland. Koch-Erpach, almost in tears because he wanted a combat command instead of a home unit command, took his farewell of us and drove off with his aide, von Wallenberg, in Koch-Erpach's white BMW sportscar. Von Lossberg, Dagel, and I were transferred to the officer reserve of the army—which at least meant a brief visit home, if not an actual furlough. Happy about that, we began another skat game.

Later in the day, a telephone call came in ordering us to recall Koch-Erpach and take over a front sector on both sides of Oppeln with the 168th Infantry and 20th SS (Estonian) Divisions. Dagel was to report to our Army Group. I called Zwittau so Koch-Erpach would get the news immediately upon arrival. Then von Lossberg and I took off by car for Oppeln. Koch-Erpach arrived at Erlenburg about midnight. He had driven all day to take over his combat corps, the assignment he wanted so badly. He need not have hurried, however, since it would be a few days before we would take over. We arrived on February 18, but did not take over until February 23. General Sieler was supposed to refurbish his battered division, but the supply of men and equipment had been delayed. Thus we were able to get a little more rest. We were supposed to rebuild a complete corps staff by replacing the people we had not been able to take out of Breslau with us. We also had to get vehicles to make us mobile for field combat because we had not been able to take any equipment out of Breslau.

The front was quiet for the moment, while the Russians regrouped for their next offensive. Our section of the front was near Neisse. During this lull, I spent one or two hours each day with the current corps operations officer. I also drove around to get to know the area and the division commanders and operations officers.

On February 23, we took over command of the corps, and I was chained to the telephone again. We now received the equipment and reinforcements we needed. Even without major action at the front, the days went by quickly. Regroupings, new formations, small combat missions, and visits by our army commander provided plenty of work and variety. The commanding general of our neighboring corps, the 8th Korps, was General Hartmann, the "Ice-Gray One" who as an oberst had commanded my home-base 24th Artillery Regiment at Altenburg, Plauen, and Jena before the war. I spent a pleasant evening at his headquarters after going there for liaison purposes. I also visited the neighboring corps on our right in order to get acquainted. Otherwise, except for short walks, I could hardly get away from my desk.

On March 10, we were reassigned. Instead of being the leftmost corps of the First Panzer Army, we became the rightmost corps of the Seventeenth Army. Our name was also changed from Fortress Korps Breslau to Korps Group Silesia for a short time and then to 56th Panzer Korps. I drove to Neisse with General Koch-Erpach to meet our new army commander, General Schulze, and to discuss the expected Russian offensive at Grottkau. As a result of this meeting, we regrouped and formed a stronger reserve. We also began construction of a defensive position southwest of the Tillowitz Forest. For this work, as well as for occupying the position, we had only civil defense units. The local Nazi Party official delayed the evacuation of the civilian population, which we demanded, again and again.

Since Generalmajor von Lossberg was too high-ranking to be the chief of staff of a corps, he was finally replaced on March 14 by Oberstleutnant i.G. von Dufving, who brought a Major Wolff with him as personnel officer. We celebrated von Lossberg's departure with one last card game—my last of the war.

Oberstleutnant i.G. Theodor von Dufving was full of energy, hardworking, and conscientious, and he had the political finesse a good chief of staff needed. He had most recently been assigned to the Training Department of the Supreme Command of the Army.

Major Wolff, in his late twenties, was an infantry combat officer who had been relegated to staff work because of arthritis. We became good friends, probably because we had so much in common—rank, age, and extensive combat experience.

The Russian offensive began on March 15, with the usual artillery and aircraft bombardment. The main attack was at the Neisse River, where the Russian superiority in numbers, artillery, and air support was overwhelming. In our corps sector, only the outermost left flank was immediately threatened, in the sector of an Estonian regiment. The first breaches of our line occurred during the afternoon, and the village of Kirchberg changed hands several times. Other parts of our corps' front remained quiet except for some reconnaissance activity. The main push was at the rightmost division of General Hartmann's 8th Korps, west of the Neisse River. The Russians reinforced in that sector, and soon they had pushed back our entire front there and our left flank lost contact with the 8th Korps. The Russians also increased the pressure on our right flank, while everything remained fairly quiet at our front at the Oder River. A Luftwaffe fighter wing abandoned the airport at Lansdorf, and Koch-Erpach tried unsuccessfully to have the concentration camp at Lansdorf evacuated.

The Russians pushed the 90th Korps back almost to Neisse on March 17, and a Russian tank unit crossed the river and proceeded toward Zülz. The Russian tanks, separated from our corps headquarters by only a kilometer and a half or so of wooded area, drove behind us to Zülz, where they united with another Russian tank unit that had broken through from the south. With that, on March 17, 1945, we were surrounded. It was not a strong line behind us, however, and the Russian tanks were in a difficult situation themselves, because they had German forces in front of and in back of them as well.

I was glad von Dufving was there, because he had the diplomatic skill we needed to get orders that would allow us to retreat. Without his skill, we would have been ordered to stand and fight to the last man, which would not have made much sense. If we had stayed, we would have lost both divisions and gained nothing. Even if the Russians had simply bypassed us, we would have been occupying a useless forest that had no roads, bridges, or anything else of value. We would have been just sitting there, and after a week or so we would have been without food or ammunition. The proper decision was to retreat and break through the Russian tanks at our rear, but Army units could never get permission to do that because of Hitler's edict that the Germany Army did not retreat. Von Dufving said we had to man a defense line that just happened to be behind us—and it worked!

We relocated our corps headquarters in a forester's house in the Tillowitz Forest and prepared a plan to break out of our encirclement. I took a motorcycle that had tank-type treads instead of a rear tire and went to the headquarters of the 20th SS Division, with which we no longer had wire communication and whose situation was completely unknown to us. Arriving without enemy contact, I exchanged situations with the division commander, General-leutnant Augsberger, and submitted the orders we had prepared for the breakout. Again without interference from the enemy, I arrived back at our headquarters, where I learned that the two leftmost divisions of our neighboring corps to the right had been put under our command for this operation because they were surrounded with us.

By staying put during the day and moving only at night, we hoped to get through the Russian lines behind us undetected. We did not know how strong the Russians behind us were, but we knew it was a tank force and we knew that tanks could not fight well at night. We prepared and issued the necessary orders to our divisions, and at dawn I again mounted the tracked motorcycle, with the usual motorcycle escort, to find out how our movements from the Oder River front positions were progressing. I learned that everything was going according to plan. Then I visited the headquarters of the two divisions that had been transferred to our command for the breakout. They were under attack and very glad to receive the orders to pull out that I had brought them. We discussed the necessary details for the operation planned for the coming night. Then I returned to corps headquarters, having to stop to take cover a few times because low-flying Russian fighter planes were firing into refugee columns on the roads.

At 11:00 P.M., I drove to Erlenberg to alert the commander of an assault battalion quartered there that he was to provide protection for the corps staff. I discussed the exact details of the operation with him and pointed out that Koch-Erpach was not to be addressed as "Herr General" during the operation, lest the Russians overhear it.

At 12:30 A.M., we assembled. The 20th SS Division was to move to the right of the 168th Division, and the two newly acquired divisions were to follow us. We moved along a narrow strip no more than a quarter of a mile wide, on a route that was chosen to avoid any large communities. Our goal for the first night was to reach the woods near Riegersdorf by morning. Our plan was to reach Altenwalde by the second morning and then to turn around and establish a new front. The two new divisions were then to break through to the south and reunite with their original corps.

It was drizzling rain when we moved out in the darkness at 1:00 A.M., on March 19. We marched in single file, using our maps and compasses and bypassing all villages. The Russian outposts remained very quiet. We let a passing Russian vehicle go by unmolested, and it never detected us. A horse-mounted Russian dispatch rider saw us and disappeared at a fast gallop.

After a while, I took the lead and guided the group, because too often in Russia I had seen infantry soldiers make mistakes reading maps. The wet ground absorbed the sound of our marching to a great extent. Those of us in the front of the column had to more or less feel our way in the darkness. Once I heard a loud moaning and panting sound in the darkness in front of me. With my pistol cocked, I carefully moved forward by myself, ahead of the column. When I saw something moving in a ditch, I called out in a low voice but heard only continued moaning. Finally I saw that it was a horse that had apparently fallen into the ditch in the darkness and probably broken a leg. I could not even relieve him of his pain with a *coup de grâce,* lest the Russians in the vicinity be made aware of our presence. Then I almost fell into a deep trench that had been dug by someone as a field position. Fortunately, it was not occupied by the Russians.

Sounds of combat suddenly broke out to the right of us. We learned later that the 20th SS Division had run into fierce resistance, and one of the first dead was General-leutnant Augsberger, the division commander.

It began to get light about 5:00 A.M., but we still had to move another five hundred meters to reach our destination, unfortunately across a deep and rather wide stream. Miraculously, we reached our objective without being detected by the Russians. We posted sentries and sent a patrol to Riegersdorf to find out what the situation was there. I went to the edge of the woods to have a look and try to see what was going on. Now and then I could see Russian soldiers on foot and an occasional Russian rider on horseback. It was obvious that we would be detected if we left the woods. Soon our patrol returned and reported that Riegersdorf had been occupied by Russian tanks.

At about 8:00 A.M., a battery of heavy 105mm self-propelled guns from the 168th Division joined us, and we changed our plans. One infantry battalion, together with the self-propelled guns, would attack Riegersdorf immediately, because the Russian tanks would be less efficient fighting within the village. Koch-Erpach and von Dufving remained at the edge of the woods to observe the battle. I took my aide, Hauptmann Kafurke, and accompanied the infantry battalion commander with the point infantry company.

One of our self-propelled guns destroyed a Russian tank at the entrance to the village, and the other Russian tanks, which were dispersed all over the village, disappeared toward the west. A second Russian tank was hit and slid into a ditch half on its side, and its crew got out and ran. We proceeded to the center of the village, where we were stopped at a church. The Russian tanks had not left the area but had taken position on a hill south of the vil-

lage, at a safe distance, from where they now opened fire
on our part of the village. Unfortunately, our battery of
self-propelled artillery had rushed at full speed on through
the village and gone on to break through to the German
lines, and we no longer had their protection. The Russian
tanks were consequently shelling every house now, causing
a lot of casualties.

When we spotted a company of Russian infantry approaching from the north, I ordered the commander of our
assault battalion to secure and hold the part of the village
we had gained. Some of his men panicked, however, and
started to run away—directly toward the Russian tanks! I
pulled my pistol and fired several shots into the air. This
stopped some but not all of them, so I shouted at them
that the east edge of the village was occupied by the Russians—which might not have been true, but it got the attention of those who had not stopped when I fired my
pistol. Now everybody settled down and dug in, and we
held the village until evening.

I returned and reported to Koch-Erpach, who decided
to wait until nightfall and once more try to "sneak
through" in the dark. To our left, in the area of the 168th
Infantry Division, we could hear the sounds of heavy combat, but we were not able to establish radio contact. Our
little piece of the woods was circled several times by a
Russian tank, but we left it alone, because to fire at it
would have given our hiding place away and would probably have drawn a whole pack of tanks down on us. I remembered the Russians who had tried to break out of
encirclement through my battery during the invasion of
Russia in 1941, and I realized now how they must have felt.

At about 7:00 P.M., a unit of eight or ten Russian tanks
attacked from the south and tried to enter the village. After two of them were hit by panzerfausts and started burning, the others turned around and disappeared. Finally, at
8:00 P.M., it was dark enough and we moved out through a
depression north of the village. I again led the column. By

11:00 P.M., we were approaching Altenwalde. In theory, we had made it, but we could not be sure that the Russians had not reached Altenwalde ahead of us. In three days, much could have changed, so I stopped the column and sent a patrol on bicycles to the village, which was still several kilometers ahead. I sent word back to Koch-Erpach that we would be delayed until the patrol returned. Then I sat down under a tree to rest and wait. When the patrol returned, it reported that our own troops were in control of Altenwalde. When I attempted to stand, I was unable to do so. I don't know whether it was the cold or the tension of the last few days, but I was unable to move my arms and legs. Some of the men put me on a bicycle and pushed me along. After about fifteen minutes, life began to return to my limbs, and by the time we arrived at the village, everything was normal again.

So we had escaped encirclement, although some of our units were still missing. We had got out with most of our men, but we'd had to destroy all of our heavy equipment, because we could not use roads for fear of encountering Russian tanks. On March 20, we established our headquarters in the house of the local sheriff, who happened to have a lot of good things in his pantry.

In the morning, I took a car and started looking for our missing units, as did a number of other officers. Major Wolff and the other half of our corps staff were missing, and the entire 168th Division was missing. Only a few stragglers had reported from the 168th Division. From their reports, I could guess that the whole division had been pushed toward the south, so I drove on through the mountains toward the southeast. I knew there was no continuous front between the Russians and me and therefore I could run into Russians anywhere, but I had to find the 168th Division. Finally, after a long search, I found some men and officers of the division. After a lot of asking for directions, I finally found division headquarters in a village. When I entered the headquarters of the 168th Division,

Generalmajor Schmidthammer looked at me with a bewildered expression.

"You are alive!" he exclaimed. "You are supposed to be dead!"

The news had circulated through the 168th Division that the corps' operations officer had been killed by a direct hit in a fight with tanks. I learned that the 168th had got through with 80 percent of its men, 70 percent of its off-road vehicles and arms, and even 20 percent of its other vehicles. This was, to me, a much better outcome than if the entire corps had perished in the Tillowitz Forest "heroically fighting." I felt certain that Schörner would be happy we had been able to save the four divisions of infantry, even though we had lost practically all our equipment except small arms. I left orders for the 168th to make contact with what remained of the 20th SS Division by means of reconnaissance screens (searching a large area with many small patrols). Then I returned to corps headquarters.

In the meantime, Major Wolff had arrived with the rest of our staff. Their experience had been similar to ours. I learned that the 20th SS Division was in our intended frontline position, but in a weakened state after suffering heavy casualties. Their combat capability had been further weakened by the death of Generalleutnant Augsberger, their popular and respected division commander.

We established a new defense line. Then we learned that our divisions had been assigned to another corps and we (the corps staff) were to be pulled out of the front to be rested and resupplied, since we had lost all our equipment.

24

PREPARING A COMPREHENSIVE combat report and war diary (complete with situation sketches and all the necessary attachments) kept me busy during our period of "rest." After a few days, we moved from a school to a mansion, since we were not in charge of any division and it would not be in violation of Schörner's order that staffs not stay in mansions. Finally, all the reports were finished, and we had only to wait for our new equipment. Since we had no command over any troops, we hardly received one telephone call a day. Our staff had worked together long enough now that it functioned smoothly. Except for my aide, Hauptmann Kafurke, I now had the longest service on the staff. Von Dufving wanted an endless list of things done (standing orders for the staff, alarm regulations, etc.). I delegated some of the assignments to aides and insisted on spending part of our rest period trying out the new motor vehicles, going for walks, and working two horses that had belonged to a former corps commander. The March weather was beautiful, and I intended to enjoy at least some of it, because what lay ahead of us was obviously going to be grim.

On March 25, our idyllic life came to an end with an order to take over a sector of the front in a mountainous area southeast of Ziegenhals. Koch-Erpach and von Dufving departed immediately to make contact. Within twenty-four hours, however, a counterorder arrived to move instead, by rail, to Löbau for refurbishment. I recalled Koch-Erpach and von Dufving. When they arrived, they decided that they and Major Wolff would go ahead to Löbau as an advance party. Now, as leader of the railroad transport, I had a few completely quiet days of rest without either the commanding general or the chief of staff to make work for me. During the day, I rode the horses, read, slept, and listened to the radio.

Finally, my train arrived and we loaded everything aboard it and rolled north. Exactly two months after leaving the General Staff College at Hirschberg, I passed it again as we went through Hirschberg on the train. At about 6:00 P.M. on March 31, we arrived at Löbau. I immediately placed a long-distance call to Leipzig and talked to Lilo while the train was being unloaded. Everything was all right at home. Two divisions were put under our command on April 1, and we assigned them to build a fallback position about thirteen kilometers behind the front.

Once when I visited a division headquarters during this period, I found myself at a "Schörner rally." Generalfeldmarschall Schörner was a rarity—a career officer who was also a dedicated Nazi, although the German Army had been deliberately trained to be nonpolitical and we were not even permitted to vote in elections. With political rallies such as this one, he hoped to reinforce the nation's power of resistance. He spoke to soldiers, officers, civilians, and workers at the front and near-front areas. It probably was impressive to many of these people to see a generalfeldmarschall with the country's highest war decoration speaking for the Nazi Party.

I visited the 57th Panzer Korps, which was in command of the front here. Its personnel seemed to be determined to live as well as possible now that the end was approaching—at least that was the impression I gathered from the number of butter-cream cakes and other delicacies they consumed every day. Von Dufving turned down my request to go home for two days over Easter, even though there was really nothing to do (although, of course, things could change quickly). On a trip to the headquarters of the Fourth Army, I met my former basic training leutnant from the 24th Artillery Regiment at Jena, Leutnant Badstübner. He was now a major in the supply service. We had tea and exchanged old memories from 1936.

As much as possible, and without telling von Dufving, I furloughed my aide, Hauptmann Kafurke, who had let his wife come to Löbau. I did not want Lilo to come, both because of her pregnancy and because we were too close to the front and a Russian offensive could begin anytime.

Slowly, our staff (especially the corps signal company) got back into shape. We received younger officers, which made us more capable of combat, but half of our telephone equipment and two-thirds of our radio equipment were still missing. Otherwise, we would be ready to take over command of a corps sector somewhere.

The only remnant remaining from the Army Korps Area VIII General Command of Breslau was Koch-Erpach, our sixty-two-year-old commanding general. Finally, he left us as well when, just as we were having a festive fish dinner in honor of his birthday, the order arrived for him to take over command of the Army Korps Area General Command at Kassel—a noncombat job. Although we had broken out of encirclement successfully under Koch-Erpach's command, Schörner was quite right to decide that he needed a corps commander with much more combat experience than that. Schörner replaced Koch-Erpach with General Weidling, a highly experienced front commander who had been awarded the Knight's Cross with Oak Leaves and Swords—obviously a very impressive corps commander. Weidling, however, was not to arrive until April 13, several days away.

Then we received orders that we were to leave Schörner's army group and join Heinrici's. We were to join General Wenck's Twelfth Army, which did not yet exist (it was just an army command with some corps staffs). It was being formed in the Harz Mountains, about four hundred kilometers southwest of Berlin. On April 11, my orders put me in charge of the railroad transport. I was to load the corps staff, about three hundred people altogether (including our communications company), aboard a train and go to the Harz Mountains. We were supposed to meet General Weidling there. Von Dufving went by car, with an advance party, planning to stop and see his family at Wittenberg on the way. I called home from the train station and gave Lilo some hope that I might be able to drop in the next morning for a very brief visit. I thought I might be able to leave the train at Eilenburg and drive to Leipzig on a light motorcycle and then catch the train again in Halle, Magdeburg, or Oschersleben—or even drive all the way to Blankenburg if necessary.

The last preparations for loading onto the train were soon completed, and I finally had a chance to have a look at Löbau. Together with several officers of our staff, I went to a restaurant to wait for our departure. The restaurant was completely void of patrons. Schörner had issued orders that anyone caught behind the lines without orders was to be put in front of a tribunal and hanged if found guilty of desertion. We had heard horror stories of innocent people being hanged by these kangaroo courts simply because they were acting under oral orders instead of written orders. Because of Schörner's orders, no soldier or officer dared to be seen in the cities behind the front, even when on duty (I was safe only because of the red general staff stripes on my trousers). Schörner's order seemed extreme to me at the time, but I later realized how important his iron hand was in maintaining discipline under the prevailing circumstances.

Finally, in late evening, I climbed into my car, which was secured on a railroad flatcar, and the train moved off slowly into the night.

PART FOUR

Tomorrow Will Be Better

1945–1949

25

IT WAS DUSK as our airplane that was to deliver me to a Soviet prison camp approached Moscow. I could not help remembering as I looked at the city from the air how tantalizingly close we had come to capturing it in December 1941. I remembered thinking when I was wounded just outside of Moscow that I would miss the victory parade in front of the Kremlin. How ironic that thought seemed now! I thought also of the many brave soldiers—German and Russian—who lay buried in the earth over which we flew.

When our airplane touched down on a runway south of Moscow (there were no buildings, just some runways), a Russian officer with an American jeep, a driver, and a guard met the airplane to take me to what apparently would be my final destination. With gestures, the officer ordered me into the jeep beside the driver, and he and the guard sat in the backseat. Darkness rapidly descended as we drove north, through Moscow, to a prison camp.

At the camp, we drove through a wooden gate that was opened for us by a guard with a submachine gun hanging from his shoulder. A sign over the gate said "Krasnogorsk 27/II." The numbers seemed to indicate that there were other Krasnogorsk prison camps. My escort officer went into a building next to the gate while I waited with the guard. Beyond the entrance gate, I could see two barbed-wire fences with a three-meter death strip of raked sand between them. The fences were about four meters high, crowned with ten-meter-high wooden watchtowers at thirty-meter intervals. I had seen this type of fence four years earlier at the Russian/Polish border.

Finally, my escort officer returned with another officer, who signaled me to follow him. In the darkness, I could barely make out several wooden barracks as we walked along a gravel street to a gate in another board fence. The guard, who had followed us, unlocked the gate, and the Russian officer and I entered the fenced-in area. Inside the board fence was another barrack like the ones we had just passed. The Russian officer led me into it and pointed at an empty bunk, which I interpreted as an invitation to settle down there. One lonely bulb hanging near the entrance cast light into an aisle formed by two rows of built-in double bunks, some of them occupied by sleeping forms.

I had only my fur-lined uniform overcoat, my canteen, and a small Army-issue food bag that attached to the belt (we had used it to carry food in when we were in combat). I deposited my meager possessions at the foot of the bunk and fell wearily into it, pulling my overcoat over me, more for security than for warmth, since it was summer. Sleep came quickly, but it was a very fitful sleep, full of apprehension and uncertainty about the future. I was certain they would shoot me after they had learned everything I could tell them.

When I woke the next morning, I was relieved to find that the barrack contained about fifteen German officers. I introduced myself to everyone, and someone went to a designated place and brought back food for all of us. I was handed a watery bowl of cabbage soup with a tiny fish floating in it and some extremely weak imitation coffee. I was repulsed by the sight and the smell of the soup; it had a strong, unpleasant fish odor. As a small child, I had been deathly ill after eating fish, and I had never eaten fish again.

"Is there nothing else?" I asked.

"This is it," an oberst responded, smiling wryly. "In a few days, you will be glad to get it."

"What do you get at other meals?" I asked.

"They are identical to this one. Other than that, we just get three hundred grams of bread each day."

So all that stood between me and starvation was this putrid cabbage soup and a little bread each day! I could not know what was in store for me—whether I would be shot after the Russians had everything they wanted from me, whether I would spend the rest of my life in Russian captivity, or whether I would eventually go home—but it was obvious that the only thing I could control now was how I handled myself in this new situation. I decided that I would do everything in my power to stay alive and as healthy as possible and hope to eventually return to my family. I took my meager portion of the fish soup and ate it, trying hard not to smell it. I swallowed the tiny fish whole.

I exchanged a little small talk with my fellow prisoners and learned that I was in a quarantine barrack and would stay here for three weeks. All of the other people in the barrack were senior officers (majors, oberstleutnants, and oberts) except for one oberleutnant. His name was Kurt von Burkersroda, and I'd had a von Burkersroda in my regiment when I was stationed at Plauen.

"He is my older brother, Friedrich," the oberleutnant told me when I asked. "He is in the main camp here, according to the Russians, and they are bringing me here from a labor camp to join him. I do not know why they are being so kind, but I am more than happy to take advantage of it."

The younger von Burkersroda was perhaps twenty-three years old and very thin, almost emaciated. It was good to know that I would have at least one acquaintance in the main camp. I had not known the older von Burkersroda well, since he had been at Altenburg and I had been at Plauen, but I remembered him from the meetings of all regiment officers.

After breakfast I wandered outside the barrack, where the bright June sun made the world look cheerful in spite of my unhappy circumstances. The quarantine barrack was the only thing inside the board fence that surrounded it. I could not see very much of the rest of the camp. I noticed an older man tending some flowers that had been planted beside the fence. He wore Bavarian short leather pants and the traditional Bavarian hat, complete with feather. He looked vaguely familiar to me, and then I realized that it was Generalfeldmarschall Schörner in civilian clothes.

He stopped what he was doing and looked at me for a moment, then said, "Don't I know you?"

"*Jawohl,* Herr Generalfeldmarschall," I responded. "You sent me to Breslau in January to help get it ready for siege."

"Yes, Breslau," he said, nodding. "I remember. Were you captured there?"

"No, I surrendered in Berlin. I was operations officer of the 56th Panzer Korps under General Weidling."

"Oh, yes," he said. "Well, the Russians did not capture me. My army group and I fought our way through from Czechoslovakia to the west and surrendered to the Americans. However, the Americans just turned us over to the Russians anyway, so it was all for nothing. If I had known the Americans would do that, I would not have sacrificed the lives that it cost to fight our way through to the west." He heaved a heavy sigh and looked down at the ground. "You might as well know that inside the main camp here, I am being criticized for continuing to fight after the formal surrender so I could get my army group to the west. They are saying that I sacrificed German lives unnecessarily. In view of what eventually happened, of course, they are right."

It seemed important to him that I understand his motives for continuing to fight after the surrender. He said he had also wanted to give German civilians a chance to get to the west, and many civilians had in fact escaped the Russians with his army group.

Schörner was known to German soldiers as "the Hangman" because of his order during the fighting at the end that any soldier found behind the lines without proper orders to be there should be court-martialed and hanged if found guilty of desertion.

The Russians must have resented Schörner's continuing to fight and kill Russian soldiers after the surrender and his taking his army group to the west to surrender, but they apparently were giving him special treatment for some reason. They kept him in the relatively spacious prison camp instead of in a cramped cell at Lubyanka or Butyrka Prison, where they kept other high-ranking German generals. For the rest of my three weeks in the quarantine barrack, I saw very little of Schörner, which led me to believe that he must have a room of his own somewhere.

Some of the other prisoners in the quarantine barrack had been in other prison camps, and I learned from them a little about life in Russian captivity.

"Be thankful you are here," the younger von Burkersroda told me. "At the labor camp I was in, the Russians routinely starved and worked German prisoners to death." His description of the labor camps did not paint a pretty picture: the depression that takes over the human soul in a climate with four months of darkness, the sixteen-hour work days and seven-day work weeks, the physical weakness that comes with being overworked on an inadequate diet, the brutality of the Russian guards (he told of gold crowns being broken off the teeth of live German prisoners by the Russian guards, of having to carry the dead out of the camp in wheelbarrows and bury them without ceremony). In the following days, whenever I found myself getting depressed about my situation, I would seek out Burkersroda and find some solace in the fact that I was here rather than in the hellish labor camps he described so vividly.

During the three weeks I was in quarantine, our number remained steady at about fifteen, although people would be released into the main camp and others would arrive, usually from Germany but occasionally from another prison camp. Krasnogorsk Prison Camp 27/II was just outside Moscow, about twenty-two kilometers from the Kremlin, which made it convenient for NKVD (later KGB) interrogators. Apparently, the Russians kept people they wanted to interrogate frequently, like Weidling and von Dufving, in Lubyanka or Butyrka Prison in Moscow, and those they wanted to interrogate less frequently at Krasnogorsk.

To my surprise, I learned that the main camp was actually run by Germans called Activists, who were collaborating with the Russians. I learned that the tower guards, the NKVD interrogators, and the camp commander (who counted all prisoners twice each day) were likely to be the only Russians I would ever see.

I could see some of the camp from the quarantine barrack. It consisted of a number of buildings on each side of a gravel street. Although most of the buildings were barracks, others included an administration building, a large assembly hall that I later learned was used for propaganda films and events, a latrine, a bathhouse, a small dispensary, a kitchen, and a laundry. The camp was surrounded by the barbed-wire fences I had seen on my arrival, the strands of which were so close together that nothing could get between them. The death strip between the two fences was lighted with floodlights at night and kept raked so that a footprint would show clearly.

I was told that a few attempts to escape had been made, but those prisoners who did escape had always been caught, and then they were badly beaten and kept in solitary confinement for weeks. Even if a prisoner succeeded in getting out of the camp, he would be over a thousand kilometers from another country. I later heard that some German prisoners had escaped from other camps and had actually got out of Russia. One was supposedly a German doctor who escaped with the help of a female Russian doctor. The story was that she did all the talking and he played deaf and dumb. I suspected that this story was just a fantasy kept alive by desperate prisoners.

The days passed slowly in the quarantine barrack. We shared our stories with one another, but fifteen stories are not long in the telling. We could walk around the barrack, but the fence was no more than five meters from the building, so our walking route was cramped and provided little outlet for the tension of being inactive and captive. Oberleutnant von Burkersroda reveled in being able to get enough sleep, which he had apparently not been able to do since surrendering at Stalingrad two and a half years ago. But for me, it was difficult to go suddenly from a life of constant action, of helping to command divisions, to a life of absolute inactivity, without a say in even something as insignificant as when I would eat. Time, of which there had never previously been enough, seemed suddenly to be the only commodity remaining in my life. I found it difficult to believe how slowly it passed, and the more conscious I was of it, the more its passage seemed to slow. Inactivity and restlessness were obviously enemies I would have to conquer.

As bad as the food was—and it never varied in quality or quantity—mealtimes were at least events that helped break up the day. Hunger was a serious factor we all had to deal with from our first day in captivity.

Each of us was left immersed in his own thoughts most of the time. Lilo and Klaus and our unborn child were always on my mind. I could not know whether they had survived the war, but my mother had told me on the telephone that the Americans were taking Leipzig instead of the Russians, and I tried to focus on that fact—it meant that their chances were good. But even if they had survived, how would they live? I tried hard to put them out of my mind, but I could not.

Losing the war also preyed on my mind. Being captured had always been a real possibility for all of us, but surrendering our country . . . I felt stunned now, almost as if I were in someone else's bad dream. The war had shattered my life and left only a deep void. Home and a normal life were things I would probably never know again. I had to learn to adjust to our total defeat and my status as a prisoner of the Russians. It was a feeling of complete desperation. Germany was divided both geographically and ideologically, and it was unlikely ever to exist again as a whole nation.

I spent much of those first three weeks going over Germany's experience of the previous six years. Where had we gone so wrong? I felt that Germany's claim to the Rhineland, the Sudetenland, and the Polish Corridor had been justified because they had been taken away from us at the end of World War I by the Treaty of Versailles. Hitler annexed Austria as a result of a plebiscite by the Austrian people. I felt that our invasion of France had been justified because France had declared war on us. Belgium, Luxembourg, and the Netherlands had not declared war on us, however, and yet we had gone through those countries to get to France. Occupying them had been just a matter of convenience; obviously, in retrospect, that was wrong. We had done it during World War I and we automatically did it again—and perhaps because we did it the first time, it seemed acceptable when we did it again. We had needed Norway for its raw materials and to protect our northern flank from England—but now that I had time to consider our actions, I had to concede that we had no right to invade and occupy Norway. It was only now beginning to dawn on me that our treatment of other nations had been arrogant—that the only justification we had felt necessary was our own need. As for the Soviet Union, we had hated the concept of communism and felt that the Soviet government was cruelly subjugating the Soviet people, but that hardly gave us the right to violate their sovereignty. Of course, we were not just fighting communism; the concept of *Lebensraum,* or living space, would have been our justification for annexing the Ukraine for its food-producing capability and the Caucasus for its oil reserves. We had operated under a "might-makes-right" theory.

As these things all went through my mind, I began to realize that I should have thought them through at the time of their occurrence—but I was a soldier, and a soldier does not question the orders of his superiors. I had unquestioningly accepted the brutal philosophy that might makes right; the arrogance of our national behavior had not even occurred to me at the time. Although such blind obedience was probably the only military way to keep soldiers focused on the task at hand, the realization that I had allowed myself to become a nonthinking cog in Hitler's military machine depressed me now. What had begun—at least in our minds—as an effort to correct the injustices of the Treaty of Versailles had escalated far beyond anything that any of us could have imagined. In retrospect, I realized that I—and countless others like me—had helped Hitler start and fight a world war of conquest that had left tens of millions of people dead and destroyed our own country. I wondered now whether I would ever have questioned these things if we had won the war. I had to conclude that it was unlikely. This was a lesson taught by defeat, not by victory.

26

AFTER THREE ENDLESS weeks, I was finally released from quarantine and moved into the main camp. A German generalmajor named Bammler met me at the camp's administration building and escorted me to my assigned barrack. Bammler was several inches taller than I and perhaps fifteen years older. As we walked from the administration building to the barrack, he glanced at my uniform.

"You would be wise to remove the red stripes from your trousers," he said as we walked.

I was surprised, because those red stripes were a badge of honor to a general or a general staff officer. I glanced down and only now realized that he had removed his own red stripes.

"Why?" I asked.

"Because the only purpose in wearing them is to set yourself apart as a member of an elite group, and there are no elite groups here."

I did not respond, but I wondered why a German general would make such a statement. The general staff was indeed an elite group, and one that took much pride in being elite. I did not pursue the subject with him at that moment, but in the ensuing days, one German Activist or another would make a point of attacking me verbally, until I finally removed the red stripes so I could have some peace.

When I moved into my assigned bunk, I introduced myself to my neighbors and we exchanged our stories. I looked for Oberleutnant von Burkersroda and found him in my own barrack. He introduced me to his brother, Friedrich, who remembered me from 1938 when we had served in the same regiment. His unit had surrendered to the Russians in the Crimea during the summer of 1943 and he had now been in this camp two years. We were to become very good friends. He told me that General Bammler was cooperating with the Russians in return for more food and better treatment and cautioned me to be very careful what I said to Bammler or to anyone else whom I did not know extremely well.

I began to watch the people around me carefully. Slowly during the days and weeks that followed, I learned more about them, not so much from what they told me as from the way they conducted themselves. I learned that how they were reacting to what was happening to them now was more important than what they had been or done in the past.

I was now able to get a closer look at the camp. Each barrack was a long, narrow building, about ten meters wide and twenty-four meters long. Two aisles ran through each barrack, with a row of bunks on each side of each aisle, and wood-burning stoves at opposite ends of each aisle (although the stoves were not being used in June). In one corner of each barrack was a separate small room for the German Activist who was supervising the barrack for the Russians.

We slept on board bunks that were in three tiers. The bunks were built for two men, but at times over the years we were so crowded that six men had to sleep in a space built for two (when that happened, we could not turn over at night unless we all turned over at the same time). We had straw bags for mattresses (the German Army used the same kind of straw-bag mattresses, but ours were fuller). A small, crude table and a window separated each set of bunks. The tables had no chairs, but we could sit on the lower tier of bunks. The barracks were dimly lit, with only four electric bulbs hanging from the ceiling, two over each aisle.

The first order of business each day, at 6:00 A.M., was to be counted. The Russian camp commander, the equivalent of a hauptmann, counted us twice a day, accompanied by a noncommissioned officer. He would say, in Russian, "Prisoners of war, good morning." and we had to answer, also in Russian, "Good morning." Then he counted us. If the number came out right at each barrack, we could go to breakfast; if not, he would count us again. The hauptmann was a stocky, peasant-looking type of person—sort of a Nikita Khrushchev without intelligence. (The Russians must have put their least capable officers in charge of the prison camps, because most of them were really dumb, sometimes even counting on their fingers. They surely had people with more intelligence than that.) In the summer, we were counted outside in the camp street. We stood in military formation, in rows of three, in front of our barracks, and the camp commander would come through with a small wooden board, count us, and write the number on the board. No effort was made to identify us. Then he would do the same with the other barracks. In the winter, we stayed in the barracks for counting if it was unbearably cold outside. Sometimes the counting was fast and sometimes it took up to an hour.

If there was an announcement to be made, the camp commander would make it in Russian after completing the count, and then a Russian-speaking German Activist would translate. An Activist would then read us the news the Russians wanted us to have—slanted and carefully edited bulletins that were of value to us only if we read between the lines. Sometimes the news they gave us would inadvertently indicate that they were having trouble with the western nations; when their relationship with the west deteriorated, their treatment of us deteriorated; when their relationship with the west improved, their treatment of us improved.

After the news, we would have breakfast. In each barrack bunk compartment (usually twelve to eighteen people), the members took turns going to the kitchen, getting the food for the group, and bringing it back. Each group designated an especially trusted member to be the food master, whose function was to divide the food into equal portions. If any was left over, the food master kept a list of who had received seconds last, and the extra was distributed fairly in this manner. Our food master was Hauptmann Pawelek, a former judge from Bremen.

After breakfast in our bunk area each day, we went to an open shed that had a metal water pipe running through the center of it. Water would squirt out of holes in the pipe and into a wooden trough underneath. We would stand there, a row of ten of us on each side of the pipe, and wash from the waist up in the cold water. The water was then turned off and we brushed our teeth (those who had not brought toothbrushes into captivity used their fingers), and then the water was turned on again briefly. I had taken a comb and a toothbrush to the camp with me, but of course there was no toothpaste. Then we filed out and the next group came in.

The latrine was a board with twelve holes over a large pit that was emptied every two weeks. It was open except from behind, so in the winter it was quite cold. The latrine was located a hundred meters or so from the barracks, and chemicals were applied to it regularly to reduce the odor.

After the counting, breakfast, and washing, those who worked fell in outside the barracks and were marched to work. Senior officers were not forced to work, because Stalin, for some reason that we never learned, had signed an order to that effect. All ranks up through hauptmann had to work, and some of the higher-ranking officers volunteered to work in order to get out of the camp. Most of the prisoners worked in the woods, cutting and trimming trees, but some also worked in factories in Moscow, and some worked in the camp (in the bathhouse, the laundry, the kitchen, and so forth). Senior officers also received a ration of ten cigarettes a day, and lower ranks received ten cigarettes a day for working. Cigarettes and food had become the monetary currency within the camp.

We were fed at 7:30 A.M., at 12:30 P.M., and at 5:30 P.M. every day. Our meals were a small bowl of soup three times a day, and two of the three bowls of soup might include a small piece of fish or meat if we were lucky. The Russians gave us two different kinds of soup: one was cabbage soup, and the other was kasha, a soup made with rye, oats, or some other kind of grain. Although the kasha was quite thick, we got only a small bowl of it. The cabbage soup would have some potatoes, some cabbage, and occasionally a small fish—complete with head and guts! I had to force myself to eat it because of its horrible fishy smell and taste. The little fish or piece of meat was the only protein we got, and as repulsive as it would have been before, we considered it a rare treat after a few weeks in camp. We had no choice but to eat it or starve, because sometimes for periods of three weeks we got nothing else, morning, noon, and night.

The Russian government provided the camp with so many grams of meat per day for everyone, but the weight was on the hoof, which meant that bones and horns and hooves were weighed. The Russian soldiers naturally took the good meat for themselves and gave us the head and the bony parts of the beef, so although we got the weight due to us, it was mostly bone. They would just throw the head of a beef into a tub of soup—hair, eyes, nose, everything! They went through the motions of removing the hair, but we quickly learned that we were better off not looking at what we were eating. If we got a little meat we were very lucky and did not complain if it had hair on it. More than once, I found a cow's eye in my soup. Occasionally we would get better meat because the Russians had canned Spam from the American Lend-Lease program of financial and material aid to the Soviet Union during the war, but they did not like it, so sometimes they would put that in our soup. That was always the best meat we got, so we were very glad they did not like it.

We were also given a very diluted kind of tea or a weak simulated coffee made from some kind of roasted grain. It looked like coffee and it had a bitter taste, so with a little imagination we could drink it as coffee. We got it or the diluted tea with each meal.

In addition to the soup and tea or coffee, we were allotted three hundred grams (eleven ounces) of bread a day, but the Russian bread was two-thirds water and one-third solid ingredients, so when it dried out (or was toasted on the barrack stove in winter) our three hundred grams became one hundred grams. In addition to the bread, we got thirty grams (a little over an ounce) of sugar, and twenty grams (three-quarters of an ounce) of fat (butter, margarine, or a substitute such as lard). We got different things at different times, always for periods of about three weeks. When a supply train came into the area, we ate whatever was on it as long as it lasted. If it had cabbage, we had cabbage soup until it was gone; if it had grain, we ate kasha until it was gone.

I bought extra food with my cigarette ration. The camp was sometimes short of food, but the cigarettes (or at least tobacco) were always there, and there were always people who would trade part of their food for cigarettes; in fact, some people deliberately ate less and less and smoked more and more so their health would deteriorate, hoping the Russians would send them home when their health got too bad. It worked for a few of the older ones, but most of those who did that just damaged their health.

Some people in the camp talked a lot about food, because everyone was always hungry. Some would tell how their mothers or wives made a certain dish, and people who did not mind punishing themselves would listen very attentively and dream of such things as succulent pork roasts and potatoes. One major loved to talk about the cabbage rolls his mother used to make; he could describe them so you could almost smell and taste them. I avoided such conversations, since they just made everyone who listened even more hungry.

I do not know how many calories we were allotted each day, but since everyone was always hungry it obviously was not enough. If we had got the rations the Russian government allotted to us and if the Russian soldiers had not cheated with the cow heads and that sort of thing, our diet probably would have been just barely adequate. As it was, the calories were inadequate and protein was seriously lacking from our diet. Yet, surprisingly, there was little sickness in the camp.

During the evenings, the Russians often played Radio Moscow for us over a loudspeaker in the barracks. We got a lot of good classical music that way, which I enjoyed very much. For me the music quickened the passage of time. I am sure the Russians did it as part of their effort to keep us docile. The Russians loved music and even allowed us to have a band; it played more for the Russians than for us, but we had concerts occasionally.

One day in late 1945, quite unexpectedly, I found myself face to face with Major Wolff! He was as surprised as I was to find an old friend in Russian captivity. It was the most pleasant thing that had happened to me since I left Germany. I learned that after I had left him at the gravel-quarry prison, he had become extremely ill—so ill that even the Russians took pity on him and sent him to a hospital. He spent several weeks in the hospital, and before he left, he had fallen in love with a German nurse. I was extremely glad to have my old friend around and was soon able to get him a bunk in my barrack. We fell into our comfortable old relationship as colleagues and friends, although I almost wished he had not fallen in love with the nurse at the hospital in Berlin, because now he just had someone else to worry about, and he fretted about her constantly.

27

THE CAMP CONTAINED prisoners from all the European countries: Bulgarians, Rumanians, Czechs, Poles, Austrians, Hungarians, Italians—people from every country that had fought as a German ally. Even though Spain had been neutral in the war, we had some Spaniards, because Spain had sent a division of volunteers to fight for Germany in reciprocation for our helping Franco in the Spanish Civil War. Of course, the great bulk of the prisoners were German.

From 10 to 15 percent of the population of the camp were junior officers (under the rank of major) who were there because of their noble or famous names, about 5 percent were civilians and enlisted men who were there for the same reason, and 80 to 85 percent were senior officers (major and higher). The German military hierarchy was generally maintained in the camp. We did not wear insignia of rank or use titles of rank, but everyone knew everyone's rank and the majority of us remained in the same relationship with one another.

I discovered quickly that Krasnogorsk was populated by very interesting people. The Russians had congregated in the camp some of the outstanding military and civilian people from all over Europe and Asia: scientists, scholars, diplomats, artists, generals, nobles—people the Russians found useful or interesting. I felt fortunate to be held captive with some of Germany's best and brightest, but it seemed to me to also make it more likely that the Russians would shoot us once they had what they wanted from us, because these were all people who could exercise great influence over our society at home.

I learned that I was there because I had been Weidling's operations officer and they wanted to piece together what had happened in Berlin, and especially in the Führer bunker. They also had Weidling, von Dufving, Refior, and others who had been in Berlin at the end. In other words, it was only because of where I had been the last weeks of the war that I was in this camp instead of in a labor camp. The Russians found me "interesting" only because of my experience defending Berlin, and that was a fluke, because if we had not lost contact with the Ninth Army as we fell back to Berlin, Weidling would not have decided to go to the Führer bunker to get the big picture of what was happening and Hitler would not have ordered us into the city to defend Berlin.

I was finding it difficult to "justify" my luck during the entire war. I had to accept it as my destiny without feeling guilt—guilt that I had gone home to hospitals and schools during the war when others had stayed at the front, guilt that I had lived when so many others had died, and guilt now that I was in a prison camp where I did not have to work when so many were being worked to death in slave labor camps.

I concluded that the Russians brought people to Krasnogorsk either because the people had information they wanted or because they hoped to recruit and train them and return them to Germany to spy and work for them. They thought anyone with a famous name would be especially influential back home, and their thinking was on a double track: if they brought them here, these people could not influence the people at home against them; and if they could recruit the people with famous names, they could send well-known Germans back home to influence people in their favor.

A few people in the camp were there only because of their names. One, for example, was a man named Truman who had operated a cigar store in Potsdam. The Russians had asked whether he was related to the American President, and he boasted that he probably was because his grandfather's brother had emigrated to the United States. His boasting won him a ticket to Krasnogorsk! Another was named Ackermann. His father had been an important German politician before World War I. He caught their attention because of his name, and they shipped him off to Krasnogorsk. Another was named Hugo Dörpfeld. His father, Wilhelm Dörpfeld, had been the director of the German Archaeological Institute in Athens and had assisted in the excavation of Olympia and Troy; he was at Krasnogorsk simply because the Russians recognized his father's name. He must have been in his fifties. He had been a pharmacist. Intelligent, mature, and stable, he had adapted well to being the son of a famous man, and we all liked him. He would not have been a threat to the Russians.

The Russians were fascinated with nobility, although they had killed or frightened away all their own. Probably 30 percent of the prisoners in the camp were from the German nobility. Most were generals or general staff officers, but there were also some civilians. A board fence had been erected at one part of the camp to block our view of some civilian prisoners, primarily the family of Polish Prince Radziwill. The Russians had brought Prince Radziwill to Krasnogorsk to prevent him from being an influence against them in postwar Poland. His family included twelve to fifteen people who spanned three generations. They had one barracklike building to themselves, and the Russians had built the wooden fence around it to provide them with privacy. They were obviously showing Prince Radziwill a great deal of deference. We knew about the Radziwill family through a Catholic priest who lived in our barrack and conducted mass for them. I do not know whether the Prince Radziwill who later became an in-law to U.S. President John F. Kennedy was one of the prince's grandchildren in that camp.

Another noble civilian was Count Schwerin. He was a widower whose very prominent family had had large estates in Mecklenburg and Pomerania. Many members of his family had been government ministers, and one was Finance Minister under Hitler. He was one of the oldest people in the camp and one of the most dignified members of the nobility. He kept very much to himself. Although he was not naturally gregarious, he became a supportive friend to me. The Russians took him to Krasnogorsk because he had a famous name and was a rich landowner. They may also have known that his deceased wife had been a Russian princess who had emigrated to Germany after the Russian revolution. I think the Russians wanted to hold people like Schwerin and Radziwill as hostages for whatever need might arise.

Eventually, I knew most of the people in my barrack personally, perhaps half the people in the camp by name, and most of the people in the camp (usually around six hundred) by sight. I knew many of their stories and why they were at Krasnogorsk. I also knew, for the most part, who was cooperating with the Russians in return for extra food and who was not.

Groups of friends formed quickly in the camp, composed of people who were drawn together by common cultural backgrounds and interests. The groups would vary in size from a half-dozen to a dozen people. These were the people we bunked with and ate with. We got to know one another well, and we did not have to worry so much about being spied on by clandestine collaborators (in addition to the known Activists). We would celebrate one another's birthdays and other holidays as a group.

Wolff, of course, became a member of my group. I trusted him completely, and in our years of captivity his natural affability and optimism helped a lot of people through this bleak time.

Another good friend and confidant was Major Friedrich von Burkersroda. He was also friendly and affable, but more important he was very steady and mature, exuding an aura of great strength of character. He was also very intelligent, and he inspired confidence in those around him. He was the sort of man anyone would like to have backing him in any endeavor. He had been a division adjutant and had been captured by female Russian soldiers, whom he described as considerably more cruel than the male soldiers. He was from an old noble family that had large landholdings before the war in what was now East Germany. Of course, they lost all their property under the Russian occupation.

His younger brother, Kurt, was also part of our group. He was little more than skin and bones and looked much older than his years. After the war, the Russians started looking for certain people, especially nobility. When they found they had two brothers from a noble family in different camps, they brought them together, probably thinking that if they did that the brothers might be more willing to cooperate with them. It did not work for them in this case, but it was a lucky break for Kurt. As an oberleutnant, he had to work at Krasnogorsk, but life was much easier for him there than it had been in the labor camp. Kurt had a quick sense of humor and an interesting, inquisitive mind. With the natural optimism of his youth, he fully expected to go home.

The von Wangenheims, another set of brothers from an old noble family, were also part of my group. The older brother, Konrad, had participated in the 1936 Olympics in Berlin, in what was known as the Three-Day Event in horseback riding. During the cross-country ride, he had fallen and broken his collarbone, but he got back on his horse in spite of it and finished the event under terrible pain. Because that had assured his team the gold medal, he was a hero in Germany. Of course, the Russians were aware of all this.

Our group also included the operations officer of Generalfeldmarschall von Paulus's Sixth Army, which had surrendered at Stalingrad in February 1943. He was an oberst in the general staff. He was a quiet sort of person, and he suffered from his experience at Stalingrad. He was in his late thirties, about average in size, with dark hair and haunted eyes. In addition to the brutal combat with the Russians at Stalingrad, he had seen too many men die needlessly of starvation, of insufficient winter clothing, and of inadequate medical care because the Sixth Army had not been allowed to retreat and could not be kept adequately supplied. He had completely given up on life, even though he had a wife and children at home, and he now just existed from one day to the next.

We had a Catholic priest in our group, the one who ministered to the Radziwills. He was one of a group of chaplains who had cooperated with the Russians by writing articles and signing statements to the effect that a Christian could also be a communist. The Russians had sent the other chaplains who had done this to other camps after they had cooperated, but ours stayed at Krasnogorsk for some reason. We knew what he had done, but he was very congenial and we accepted him. We had long discussions with him about why he had cooperated with the Russians. He was able to rationalize to himself that he needed to do whatever was necessary to stay alive in order to minister to the other prisoners. He also acknowledged that they could break him and force him to sign their statements, so he complied without forcing them to do so. He felt he was just being pragmatic. But a communist was an atheist by definition; how could an atheist also be a Christian? He also traded on the "we no longer have a country" theme that was common among German prisoners who cooperated with the Russians for better food and treatment. He was a survivor, a good talker, and very good at rationalizing whatever he wanted to justify.

Hauptmann Arthur Pawelek, the former judge who

was now our food master, was at Krasnogorsk because of his former influential job and his prominent family. The Russians especially feared such people, because they might influence others against them. He was tall and slim, a nice person, friendly, and supportive of everyone. He wanted to survive and he wanted everyone else to survive, but he would not compromise his principles to do it. He took forceful issue with those who rationalized collaborating with the Russians because they "no longer had a country." He felt strongly that since it was our generation that had helped to destroy Germany, it was our responsibility to rebuild it. He was generous with all of us whose homes were in East Germany, giving us his address in Bremen (West Germany) and offering to help all of us get a new start if we ever got out of Russia.

Count von Schwerin was also a member of our group. Although he was more than twenty years older than I, we became close friends. With deep-set eyes, he quickly developed a gaunt look as he lost weight on our diet. He traded his cigarette ration for extra food, just as I did. (The Russians treated the older civilian nobility like senior officers —they received a cigarette ration and did not have to work.) He was a walker, walking kilometers every day around and around the camp.

Except for the chaplain, these were close friends with whom I felt I could discuss anything. We had many long discussions on an endless number of topics. This ability to discuss things helped us maintain our sanity. It was one of the few weapons we had against the constant propaganda and the oppression and boredom of our situation.

28

ONCE A WEEK we got a bucket of warm water to take a bath with. We called that day Banya Day (*banya* is the Russian word for "bath," but for us it was a word for all the pleasant little things that we missed). When we had our Banya Day, we went into the bathhouse and got a tiny piece of soap, which had to last us a week, until our next Banya Day. The soap was a brownish substance that did not work very well. We got a wooden bucket that held perhaps two gallons of warm water. We took the bucket of water to a room, where we undressed and washed; then we rinsed off in a cold shower. We had small towels that we kept from one Banya Day to the next. We could have a bath only once a week, because only so many people could go through the bathhouse in one day. Once a week for each of us was probably the most they could accommodate; as it was, we had to rush so everyone could get his turn. We also got a shave at the same place on our Banya Day; the Russians kept the razors locked up, of course, but we were shaved by a barber (a German prisoner) when we had our bath each week.

Our haircuts amounted to being shaved bald with clippers from time to time. This, at least ostensibly, was to prevent lice. If one person had lice, they shaved everybody. It was an indignity at first, but we got used to it. I got someone who could sew to take the material of the red stripes from my pants and make me a skullcap like the Pope's, and whenever they shaved me bald I wore the skullcap until my hair grew out again. The German Activists did not like that, because it was made from the red stripes of a general staff officer's trousers, but I did it in spite of them.

Probably the worst aspect of prison life after the loss of freedom and the hunger was bedbugs—millions and millions of them. There were so many of them that they went right on biting in the daytime. There was no point in trying to kill them, because there were so many. The biggest ones were almost as big as ladybugs. In the winter, when we were counted inside, we could see the bedbugs crawling on the bunk posts as we stood at attention. We finally persuaded the Activists to mention it to the Russians. After that, we had to move out every two or three months so the Russians could fumigate the barracks and kill the bedbugs. Then for a few days we would have some relief, but the bedbugs would gradually begin to build up again. The Russians just could not get rid of the bedbugs completely, and for those prisoners who were allergic to bedbug bites it was pure hell. During the worst times, some of the men would be literally covered with bites.

I found a way to sleep without being bothered by them. I bought a horse blanket for ten cigarettes and sewed it together like an envelope, with an opening toward the center from both the top and the bottom. I would get into it so that the only opening, at the center, was beneath me. It was difficult to breathe through the thick blanket, of course, but it was far better than getting bitten by bedbugs.

We wore the clothes we had brought into captivity with us. I had my uniform, with the riding pants, blouse, and boots. I also had the long pants that our mechanized troops wore, which I had worn over my riding pants when I surrendered. Apart from that, I had two extra sets of underwear and two shirts. We had to take the badges of rank off our uniforms, and we were not allowed to wear any decorations. The Hague Convention would have allowed us to wear our decorations, but the Russians would not permit it, because all the decorations had swastikas on

them, and we understood their feelings about that. We did
not feel that Stalin and communism was any improvement
over Hitler and fascism, but we did not want to provoke
them needlessly.

At first, I had only my riding boots for shoes, so I wore
my riding pants. Later, I bought a pair of homemade
wooden-soled sandals, and then I wore the long pants and
saved my boots and riding pants. The wooden shoes were
just blocks of wood carved to the appropriate shape, like
Dutch wooden shoes, with a strip of cloth across the top
and nailed to the sides of the sole. They would hardly be
good for marching, but they were adequate for our use in
the camp. In the summer, we did not wear socks. We wore
just the wooden-soled sandals and saved the socks for winter. The Russians provided no clothing at all in the beginning.

Later, when ours had worn out, we received Russian
Army underwear—flannellike long johns, but very primitive. Our underwear was laundered once a week by prisoners. We could not wash any clothing except underwear. In
the winter, the Russians gave us old shirts and quilted jackets that had been worn out and discarded by the Russian
Army. We got them with patches, but they were at least
washed and they were warm. Russian shirts had no shape
and no buttons (there were no buttons on any Russian
Army clothing)—they were just straight down and short,
with ribbons that tied.

No German soldiers arrived at the prison camp with
wounds that required medical attention. Those who had
such wounds were treated in Germany before coming to
the camp. Many people had old wounds (for example, several people could not walk without a cane), but nobody
had open wounds. Fortunately, none of my wounds gave
me any trouble.

If someone got sick, the camp had a dispensary that
was operated by German doctors and medical corpsmen
who were prisoners. The Russians feared epidemics and

tried to prevent them. We had regular delousings, and we had regular health inspections by the Russians every three months. The health inspections, however, amounted to nothing more than stripping naked and walking past a table behind which three Russian doctors sat (two of them were usually female doctors). They just looked us over to see if we seemed healthy. They would stop someone and question him only if he did not look right. Sometimes they would have us turn around, and sometimes they would even pinch us to see how much fat we had. If someone had a lot of bedbug bites, they would see that and be concerned about the possibility of a skin disease. Otherwise, the examination did not amount to much.

From time to time, a Russian camp commander would try to force senior officers to work. However, we knew the number and the date of the order Stalin had signed specifying that senior officers would not be forced to work, and whenever they tried to tell us we had to work, we quoted that order to them. The first time this happened, we were ordered outside to fall into formation. Then the camp commander told us we were going to work. We quoted the Stalin order to him, and he began shouting at us, "You are war criminals! You will do as you are ordered!" Then a German oberst who knew all the details of Stalin's order quoted the order again in greater detail. The camp commander continued shouting for a while and then gave up. We suspected that he got so much money for every prisoner who worked. He could not force us to work in defiance of Stalin's order, but he could vent his spleen, and he did.

Nobody was overworked in our camp, unlike the German prisoners in Russian labor camps (where senior officers *were* forced to work). Our people worked an eight-hour day, and for this they received a meal and ten cigarettes. Those who worked never complained about it. If they worked in the forest, they could bring back wood and sell it to other prisoners in the camp. If they worked in the factories, they could steal things like small pieces of metal and Plexiglas and sell them in the camp to people who could make useful things of them. They also made contacts with Russian workers in the factories to whom they could sell things that were made in the camp—such as cigarette cases, small picture frames, and chess sets—acting as middlemen between seller and buyer. They worked only six days a week; Sunday was not recognized as having any religious significance by the Russian government, but they recognized it as a day of rest. Those who did not work or stay occupied—those who just lay around and thought about food and home—began to deteriorate. Such prisoners would lose any capacity for generating or accepting ideas within months.

Those of us who did not work occupied ourselves in a variety of ways. We had experts among us on every conceivable topic—theologians, diplomats, accountants, lawyers, writers, businessmen—so we would informally organize lectures. Someone would say, "Let's talk about horticulture," and a former professor of horticulture would lead a discussion about plants, flowers, trees, how and when to plant them, how to treat them, and so on. Other lectures were held in accounting, economics, history, and other subjects. Such discussion groups were scattered all around the camp, outside in the summer, inside in the winter. We had to keep the numbers small, because the Russians, through the Activists, would not allow large numbers of people to congregate. The Activists kept everyone under close surveillance at all times, because the Russians were always afraid of insurrection.

We would sit in one of the bunk compartments, where there was room for eight, with four on one bunk facing four on the opposite bunk. Depending on our interests, we could join one of these study groups. We might have a series of lectures on one subject every Tuesday. Perhaps ten to fifteen lectures would occur during a day. Those of us who attended the lectures were able to keep our intellects sharp and acquire knowledge. The people who gave lectures did it to maintain their skills and knowledge. They lectured from memory, of course, because we had no textbooks. I continued my language studies, polishing my French and English and beginning to learn Spanish. I practiced my Italian with Italian prisoners. I even added some studies in law by attending the lectures by Hauptmann Pawelek, the former judge.

We also played cards, although playing cards was supposedly decadent and forbidden (cards were forbidden in the Russian Army, so that ban was automatically extended to us). We got around it by telling them that our wooden cards were dominoes. They were not stupid enough to believe that, but they pretended to, because playing cards helped to keep us occupied and quiet. To make playing cards, we would buy thin plywood from those who worked in the factories. We made the cards about two by four centimeters. We would sand the plywood until it was smooth (with sandpaper stolen from the factories), then carve the numbers and symbols in the wood and color them with red and black ink that was stolen from the offices by those who worked there. The cards would bend just a little, but they were too stiff to hold, so we made little stands the cardplayers could put them on.

We staged a bridge or chess tournament in the camp every few months. Although our chess tournaments were limited to the camp, so many nationalities were represented that we called them international tournaments. A tournament took several days, and each "nation" sent its best players. A Hungarian oberst and I played the final game in tournaments many times, and I was chess champion at Krasnogorsk during my whole time there. The Russians helped organize these tournaments, because they loved chess and they wanted to keep us occupied. When an important Russian visitor came to visit the camp from Moscow, they would ask me to play a game of chess with him if they knew he was a chess player, as many Russians were. I always got some extra cigarettes and a cup of *good* tea for doing that, and it was usually quite friendly (only one of them became angry and abusive when I beat him).

Another way we occupied ourselves was by making things that we gave to one another as gifts at Christmas and on birthdays. We could buy wood from the prisoners who worked in the forest, and we could buy tin from those who worked in the kitchen. The Oscar Meyer cans the Spam came in served us very well for many purposes. The prisoners who worked in the kitchen would get the cans, because the Russians did not realize their value to us. The kitchen workers would then sell the metal to those who had handicraft skills. We used the cans not only for material, but also for blades for carving knives. (The Russians allowed us to have small carving knives; the blades were too small to constitute a dangerous weapon.) To make a knife, we would cut a piece of metal into a small triangle, put it into a wooden handle, and then sharpen it on a piece of rock.

People carved chess sets, cigarette boxes, and things like that. One prisoner even made clocks, with all the wheels and gears made of tin from Oscar Meyer cans! We called them Oscar Meyer clocks. The people who were good at crafts could make such things, and prisoners who worked in Russian factories could take them to the factories and sell them to the Russian workers on commission. I still have a fold-out set of picture frames and a carved cigarette case that were given to me as gifts and an aluminum cigarette case that I won for being chess champion.

There was no reason for us to be bored. Some people put enormous psychological pressure on themselves by just lying around all day thinking about food and living from meal to meal. We were *all* always hungry, but I kept my time filled so there was no time to brood about it. I tried to keep myself occupied with studies and lectures, with crafts, with music, and with bridge and chess. All this may sound like fun and a good time, but it was really just a desperate attempt to survive and not give up. Even though this prison routine continued for nearly five years, I refused to allow it to become boring. Only when I thought about home did things get really bad for me; otherwise, my days were filled and I kept myself occupied. When I felt myself becoming depressed, I had only to remind myself of all the other German soldiers of all ranks who were being worked to death in the brutal labor camps.

I had always been athletic, and I established an exercise routine for myself. In summer, I would walk throughout the camp for an hour, and then I would do calisthenics for thirty minutes. In the coldest part of winter, I would suspend the walking and just do the calisthenics. Many others did various kinds of exercises also. Our limited diet made us tire quickly, and for this reason some people did not exercise, but I did all right with the extra food I was able to buy with my cigarettes.

Paper was of tremendous value in the camp. It was not just in short supply—it was practically nonexistent. Even the Russians did not have it. When they counted us, they marked the numbers on a small wooden board, because they did not have paper. Then after the numbers tallied and had been reported, they scraped the numbers off with a knife and used the board again.

Sometimes, when cigarettes were scarce, we got "Red Star" *makhorka* tobacco instead. But, of course, we had no cigarette paper. The only people among the prisoners who could get newspapers were the Activists and those who worked as translators (the newspaper was intentionally made so it could double as cigarette paper). The translators were allowed to read the Russian newspapers *Pravda* and *Izvestia,* so they had paper they could use to roll cigarettes. The Activists and translators would share their newspaper with friends, but others would have to buy it from them or try to fashion pipes for their tobacco. One page of newspaper was worth six hundred grams of bread. The only other paper we ever got was the paper the tobacco came in—and it was almost more precious than the tobacco. If our group was twelve people, we would divide the paper into six pieces and take turns getting it. We kept a list so that nobody was left out. The paper was too thick to roll cigarettes in, but it was workable for writing. It was white with a red star and a hammer and sickle on it.

Time was different in the prison camp from in the outside world. To a large degree, time conditioned and ruled the outside world, whereas in the camp time had no meaning at all. Units of time like a day, a week, or a month were meaningless, because nothing was happening and nobody was going anywhere. Except for Sunday, when no one marched off to work, every day was like every other day. Our routine was carefully organized. Our food was distributed at the same time every day, and in the monotonous void of our daily lives the meals, as bad as they were, afforded certain stimulus for the eye and the brain.

In May 1946, exactly one year after I had surrendered in Berlin, the Russians finally permitted us to write home. I was permitted to write a postcard, with another postcard attached to it for an answer. I was allowed only fifteen words in my postcard, and Lilo was allowed only fifteen words in her response. I wrote that I was well and healthy. Waiting and hoping for a reply was sheer agony. Finally, after more than two months, I got Lilo's reply on July 24. It was a day sent by heaven! Only when I received it did I know for certain that she and Klaus had survived the war. She knew that I was alive, because the old retired general who had been released from the gentlemen's prison in Köpenick delivered the letter I had written her from there. Lilo wrote that she and Klaus were well and that we had a second son, whom she had named Alexander and who had been born exactly one year earlier—on July 24, 1945! She had sewn a photograph of her and our sons onto the back of the postcard, and I blessed her for her ingenuity. Receiving that photograph was like getting a new lease on life. I still had a small oval locket with a picture of Lilo that

I had saved through countless searches by Russian guards. When I got the postcard with the new family picture, I cut it to size and put it on the other side of the locket. The locket stayed around my neck during all the rest of my period of captivity.

The elation of knowing that my family was alive was just as quickly squelched as my eyes fell upon the barbed wire that kept me from them. Knowing they were alive made me miss them all the more. Until now I'd been steeling myself against news that they had not survived the war. Until now, I had survived one moment just to be able to survive the next one. Now I had something to live for beyond survival. Until now, I had looked upon each new day as a small miracle and a gift. Now that I knew I had a family waiting for me, each day of life became even more precious.

From May 1946 on, we were allowed to exchange postcards with our wives twice a year, although I won an extra postcard as first prize every time we had a chess tournament. The postcards provided me with a motive to win. However, when things went badly for the Russians in the Cold War, they would hold our return postcards and not give them to us, so we could not count on receiving them.

Not knowing whether I would ever see Lilo and our sons again was the worst part of captivity. Sometimes the Russians told us, "You are war criminals—you will never go home." Then when things were going better for them in the Cold War they would tell us we would be home by Christmas. Sometimes their deliberate psychological machinations would get the better of me and I would become despondent, but with time I finally just adopted the philosophy of the Russian peasant: "Tomorrow will be better." It helped me to accept the uncertainty of captivity.

It also taught me the value of patience, a lesson that has served me well throughout my subsequent life. Patience is also a characteristic of the Russian peasants, and now I know why.

29

THE RUSSIANS INTERROGATED us regularly during the entire term of our imprisonment. A guard would come and take us to the administration building for interrogation.

During the average interview they would ask questions like "What units were you in?", "What did you do?", "Where were you in Russia?", "On what dates?" They knew the names and numbers of all our military units, and they also had a pretty good idea of what had happened and where. German prisoners who had been at Russian villages that had been destroyed and in which civilians had been killed were in for a very bad time from the Russians. Anyone who had been part of a unit that had participated in such an action did not have a real chance of escaping execution or being slowly starved and worked to death.

My interviews were different in the beginning, because I had been operations officer of the 56th Panzer Korps during the defense of Berlin and had been in the bunker at Führer Headquarters at the end of the war. The Russians wanted to piece together exactly what had happened at the end, so they had rounded up everyone they could find who had been there. The first information they wanted when we surrendered in Berlin was about Hitler, Goebbels, Bormann, and other important people in the Nazi hierarchy. They wanted to get the leaders they believed were in Berlin at the end. Their next interest was their own research into German warfare and combat theory. They wanted to know about that from everyone on every level.

The Russians also thought the German government had laid plans for an underground resistance in Germany after the surrender. There had, in fact, been talk of guerrilla resistance, and apparently there had been some planning (the guerrillas were to be called "werewolves"), but as far as I knew it had never come to anything. The Russians were very much concerned about it, and it was one of the things they asked me about. Of course, all I knew was vague rumors.

Another thing they wanted to know about was what they considered to be "war crimes," mainly in Russia but also in every Eastern European nation they dominated. During all interrogations they wanted to know whether we had been in an area where partisans had been executed or anything of that nature had occurred. If they found something, they would bore deeper and deeper into it.

My interrogator at Krasnogorsk for most of the interrogations was a Colonel Stern. He was a little taller than average, well groomed, Central European in appearance, and slender. He was handsome, intelligent, and well educated, a cultured man who spoke German without an accent and always wore civilian clothes. He was quite different from the camp officers, who were all rather crude peasant types. He interrogated me about every four weeks in the beginning, when they wanted to know about Berlin. He was Jewish, and during my first interrogation he asked about Auschwitz.

"You are the second Russian officer who has asked me that," I said, more than a little curious about it. "The first one, in Berlin, became angry and said, 'Don't pretend you don't know!' What is it that I don't know?"

Stern searched my eyes for a long moment before responding. "The concentration camp at Auschwitz was one of several extermination camps where millions of Jews and Eastern Europeans were put to death," he said with obvious contempt. "And I do not believe that you did not know about it either. After all, you were right there at Führer Headquarters."

I was sure that this obvious lie was a trick of some kind. What he was saying could not possibly be true, but I decided to play along with him until I found out what he was up to.

"I had time for nothing but combat in Berlin," I said. "There was not even adequate time for that."

Although it was not easy, I eventually convinced him that I had no knowledge of Auschwitz or any other extermination camps.

"But you knew about the concentration camps?" he asked finally.

"Yes, I knew of Dachau as a place where the government detained political agitators, Jews, and homosexuals. This was reported in the newspapers, but nothing about people being put to death."

After that, Stern never raised the subject again. He asked me very specific questions about military events in Berlin. I never had any really unpleasant encounters during my interrogations. He never took notes, so I was sure he was after just small bits of information. He was curious about dates, about the fighting between the Oder River and Berlin, about the fighting in Berlin, and who the commanders were. After I convinced him that I knew nothing about the death camps, the questions he asked concerned only military history.

After my interrogators had satisfied themselves about what had happened in Berlin, they wanted to know about the fighting in Russia in 1941. They wanted to know where I was, when, and with which units. They were also very interested in knowing whether any Russians had cooperated with us. Of course, many Russians behind our front worked for us in hospitals, supply depots, and the like. The Russians always wanted to get their names, but they knew I was always at the front when I was in Russia and they always dropped it when I said I had never known any.

All interrogations included a common set of questions, and if someone slipped and said something different from one time to the next, the Russians became suspicious and accused him of lying. Then they would really bear down on him to find out what he was hiding. They caught many people that way, and it was horrible for those who got caught. Those who were trying to hide something, those who said something dumb, those whose unit caught the Russians' attention, or those who they thought might become an agent for them were interrogated more frequently than the rest of us.

The interrogators were all NKVD agents, and all except Colonel Stern wore Russian Army uniforms, but with different-colored hats. Once when I was being interrogated by another interrogator, the interpreter was a pretty young woman lieutenant. At one point, the interrogator left me alone with her. I had just said I had been in Italy, and while the interrogator was gone she told me that she had been in Italy also. We talked about Italy, and she asked if I knew the Italian song "Parla mi d'amore" ("Speak to Me of Love"), and she sang a few words of it. We talked very cordially for several minutes, but when the interrogator returned she became sober and businesslike again. It was obvious that she had been in Italy as a spy, because normal Russian officers did not go to Italy before or during the war. That was one of the very few instances when I saw ordinary human behavior from a Russian, although Colonel Stern was capable of showing a little human behavior in a one-on-one situation.

I quickly learned enough Russian to understand my interrogators' questions, although I never let them know that, because pretending ignorance gave me time to prepare my answer while the interpreter translated the question. This was important, because sometimes just a single word about cutting trees for bunkers or even firewood in

Russia, or feeding Russian grain to your horses, or having blown up a bridge during a retreat in Russia, could later mean a sentence of up to twenty-five years in a labor camp. That was a little game they invented later, when they wanted an excuse for not sending certain people home. Fortunately, my story was believable and always consistent. I convinced my interrogators that I never had problems with supplies during the invasion of Russia because we were always on the post road and our supply columns were able to keep up. My story was logical and I never slipped up, so they believed it. I was lucky that I was always along a major supply route during the invasion of Russia, that I was in the hospital and at school a lot, and that I was never in the wrong place at the wrong time—where a village had been destroyed, for example.

I was always extremely careful about what I said during interrogations. I made it a policy never to admit that people in my artillery battery had ever killed a chicken in Russia or used Russian firewood or hay, but I was always careful never to lie to them about anything other than that. They would ask you the same question again next year, but from a different angle, and they would catch you if you tried to lie. I never said a word more than was absolutely necessary, but no less than would provide a reasonable answer. I tried never to be openly hostile toward the Soviet Union, but when asked I always insisted that Germany had to have good relations with all countries in order to get along in the postwar world, even though Russia was obviously her most powerful neighbor. If pressed, I told them frankly that I did not believe that communism was the best form of government for Germany, but I was careful not to criticize their system or praise fascism.

After an interrogation, we had to sign a transcript of it, and anything in it could be used against us. Once, however, an interrogator ordered me to sign a transcript that was written in Russian, and I refused to sign it because I could not read it. The interrogator became angry and started shouting, so I wrote "I do not understand the Russian language" and signed that. Then he got even more angry, but I refused to sign it any other way, because if I had it could have been my death warrant.

Another objective of their interrogations was to get information on people in order to determine whether they might be candidates to become spies for them.

We had a continuous coming and going of prisoners from Krasnogorsk to and from Lubyanka Prison and Butyrka Prison in Moscow. I was lucky that I was never taken to either of the political prisons and could spend all my years of captivity in prison camps, where the area we had to move about in was about 300 by 150 meters instead of a four-by-five-meter prison cell that sometimes housed up to six people. In the camp, we were under the constant surveillance of the Activists and the Russian guards, but we could at least move about and go outside the barracks. Especially important inmates were kept separated and isolated at Lubyanka and Butyrka so the Russians could maintain complete control over them. When the Russians thought they had all the information from someone in Lubyanka or Butyrka, they moved him from his prison cell to Krasnogorsk. They still interrogated everyone at regular intervals, however, and when they discovered something about someone that they had missed the first time, they took him back to Lubyanka or Butyrka.

Every week, newcomers arrived from the political prison cells, always with pasty-white faces, because they never saw the light of day in their prison cells. For a period of time after arriving at the camp, they would be afraid of everything and everyone. They would be very quiet and extremely suspicious. These people were easy prey for the Activists and the spies. They usually either succumbed to the attempts of the Activists to make them collaborators or went the opposite route and took a foolish stance of open resistance—in which case they eventually disappeared.

Von Dufving, Refior, and Weidling were all in

Butyrka, as were many German generals and general staff officers. When the Russians finished with most of them, they sent them to our prison camp if they did not consider them dangerous; otherwise, they sent them to the labor camps. Refior was released to our camp, and von Dufving was sent to a labor camp. In the labor camp von Dufving was eventually sent to, the Russians apparently intended the prisoners to die, considering their exposure to the weather, the hours of hard work, the quarters, and the inadequate food. It was also near the Arctic, where it was dark several months of the year and extremely depressing. Von Dufving survived two years there.

30

THE FIRST CHRISTMAS in captivity, in 1945, everyone in my group saved a small portion of his bread, sugar, and fat each day for two weeks to make a cake. Because the bread was two-thirds water, we could mash it up with a little sugar to make the cake. Then we mixed sugar with butter or margarine or lard—whatever form of fat we were receiving at that time—to make a sort of icing for the cake. Someone else in our group made the cake, and I made the icing and decoration.

On Christmas Eve, we all got together as a group to celebrate. Meanwhile we had to guard the cake carefully to prevent it from being stolen, because everybody was so hungry. The taste of the cake was pure heaven for us after the prison food. We sat together in our bunk compartment and reminisced about past Christmases at home and about our wives and children. We sang a few Christmas songs, and the chaplain in our group conducted a little service (it had to be done very quietly, because the Russians would not tolerate religious services). We exchanged gifts that we had made or bought for one another, things like cigarette cases, in an attempt to maintain a semblance of civilized life in prison (those who had the skills to do so made things, and those who did not have the skills bought things with cigarettes or food). After the singing and celebration, Christmas Eve was a very quiet and sad time in the camp, because we were all lost in remembrances of a much happier past. Christmas was the worst day of the year, in terms of longing for home.

31

URING THE NUREMBERG trials, the Russians wanted to blame the massacre of Polish soldiers at Katyn on Germany even though the International Red Cross had already filed a report that the Russians had clearly committed the crime. To prove their case, they needed a "foolproof" witness, so they cast about for a German enlisted man they could coerce into testifying that he had been part of the execution squad. They found their candidate in a labor camp and brought him to Krasnogorsk for coaching. He was a big farmboy, fun-loving and much too trusting. He was not intelligent enough to realize that his actions endangered his life. He was from near Nuremberg, so they promised him he could visit his family if he would cooperate with them. It was easy for him to rationalize what he did, especially when the Russians pointed out that the country he had sworn allegiance to no longer existed. They gave him better food and a new uniform and made him feel important.

They coached him for weeks, probably until he honestly believed what he was saying. (None of this was common knowledge to us at the time; although he talked to some of his friends about it, the rest of us learned about it only after the fact.) Then one day he was gone, and a few days later when we were read the news, we learned that he had been presented as a prime witness for the Russians at the Nuremberg trials. He described in great detail how his infantry unit had carried out the Katyn massacre. The western countries ignored the testimony, however, because of the Red Cross records, so the elaborate lie the Russians had constructed around him did them no good.

After being inundated for days with news of the Katyn massacre and how the German Army had cold-bloodedly mowed down more than four thousand innocent Polish officers, we suddenly heard no more about Katyn. A few days later, their star witness returned to the camp. He was still almost as cocky as he had been before—but not quite, because he had not been permitted to see his parents as they had promised. Perhaps if they had succeeded with their big lie, they would have at least let his parents visit him. As it was, he got nothing for his treachery except better treatment in the camp. He was probably put in a jail cell in Nuremberg and kept there except when he was testifying. They had also told him that if he did a good job they might release him after he had testified. He should have known they could not release him after he had lied for them.

When they returned him to the camp, he still got more and better food, and he still had his new uniform, but in the following days and weeks he began to complain to others that the Russians had not delivered on their promises. When his complaining was reported to the Russians, they stopped the better treatment. He ate what we ate, and they took back his new uniform. Then he complained even louder, which was unbelievably stupid. So he disappeared. They love what a traitor can do for them, but they despise him as a person.

During the Nuremberg trials, we got daily reports about what was happening. We learned the details of the Nazi extermination camps and finally began to accept them as true rather than just Russian propaganda. There had been unanimous skepticism among us about the extermination-camp stories because of the attempts of the Russians to blame their own slaughter of Polish officers at Katyn on us. After that, we just assumed that these stories of horrible atrocities in the German concentration camps were just so much Russian propaganda. But when it became clear that the Western Allies as well as Russia were prosecuting the Germans responsible for the atrocities, it was evident that there might be some truth to the stories—although we still found it impossible to believe that six million Jews could possibly have been put to death.

We knew that the Jews had been persecuted by the Nazi government, however, and that they had been rounded up and sent to concentration camps just because they were Jews. Anti-Semitism had a long history in Germany, and Hitler used it to his political advantage by blaming everything negative on the Jews. So it was not difficult for us to believe that some of the Jews might have been killed, but the figure of six million stretched credulity too far for us. Nevertheless, we slowly, sadly, began to realize that the Nazis had indeed committed terrible crimes against humanity.

I had known about political concentration camps like Dachau, where people were sent for what was known as "political reeducation." But those people returned and resumed their roles in German society, and when they returned they did not oppose the system any longer. This was common knowledge. Germany had no tradition of the freedom of speech that Americans cherish so much, and we did not see anything unusual about people being sent to Dachau for "reeducation"—especially since it was helping to maintain stability. There were jokes about Dachau then just as there are jokes about being sent to Siberia today. Union leaders and communists who fought against the Nazi program were sent there, as well as Jews and homosexuals. But nobody was killed there, at least that we knew of.

In contemplating these things, I often went back to my teenage years in the middle thirties, when Hitler had been immensely popular with the German people—when no one in Germany could have even dreamed of the nightmares to come. Hitler had brought political and economic stability to Germany, which appealed greatly to the average German. In effect, he had reunited a German people who had been divided by literally dozens of political parties during the democratic Weimar Republic established in Germany following World War I.

A major factor in Hitler's popularity was the restoration of national pride. All during the twenties and early thirties we were constantly being told by the rest of the world that we had started World War I (which we felt was not true) and this was what we got for it. And we were constantly being told by the German government and press that the Versailles Treaty took away big pieces of German territory and gave them to other countries. So Hitler's moves that were restoring some national pride were generally appreciated by the German people. Hitler disavowed the Versailles Treaty, which had hurt Germany so badly economically, and his moves to recover land and German population that had been taken away from Germany were popular with the people. The treaty had also limited Germany to a 100,000-man army, making it impossible for us to defend ourselves. So Hitler's expansion of the military forces after tearing up the Versailles Treaty was also widely popular. Hitler dominated Germany because he was effective in his early years and because he offered Germans their national pride back. Never in our wildest dreams could we have anticipated the atrocities his government was to commit.

Losing the war, losing my freedom, and losing my country were things I could think through and understand. War is a calculated risk, with a winner and a loser. I could understand the penalties we had to pay for losing. But we had thought of our participation in the war as noble and honorable. Now we could only be ashamed that our noble venture to right the injustices of the Versailles Treaty and regain what we thought of as rightfully ours had led to the inhuman horrors of extermination camps. There was no way to rationalize attempting to exterminate a whole race of people. I remembered the government propaganda that there was a worldwide Jewish conspiracy to take over the positions of power in all the countries of the world. In the 1920s and 1930s, Jews held high government positions and they were the bankers and the industrialists—they controlled much of Germany's wealth, and the Propaganda Ministry harped on that constantly when the Nazis took over. But even if the government had indeed felt threatened by such a Jewish "conspiracy," it was madness to think that an entire race of people should be exterminated. I was sickened by this news. I finally decided that my inability to come to terms with it was going to chip away at my mental and emotional strength, which was already being tested severely, so I filed the issue away in a dark corner of my mind and did not participate in the discussions taking place on the subject. I had to accept the fact that it had happened so I could get on with the business of living, but I did not have to like it or discuss it. I simply forced myself to concentrate on the here and now, so that I could survive each day as it came. As a professional soldier, I could not escape my share of the guilt, because without us Hitler could not have done the horrible things he had done; but as a human being, I felt no guilt, because I had had no part in or knowledge of the things he had done.

Having to accept that my government had, in fact, murdered huge numbers of Jews threw me into a deep depression. I still found it difficult to believe that Hitler was personally responsible for such actions, but they could not have been done without his acceptance of them. In all of my experience, only old Herr Hoffer had been able to see that Hitler would lead us to ruin. "At what cost?" he had asked. I knew now that even Herr Hoffer could not possibly have foreseen the horrible cost that Hitler would extract not just from the German people but from the world. And it was our blind and unquestioning faith in him that had enabled him to do so.

32

THE POPULATION OF the camp fell politically into three groups: the Indifferent Majority, the Opposition, and the Activists.

Most of the prisoners belonged to the Indifferent Majority. Under pressure from the Activists they would usually do what the Activists wanted, but for the most part they avoided conflict and took the path of least resistance.

I was part of the Opposition, but we had to remain largely silent. Overt opposition could lead to our extermination for "fascist activities" or "war crimes." But we refused to participate in anything political and refused to give reasons, and we got away with it. As long as we kept quiet, we were not tortured or singled out for abuse, except for being hassled by the German Activists.

The Activists (who were also called Anti-Fascists) were open collaborators; they ran the camp and controlled the jobs. They took their orders from the Russians, reported to the Russians, and spied for the Russians. The Russians called the Activists *natchalnik*, meaning "chief" or "superior," and we called them that sometimes. If we wanted anything from the Russians, such as alleviation of the bedbug problem, we had to ask the Activists instead of the Russians, because only the Activists could talk to the Russians. To maintain their standing as Activists and therefore retain their privileges of more and better food and all-around better treatment, they were required to acknowledge, accept, and espouse the Russian point of view on everything.

Some Activists were not as radical as others and tried to maintain a relatively good relationship with members of the Opposition by discussing things objectively. Mostly these were people whose families lived in the Russian occupation zone of Germany and who felt they had no choice but to go along to some degree, but they wanted to avoid the label "traitor," which the Opposition gave to Activists. A smaller group of the Activists were real agitators for the Russians; they did the political work, were barrack commanders, propagandists, etc. They praised and made excuses for everything that came from the Russian authorities. Only in very rare cases were these people actually converted communists; they behaved as they did either just to get better treatment or because they felt guilty about something (such as being an *actual* war criminal). These people were dangerous because of their fanaticism.

Whenever there was something unpleasant to be done, the Russians did not do it themselves—they had their collaborators, the Activists, do it. For example, if there was an escape attempt, they would call in the Activists and tell them, "This has happened, so now you all have to stand out in the cold for an hour." The Activists would then do their bidding, and we all would have to stand out in the cold for an hour. They had all the power, and the rest of us were at their mercy.

Activists held pro-communist lectures we were all required to attend, they performed as actors in political plays we were required to attend, and they wrote inflammatory articles we were required to read. The Activists also circulated political resolutions on subjects over which the Russians were at odds with the west. A resolution would be a one- or two-page statement of support for the Russian position on the issue. The Activists would pressure everyone to sign these documents. They would say, "It is for peace. The Soviet Union wants peace for the whole world, and the western powers are warmongers. Are you for peace or for war? If you are for peace, you will sign this resolution.

If you do not sign it, you are for war." At the time of the Berlin Blockade, for example, when the Russians tried to close the access routes to Berlin to the Western Allies, we were pressured to sign a resolution supporting the Soviet blockade of Berlin. The purpose of the resolutions was obviously to control our minds, since the resolutions were of no practical value to the Russians after they had been signed. Probably 80 percent of the prisoners signed these resolutions for fear of the consequences if they did not.

The Activists were not all low-ranking or unintelligent people. Some of them were generals and Ph.D.s; in fact, they were often the worst of the lot. A Dr. Nawrocki, for example, was one of the more active and dangerous of them. He harangued prisoners to sign "resolutions" and worked constantly to agitate other prisoners and convert them to collaborators for the Russians. A former university professor, he was in the camp because the Russians perceived him as an intellectual and therefore potentially dangerous, and he was determined to convince them that they had nothing to fear from him. He outperformed the Russians in his propaganda attempts. He was completely self-serving, and disdainful of everyone else. Supercilious and arrogant, he seemed to have learned nothing from Germany's defeat. He looked forward to a high-ranking job for himself in the communist regime in East Germany after his release.

Another such Activist was my barrack commander, Generalmajor Bammler, who had been a general staff officer in intelligence work in peacetime and during the early part of the war. After Germany occupied Norway, he became chief of staff to the supreme military commander in Norway. Later he was transferred to the eastern front as a division commander, and he was captured there in 1944 when Army Group Center collapsed. Bammler was in his middle forties and over six feet tall. He was always looking out for his own welfare. He not only did everything the Russians asked him to do, but he did anything he thought they *might* want. He was not just interested in getting home, but like Nawrocki was ambitious to play a leading role in the new government of East Germany.

He became one of the most active, cunning, unscrupulous, and dangerous leaders and organizers in the service of the NKVD. He signed everything the NKVD personnel asked him to sign and wrote inflammatory articles for them, and he tried with all means at his disposal to force others to do the same. He collaborated with the Russians in gathering or fabricating the evidence used to convict many of the people who were later convicted by the Russians and sentenced to long prison terms. If he is still alive, he has the fate of many men on his conscience.

We all knew, of course, that he had not had a sudden conversion to communism, but that he had something on his conscience and was just trying to save his own hide—at the expense of *everyone* else if need be. And, of course, the Russians knew that too. It may be that as chief of staff to the supreme military commander in Norway he had ordered the execution of partisans or people who supported the partisans. This constituted a very real and serious war crime to the Russians. He knew, of course, that the Russians were aware of what had happened in Norway and that he was at least partially responsible. Norway was long, narrow, mountainous, and difficult to control. If partisans blew up a hydroelectric dam in his area, he would have had to respond to it. As a soldier, it would have been his job to keep the area operating smoothly. The Russians probably were not concerned because they considered Norway to be a Cold War enemy. If he had done the same things in an Eastern European country under their domination, I am certain they would have had him executed. Therefore, he was afraid that the Russians would return him to Norway to stand trial. He probably thought that collaborating with the Russians might save his life. Bammler, in exchange for better food and other privileges, sacrificed all conviction, dignity, and self-respect. Although he pretended to be a converted communist, I am sure that the Russians did not believe that any more than we did.

We also had a major in the general staff who was an Activist. He was a very good bridge player, and he and I often teamed up as partners because the two of us could beat almost any other team. He had been operations officer of an infantry division and had been captured at Stalingrad in 1943. He had become embittered by Hitler's refusing to allow them to fall back and regroup at Stalingrad, and he had turned on the government just as Generalfeldmarschall von Paulus had. He felt strongly that he was a man without a country and that he owed no allegiance to anyone, and he felt neither guilt nor shame for cooperating with the Russians in exchange for a job in the kitchen and better treatment. Although as far as we knew he had never harmed any of us, we were very careful around him and avoided providing him with any information that could be used against us. He was not a gloomy or depressing person in spite of his dark conclusions about his fate. In fact, he was almost cheerful much of the time. He was sometimes called in for interrogation at night, and that usually meant that the person being "interrogated" was actually reporting to the Russians.

Another Activist was a young officer named Count von Waldersee, who was in the camp because he came from a well-known noble family. His grandfather had been a Prussian generalfeldmarschall and Chief of the General Staff. The grandson was in his early twenties, tall and blond. In spite of his noble background, he was easily bluffed and cowed. He was especially afraid the Russians would never let him go home because of his grandfather, so he cooperated with them to convince them he was on their side.

A separate Anti-Fascist Active (group of Activists) was established by the Russians for every national group. Each Anti-Fascist Active adapted the orders of the NKVD's Political Department to its own national mentality and then carried them out. Each national group of Activists was controlled by a leader and several close associates. An Extended Active, to which all Activists belonged, exercised control over the national groups. Through this group, the Russians came to know everything that was going on in the camp in the shortest possible time. The Activists considered it their "anti-fascist duty" to watch everybody and everything going on in the camp and report everything immediately to their Russian superiors. A few of the Activists refused to collaborate to that extent—a very dangerous thing for them to do, because to the Russians, that was "supporting the reactionary forces" in the camp—a very serious offense. On the other hand, some of the Activists could not seem to do enough to get in good with the Russians.

The Russians also sometimes used different national groups against each other. One of the national groups of Activists was the Austrians, who conveniently forgot that Austria had voted 90 percent in favor of being incorporated into the Reich in 1938. Encouraging the Austrians to pretend they had been enslaved and that they hated the Germans gave the Russians a large pool of people they could use to help keep us under control. The Austrians wore little red-white-red flags on their sleeves to distinguish them from the rest of us.

33

CONTROL OF THE Krasnogorsk prison camp was in the hands of the NKVD's Operations Department, although its people always remained very much in the background. Reporting to the Operations Department of the NKVD was the Political Department, to which our interrogators belonged. This department controlled the political and intelligence activities in the camp by issuing directives to the inmate Activists. It also controlled access to the newspapers *Pravda* and *Izvestia,* the radio news broadcasts, the propaganda films we were shown four or five times a year about the inevitability of communism, and any cultural activities like concerts and plays.

Everything the Russians did was directed toward one great goal—to strengthen their own forces for the coming battle with "capitalism" (meaning the non-Soviet-dominated part of the world) and to weaken their adversaries in any way possible.

The sheer volume of the constant propaganda the Russians heaped on us had a depressing effect on us. Their political slogans were posted everywhere in the camp; it was impossible to open our eyes without seeing them on the walls no matter where we were—in the barracks, in the laundry, in the bathhouse, in the latrine, in the administration building, *everywhere!* Their theory was that if something was repeated over and over and over, it would eventually become an unquestioned fact in one's mind. That is how they maneuvered people to the point where for them "The Soviet Union is for peace and the United

States is for war" was not an opinion but an unquestionable fact. (The constant theme throughout all their propaganda was how peace-loving the Soviet Union was and how war-mongering the United States was. To my chagrin, this heavy-handed brainwashing seemed to work. They actually got people to the point where to question something like that seemed wildly illogical.) They also showed us outrageously distorted political films to try to influence our thinking.

The Russians at one time brought in professors from Moscow University to give us lectures in their versions of history and political philosophy. They gave it up after a few months, however, because we asked questions instead of just accepting what they told us. If you applied a western mind to their doctrines, the doctrines did not stand up under questioning. It was like religion: you had to accept their doctrine on faith or not at all. No doubt existed in their minds that *everything* Marx and Lenin said was unquestionable truth. It was impossible, in their minds, for either man to have been wrong. We found that they were so incredibly set in their thinking that they could not even comprehend that other people could think differently. When we pointed out fallacies in their logic, they could not cope with it. They felt ridiculed by our questions and our insisting on logic. We had professors of their own rank among us who posed questions they could not even comprehend because of the mental straitjacket in which they had bound their minds. So they discontinued their series of political lectures, although they had apparently found such lectures successful with German communists. All the people who formed the first East German government had been given this kind of "education" in the same camp we were in before it had been converted to a prison camp. The difference was that the German communists blindly accepted their theories on faith, and we did not.

The Russians' main objective seemed to be to produce spies who would work for them after returning home. They were looking to the future. They wanted people they could blackmail, who would return to West Germany or other Western countries and appear to be beyond suspicion and could therefore get into important positions. The more important the victim's former position, the greater his intellectual powers, and the more unsuspected his political conduct during captivity, the more valuable they felt he was to them. But the victim first had to be made to cooperate. They tried especially to recruit people who had never been sympathetic to the communist cause, because they would be less suspect back in their home communities. We were able to gain some insight into the recruitment methods used by the Russian intelligence service from our own experiences during interrogations, from conversations with other prisoners, and from direct observation of people and events.

The clandestine informers (as opposed to the known Activists) were coerced to play another role in addition to spying for the Russians: to select from among their fellow prisoners those who might be suitable for future deployment as Russian agents once they had been returned home. In this role, they tried to find out about a potential victim's family and financial circumstances as well as his ideological attitudes—all this in order to draw conclusions about whether he could be coerced to work later as an agent for the Soviet Union. The final decision about such a person was made by the Russians, of course, but all the preparatory work was done by German informers. Only very clever informers who had a profound knowledge of human nature and the trust of the Russians were suitable for such work.

With the help of the Activists and the other informers, the Russians had no difficulty getting sworn—but false—written testimony against any prisoner, based on which the prisoner could be convicted for "war crimes," not only in Russian courts but even in the courts of the prisoner's own country! After they had selected a victim by close scrutiny of his qualifications, the Russians put him under steadily increasing pressure until he thought the only way he could go on living was to sign the document they wanted him to sign. The document always incriminated some innocent fellow prisoner of a false war crime, *but exonerated the victim himself.* Of course, the victim knew that others had signed similar documents incriminating him (if necessary, the Russians would show him the documents that incriminated him falsely). Once this had been accomplished, the victim was asked whether he would be willing to perform certain tasks for them upon returning home. If he refused to cooperate now, he would disappear into the Russian penal camps, from which he would not return; if he refused to cooperate after he had returned home, the Russians would produce the signed documents that would convict him in the courts of law in his own country.

The Russians found it easy to put us under pressure. We had invaded Russia, and they constantly preached to us that we were "war criminals." It never stopped: "We did not invite you here. You invaded Russia. You are all war criminals." And it was true that we had invaded Russia; we could not deny it. We were not responsible for our government's decision to invade, but we certainly could not deny that Germany had started the war against Russia and that we had been our government's instrument of war. We knew they could do whatever they wanted to us; we were completely at their mercy. Their murder of over four thousand Polish officers at Katyn was a chilling reminder of what they were capable of, and our feeling of utter helplessness was overpowering. I had already been subjected to it in the two prison camps in Germany, but it was more difficult to endure here because we were so far from home and everything was so foreign to us. In combat we had been strengthened by a sense of duty and military unity, but in this new situation nothing was clear, there were no rules, and everything had to be learned by trial and error.

They tried to put an enormous burden of guilt on each

of us, drilling into us the guilt of every *individual* German and the right of the Soviet Union to protect itself by any means against a repetition of German aggression and arrogance. (Of course, Russia had *actually* done to Poland, Latvia, Estonia, and Lithuania what Germany had only *attempted* to do to Russia, but we tactfully did not point this out to them.) We were constantly reminded that it was only due to the unprecedented generosity of the Soviet government that we were allowed to *live at all.*

The Russians preferred people without strong political convictions. Although such people would never be avid Marxists, neither would they be fanatical in their opposition to Soviet policies and objectives, so they would not risk everything in order to harm the Soviet Union. To pressure people to agree to cooperate with them, the Russians did such things as keeping them in solitary confinement for months (sometimes in total darkness), withholding food for long periods of time, and conducting interrogations that lasted for days on end (twenty-four hours a day, by a shift of interrogators) without rest or sleep. Sleeplessness and lack of rest rob the prisoner of his reason, producing a form of semiconsciousness in him. And when such cruelties are combined, it becomes too much for any human being. The victim is eventually worn down to his breaking point. We knew they could break anyone they wanted to break.

One person chosen for such treatment was Oberst Heigl, who had been in intelligence work in the Luftwaffe. His father had worked in the German military mission in Madrid, Spain, prior to the war, and he spoke Spanish fluently (I learned Spanish from him while in the prison camp). The Russians were eager to recruit him as a spy because of his intelligence background and his father's diplomatic background. He had a naturally cheerful disposition, but the Russians made his life miserable with their attempts to recruit him. In spite of his cheerful nature, he was despondent much of the time because of his frequent interrogations and the pressure they put on him.

He was one of those they interrogated for days on end —day and night, without letup. They put him in solitary confinement in total darkness for weeks, from which he would return pasty-white and disoriented, as well as depressed and subdued. He would have been a fine human being if they had left him alone. As it was, we had to be careful of him, because we knew he would eventually have to give in to them if he had not already. We understood the psychological pressures he was being subjected to and the personal agony he was experiencing.

Hunger, desperation, fear, and hopelessness helped break many prisoners. Some people were more affected by hunger than others. Some just thought of nothing but food all day long, and then they ended up throwing away their pride. Diplomats, generals, noblemen, war heroes—it was not possible to predict who would sell his soul for a little more food. I have seen generals going through the garbage cans behind the kitchen building, looking for potato peels! I was hungry too. We all were. But I could always find a way to put it out of my mind.

Courage and cowardice were very different in the prison camp from on the battlefield. In the camp, I witnessed behavior by people I would not have expected it from on the basis of the person's war record. But nobody can predict how he will react to either combat or captivity.

We had a Luftwaffe fighter pilot in the camp, Oberstleutnant Graf, who had shot down almost four hundred enemy airplanes in combat. As one of the most successful fighter pilots in the German Air Force during the war, he had all the highest decorations for bravery. In his fighter plane, he could not have been a coward. Yet he just could not take the psychological stress of life in the prison camp, and he caved in to the Russians. He did everything the Russians asked him to do, because he was afraid they would never let him go home or would punish him in some other way if he did not. A cold and distant man who seemed to look defiant and apologetic at the same time, he was a loner with no close friends. He obviously felt he was doing what he had to do to survive and return home. He worked in the kitchen—his reward for cooperating with the Russians—so he ate better than the rest of us, although food did not seem to be his primary motivation.

He did not behave defensively, and he would rationalize his actions if provoked to do so. He could put up a good argument about not feeling loyalty to a country that no longer existed, but when he gave in to the Russians he lost his self-respect and the respect of his peers. An obviously intelligent man, he would probably have gone far in a victorious German Air Force. He never became an Activist, but he lent his name to articles that were published throughout the Soviet Union criticizing the German Air Force and the air forces of the western nations and praising the Russian Air Force.

Of course, the opposite was true. The German, British, and American air forces were highly skilled and efficient, whereas the Russian Air Force was, by comparison, inept. I think he would have been better off if he had said, "No, it is not true. I shot down over three hundred of your airplanes and fewer than one hundred British and American airplanes. I am sorry, but I cannot sign this article that says the opposite." They would have thought better of him if he had.

Of course, the record showed the difference in the skill of the western fighter pilots compared to the Russian fighter pilots, and it did not hurt the Allied air forces for him to sign the articles—but it hurt him in his own self-esteem and in the esteem of this fellow prisoners. It also helped the Russians by increasing the confidence of their fighter pilots (the Russian pilots were impressed because they knew he was one of Germany's most decorated pilots). Most important, his signature on such articles was of value to the Russians in their propaganda efforts. He might have thought they would torture him if he did not cooperate, but all our experience indicated otherwise.

I never agreed with the Activists that you had to collaborate with the Russians in order to get along with them. The interrogators always knew my stand. I did not get any privileges, of course, but I did not get singled out for abuse either. I admitted freely that Hitler had been a disaster for Germany, although that had not become apparent to me until late in the war. But I also told them that with my education and cultural background I could not accept their system either, and they seemed to respect that. The Germans who became turncoats did not get anywhere with the Russians. In fact, the Russians just assumed that they had something to hide and started bearing down to find out what it was.

For example, an oberst in our camp had been in Yugoslavia during the war and had been part of an action there in which partisans had been killed. He became an Activist and an ardent supporter of the Russians to try to protect himself, but that just made them suspicious, and they turned the pressure on and learned of his background in Yugoslavia. He had been a regiment commander whose regiment had wiped out villages for supporting the partisans. About forty years old, he was a serious and conscientious man, and he felt he had done only what had to be done if order was to be maintained in Yugoslavia. He had a wife and four children at home, and he wanted desperately to return to them. He disappeared one day, and a few weeks later we heard in the daily news broadcast that he had been convicted of war crimes in Yugoslavia and executed.

The best way to avoid this dangerous game was to convince the Russians during their screening sessions that you were unsuitable for their purposes because of your political views, your philosophical views, or your general attitude. Of course, it was not easy to do that without at the same time appearing to be an "enemy of the Soviet

Union"—for which they would punish anyone severely. I managed to do it simply by sticking honestly and openly to my beliefs, but being careful not to attack theirs.

It was possible, by careful observation, to identify many of the future agents who had been recruited by the Russians. They got good jobs or other little privileges without any assistance from the Activists—and sometimes even over the opposition of the Activists. It was also obvious that they were at the administration building from time to time when no wave of interrogations was happening. But the most telling sign was a certain insecurity and constraint in their dealings with other prisoners that was especially perceptible to one who had known them for some time. To those who knew them well, there was just something different about them. Though the Russians camouflaged everything connected with these matters in a very sophisticated way, we knew.

Because of the many informers, we had to be careful what we said to anyone who was not a very close friend. If we said something against the Soviet system and it was reported, we would be called in for interrogation—and at the very least it would be unpleasant. Of course, it was foolish to knock the Russians' system when we were at their complete mercy, but some people did it. To me, those people were foolish rather than brave. If the Russians thought someone's attitude was a serious problem, or even potentially serious, they would threaten the person or move him to a labor camp. They were especially likely to move a person to a labor camp if they thought he was someone who could influence the mood of others in Krasnogorsk. They would not tolerate active opposition to their system. Even if someone just complained about the food or not being able to write letters and someone reported it, the Russians would summon that person for interrogation and threaten him.

The Russians themselves never tried to convert me to communism, although Generalmajor Bammler did. He

knew that I had no respect for him and that I was opposed
to what he was doing, but he tried anyway. He called me
into his little room and started talking about the general
staff and trying to convince me that it would be better to
give up any opposition because that was all over and now
Germany had to work with the Russians in order to continue to exist as Germany. He said, "You must see that you
will not get anywhere if you are hostile. Our time is over,
and if you want to get home you had better cooperate. Of
course, there are some things we do not like, just as there
were things we did not like in Germany," and so on.

From time to time Russian officials came to the camp
from Moscow to get a personal impression and examine
the selections that had been made. During the inspections
by these officials, massive interrogations would be staged
to hide the identities of those few recruited prisoners they
actually wanted to interview. Most of these interrogations
were about trivial matters.

I tried to put my broken world into perspective and
understand this new world about me. I systematically studied the literature the Russians made available to us. I listened to their lectures, I talked to German communists, I
studied the books in our library by Marx, Lenin, and Stalin.
I read other literature as well, but I could not convince
myself that bolshevik socialism was anything more than a
clever scheme to keep a small group of elitists in power. I
felt that if Germany accepted their political system, we
would be exchanging a bad system for a worse one.

I had philosophical discussions with other prisoners
who were supposed to be experts in political philosophy,
some of them among the elite of German intellectuals,
about communism and other political philosophies, but
they were usually disappointing. Most of these people
seemed broken by the experience of the last several years
and conditions in captivity. Some had just become apathetic. Others became dreamers, thinking only in unrealis-
tic terms and losing all measure of reason. All of us were

affected by our total isolation and lack of outside stimulus. Only a minority managed to sort through the communist influence and maintain sound judgment.

Trustworthy companionship was my salvation against the Russians' constant attempts to take over my mind. The maintenance of a strong mental attitude was critically important to us. I had close friends with whom I could talk and even discuss dangerous things, intelligent people who shared my social, cultural, and educational background. When one of us tended to become negative or defeatist, the rest of us would sense it and move to help that person overcome his mood. Also very important to maintaining a healthy and independent mind was having access to the other intelligent and stimulating people who populated the camp. The value of being with such people was worth more than a larger food ration.

34

DURING THE WINTER of 1946–1947, the Russians made a movie about the battle for Moscow that took place in December 1941, and they forced all of us who were in uniform to play the role of the German Army in that movie.

Having been part of the real battle, I was not a willing participant in their movie, but of course I had no choice. They set up propeller-driven airplanes to whip the snow into our faces and create the effect of a winter gale. Of course, the sorry state of our uniforms made us a rather pathetic-looking "army," but that probably fit neatly into their propaganda objectives.

One day in early 1947, Refior arrived at Krasnogorsk from Butyrka Prison. He was a tall man and he had been quite fat, but of course he was now as skinny as the rest of us. He told me that Weidling and von Dufving were still in Butyrka. We did not talk much. We had never had any particular liking for each other, and now he quickly showed signs of becoming an Activist, so I avoided him. I remembered his love of ham and asparagus tips, along with strong coffee and liquor. I had no doubt he would become an Activist.

The camp had a small library of books we could read, and at one point during 1947 it was expanded by a big shipment of books that had been taken from a city library in East Germany. Several big boxes appeared at the camp, and the Activists began to behave secretively. We learned that the boxes contained books. Of course, the Russians had to sort out any books that did not support their system, so the Activists went through them and removed all of the books they thought we should not read. The Activists were not all terribly intelligent, however, so they let some books slip past them; of course, they probably also eliminated some books that would not have opposed the Russians' theories. But we still had plenty of books to read, mostly German literary classics and some of the philosophers on whose work Marx and Engels had built.

I spent a lot of my time reading. I felt that it was important to keep my mind as active and alert as possible. Those who did not do so became lethargic and in time seemed to just vegetate. They would sit with their heads in their hands and stare straight ahead. We learned to let them stare and pay them no heed. We called it "dozing." I read French, English, Spanish, or Italian books whenever possible to improve my language skills. I tried to get a good understanding of the Russians' social and economic philosophies. Their philosophical theory of "dialectical materialism" did not sound very logical to me.

In June 1947, the Russians decided to move most of us in the Krasnogorsk Prison Camp to another camp. We had been kept close to Moscow so we would be near the political prisons where more important German prisoners were kept. When they had everything they thought they could get from us, we were sent to another camp to make room at Krasnogorsk for new people who were now of greater interest to them. Of course, they could easily call any of us back at any time if they felt they needed us.

On the night before we were to leave, our names were called and we were told to be ready to leave the next morning, although we were not told where we were going or why. They searched us before we left the camp, which had never happened during our two years at Krasnogorsk. It was not a matter of guards taking watches and rings and anything of value (although there were a few instances of a guard seeing something he liked and taking it, saying "Not allowed"). They were looking for written material. The Russians were always terrified of the power of the written word. They feared our minds.

Russian soldiers marched us to railroad tracks, where we waited for a train to arrive. A freight train finally arrived, and we were loaded aboard it. The boxcars did not have windows, but they had ventilation slits near the roof that let in a little light. Straw had been spread on the floor for us to sit and lie down on, and a toilet (a bucket under a board with a hole in it) was in the middle of each car. Probably five hundred of us boarded the train, with perhaps forty in a car; the Russian boxcars were bigger than they were in Western European countries because they had wider tracks. We were on the train for two days, stopping at villages for food and water.

We disembarked at a railroad station in the region of Tambov, approximately halfway between Moscow and Stalingrad. We then marched an hour and a half from the railroad station to the new camp, which was called Morshansk. There we were searched again and assigned to barracks. Morshansk, which was in a large forest, was larger than the Krasnogorsk camp, but it was also more primitive. All the buildings, for example, were made of logs. The character of the camp was the same as that of Krasnogorsk: it was not a labor camp, but a political camp that specialized in psychological pressure. The barracks were not quite as crowded, because it was a larger camp, and there was a little more space in which to walk and jog. In addition to the five hundred or so of us, Morshansk had several thousand Japanese soldiers, about one hundred Polish prisoners, and perhaps one hundred German women prisoners (in a separate part of the camp).

We continued on our slow journey to starvation with the same fare we had received at Krasnogorsk. And, of course, the same German Activists who had ruled us at Krasnogorsk continued to do so at Morshansk. As far as our daily routine was concerned, Morshansk was identical to Krasnogorsk. Our lives were impoverished not only by our loss of freedom but also by the monotony of our routine. The passage of time, in effect, stopped for us as we watched the days, the weeks, the months, and the years slip away meaninglessly. In the outside world, a normal human being would be going through changes that would constitute progress in his life. In the camp we had to make an effort to keep from stagnating, although compared to the labor camps our "stagnation" was probably luxurious.

When a person follows the same exact daily routine for too long, the monotony makes time tedious and tiresome. I would begin the day in the early morning, and almost before I realized it I would find myself in the afternoon. Then twilight would fill the land with shadows, and the morning would have suddenly turned to evening. At times I wondered whether I had spent the day in a trance, and at those times I sometimes questioned my own sanity. Then I would force myself to concentrate more on engaging in activities—chess, bridge, lectures, crafts.

Although a day was twenty-four hours, it equaled nothing. A month was no time at all in our lives. The end of one year and the beginning of the next were as alike to us as any other two days selected at random. Thus did the years pass. We did not keep a conscious count of time as does the person who values it. Our lives were so regimented and routine that at times I wondered whether any of us would ever again be able to function in a society that required us to be responsible for ourselves. We lived a hermetic existence within a timeless vacuum. Yet I found it a learning experience. I feel that I gained an understanding of life that I would not have acquired under normal circumstances, especially the value of patience.

At the end of 1947, the Russians sent some of the older prisoners home, and Count Schwerin was among them. I was very happy for him. He planned to go to Bremen, and he offered to help me get a start there if I was ever released and could get to West Germany.

We stayed at Morshansk until the middle of 1948, and then we were moved again—this time to Mikhailovka, about four hundred kilometers northeast of Moscow. As always, we were not told why we were being sent there. It was near Gorki, on the Volga River. Physical living conditions were better here than they had been at Morshansk, but the psychological pressure got worse; for example, we were denied our semiannual postcards the first year we were there.

Mikhailovka held about a thousand prisoners, and here there were no civilians or enlisted men—only German officers. Mikhailovka was neither as spacious as Morshansk nor as crowded as Krasnogorsk. Although our interrogations continued at Mikhailovka, nothing out of the ordinary occurred at first.

I was not forced to work in any of the camps, but at Mikhailovka the Russians asked sometimes whether anybody wanted to go to a little island in the Volga River to cut reeds for baskets. Some of those who had gone came back and said it was interesting, that it was not much work, and that you could swim in the Volga. So some friends and I volunteered. We had to march perhaps an hour, with a few guards, to get there. It was almost like an excursion from school. The guards were friendly, and when we arrived we had to cut only as many reeds as we could carry back and then we were free to swim. It was something different, and it was the only time I did that.

At one time during the year and a half that we spent at Mikhailovka, about forty senior officers were taken to a much smaller camp at Ivanovo, not too far away. I was among the selected group. We went by train, as usual, but because forty of us were not enough for a special train we went by commercial train. When we had to change trains, we had to wait about two hours for the second train to arrive. We were accompanied by a Russian captain and a noncommissioned officer; the captain left us at the station with the noncom and disappeared into the village. On the other side of the tracks was another platform with about forty Russian civilian prisoners—men, women, and children. They had at least twelve guards with submachine guns and they were not allowed to move at all—and here we were, all young men, and only one guard. Of course, there was no place for us to go, many hundreds of kilometers from any other country, and with the language barrier escape would have been impossible. But it was terrible to see the way they treated their own people. They were surely political prisoners, since so many were women and children.

Then we arrived at the camp near Ivanovo and learned that we were there to work. Most of us refused, because of the Stalin order, which we quoted to them. They thought we would prefer to work, because the camp was just one barrack with a fence around it and we had nothing whatever to do if we did not work, but most of us refused on principle. The Russians did not harass us. Those who wanted to work did, and the rest of us did not. If they had asked at Mikhailovka, they could have taken only those who wanted to work, but they did not operate that way. It was apparently just a temporary thing they wanted done, and we were there less than two months.

Beginning in early 1949, we were finally allowed to receive letters (we could not write them, but we could receive them). Since Lilo was in East Germany she knew she could write to me, because the Russians publicized how generous they were being. For a while, she could write to me once a month, but I never received all of her letters, because the Russians used them as a weapon against us. If someone did something the Russians did not like, they would tell him when a letter arrived from his wife, but they would not give it to him. They also used this as a form of coercion, to get people to cooperate with them—and they used the letters, including those they never gave us, to gather information about what people were thinking in Germany. They also censored our mail, deleting anything negative about them or their system. If Lilo wrote anything about hunger in East Germany, for example, they would either cut it out or not give me the letter.

After we had been at Mikhailovka about a year, a rumor circulated through the camp that a military commission was coming from Moscow to put some of us on trial for "war crimes." The rumor was true. The camp commander was very nervous about the arrival of the commission, because the arrival of such a commission from Moscow was always important. Everything had to be cleaned, like a military installation before an inspection.

The trials began during the summer of 1949. The Russians, of course, were not humane enough to post the names of those who would be tried so each of us would know from the outset whether he was on the list. Instead, they called only a small group at a time, and the people in the group went in one at a time. This went on for weeks, with everyone under the stress of not knowing whether he would be in the next group. Fortunately, I was not called for trial.

Of the one thousand prisoners at Mikhailovka, about half were called for trial, mostly senior officers. Everyone had been interrogated at least twice a year since 1945, and the Russians had kept transcripts of all the interviews. They had always been especially interested in our military experiences in Russia during the war. They compared the transcripts of our different interrogations, and if there were any discrepancies they wanted to know why. They did not consider that memories could grow dim or that differences between the Russian and German languages could cause translation problems. The people they called were all convicted of war crimes and sentenced to five, ten, fifteen, twenty, or twenty-five years in a labor camp.

A "crime" was eating a Russian chicken during the war or feeding your horse Russian grain or hay. That was considered stealing socialist property, and for that people were sentenced to a minimum of five years in a labor camp. Of course, Mikhailovka held no real war criminals. People who had executed partisans or committed similar crimes had been sorted out and dealt with back at Krasnogorsk long ago.

35

AS I BEGAN my fifth year in Russian captivity, I finally decided that I would never return home. Those who had been convicted were being sent to labor camps, and I concluded that the rest of us would spend our remaining lives in the prison camps. I therefore decided to learn the Russian language properly. Most of us knew some of the language, the daily things you had to know just to survive. If you were going to another camp, for example, you had to be able to understand what the Russian soldiers wanted you to do so you did not get shot for not following orders. Now I decided to learn the Russian language systematically, grammar and all. We had ethnic Germans from Estonia and other Baltic areas, and many of them spoke Russian as their first language. I began to study Russian with them in earnest.

Having finally accepted the conclusion that I would never return home, my thoughts automatically turned to my two sons. It occurred to me now that without a father to guide them, they could be brainwashed into growing up as communists. That would be the final irony! We had told ourselves that one of the reasons we invaded Russia in 1941 was to free the Russian people of communist oppression. How many of the children of the German soldiers who took part in that invasion would now be raised under communist rule, and how many of them would be communists? I knew very well how insidious and overwhelming ceaseless propaganda can be. If I were home, I would be unable to do anything about the Russian occupation of

East Germany, but I would be able to give my sons a balanced perspective against which to evaluate communism.

At the beginning of December 1949, we began to get rumors that those of us who had not been convicted and sent to labor camps were going to be sent home. I did not put any faith in such rumors, because we had been promised so many times before that we would be home by Christmas that it would be foolish to believe such a rumor now. Then, about mid-December, the Russians read a list of those who were to go home. We still refused to believe it, because we had been lied to so many times before, and this was exactly the sort of psychological game the Russians loved to play. We could not help hoping, of course, but we were afraid to believe. Then we were inspected, however, and those whose clothes were too shabby even for the Russians got something better. My clothes were still okay. I had my boots and riding pants, and I still had my fur-lined overcoat, so I did not need clothing. Of course, we all had the caps with earflaps that the Russians had provided.

Even though we were afraid to do so, we slowly began to believe that we were really going home. Finally the day came when they told us to be ready to leave the next morning. We fell out the next morning and were searched. A guard took a chess set I had made, because I had two of them and he said I could use only one. They marched us through the camp gate, and the small number of guards seemed a good indication that we were not going to another camp. I do not remember how far it was to the railroad station, but we marched to the train. They loaded us into boxcars again, just as they always had when we moved from one camp to another. The guards were friendly this time, however, which was another good sign, and in the boxcars there were boards for us to lie and sit on instead of just straw on the floor. Since it was winter, we also had a stove in the center of each boxcar. And then the final proof that we really were going home—they did not lock the boxcar doors! We could not keep ourselves from starting to get excited now. Even though it was bitter cold, we left the door open a crack, for fear that it might be locked again if we closed it.

This trip was more comfortable than any other trip we had ever made as prisoners, and we were excited and in a great mood. We talked about the coming Christmas and what we planned to do, and we talked about our families. We sang our old Army songs, songs about girls, and Christmas songs. The trip took several days, and we stopped in villages for food and water, as usual.

Sometimes when the train stopped, the Russians came aboard and called out some names of people—who were then taken off the train and returned to prison! They did not do it at every stop, and it was not many people—but it planted terror in everyone's heart. The Russians seemed to be pathologically addicted to psychologically tormenting us.

I tried to visualize Lilo, Klaus, and Alexander, but I found it difficult. They were just the photographs in my locket, and I could not visualize them as flesh-and-blood people. Klaus would not remember me, of course, and Alexander had never seen me. Reaching home would be like being born again. I planned to stop only briefly in East Germany and then go on to West Germany if I could possibly find a way to do it. We knew about the division of Germany, and I did not want to live in the Russian-occupied zone. I had seen all of communism that I wanted to see!

When we arrived at the border between Poland and East Germany, we got our release papers. At the same time our train arrived there, another train arrived from somewhere else with women prisoners. That was the first contact we'd had with women, except for the Russian doctors in the prison camps. The women had been working in mines (even though the Russians had promised in Berlin when we surrendered that all the women would be allowed to go home). We had used thousands of civilian female telephone operators in the signal corps, and the Russians had taken them to Siberia to work in the mines. They had spent the same number of years in much worse camps than we had been in. Although they were young women, they no longer looked it. They had not had enough food and they had been worked hard, and none of them looked young or pretty, even to men who had not seen women in nearly five years.

East German soldiers had to process us in a big room at the railroad station in which old desks had been set up for that purpose. They were unfriendly, almost surly. We stood in line before one of the desks, and when it was my turn, the soldier at the desk asked, "Where are you from?" I told him I was from Bremen, West Germany. I had made up my mind to get to West Germany, beyond the reach of the Russians, even at the cost of getting Lilo and the children out after I was free. The people processing us had no papers on any of us, so they just had to accept whatever we told them. When he asked for an address in Bremen, I gave him the address of Judge Pawelek from our group. Then he wrote me a railroad ticket to Bremen. He also gave me "discharge pay" of 300 deutsche marks, my release papers (written in Russian, German, and English), which said that I had been released from Russian captivity, and the railroad ticket home.

Then we got some food and got on another train. It was a special train for prisoners returning home, but it had passenger cars instead of boxcars—an unbelievable luxury for us! We were all wearing parts of our German uniforms, supplemented by Russian clothing, such as quilted jackets. And, of course, we all had those Russian caps with the earflaps. I was wearing the same uniform (boots, riding britches, blouse) I had worn into captivity except for my cap. In addition to the chess set I had made, I also had a cigarette case carved from juniper wood, the fold-out picture frame a friend had made and given me for Christmas one year, and a little box made of aluminum that someone had made and I had won in a chess tournament (it was engraved "Chess Master of Krasnogorsk"). The East German soldiers were overworked, because two trains of prisoners had arrived at the same time, and they had a huge job just to process us. We were the first group of senior officers and the first general staff officers the Russians had released.

Being back in Germany gave us no sense of relief yet, because it was still the Russian-occupied sector of Germany; we could still have been pulled off the train and sent back to prison. The prisoner train I was taking to Helmstedt, at the border between East and West Germany, stopped at Leipzig, because it was a rail center.

Entering the suburbs of Leipzig was like flashing back to my childhood. Always when I had returned from summer vacations as a child, the most exciting thing about getting back home was the familiar experience of seeing the first Leipzig streetcar. The streetcars of different German cities were different colors and shapes, so a city could be identified by its streetcars. Leipzig streetcars were still green-and-beige! When I saw the first one, I was overwhelmed with emotion. I knew I was home, and all those childhood memories came rushing back. Familiar buildings began to appear, and finally the familiar old platform at the railroad station. The station, like much of the city, was still very much damaged from the war. Coming through the suburbs, we saw many destroyed and damaged houses—even now, four and a half years after the end of the war.

Leipzig was a one-hour food stop for the special prisoner train I was on. I talked to the railroad people and learned that a prisoner train was scheduled through Leipzig to Helmstedt every day for the next several days, and that I could catch it any day. If I tried to use my special train ticket (strictly for prisoners of war) for any other train, it could have been dangerous, but I could use it for another prisoner-of-war train. Since there were no guards in charge of us or the train, I decided to catch another train on another day—but I planned to go to the station every day to make sure the prisoner trains were continuing.

I went to my mother's apartment so I could take a bath and change to decent civilian clothes before going to Lilo's apartment. My mother did not expect me, of course. I had no way to let anyone know I was coming home. I just rang the doorbell. She could not believe it when she saw me. She gasped, and I thought for a moment she would faint. Then her face lit up, and when I stooped to embrace her, she began to sob uncontrollably. Tears rolled down her face as we stood clinging to one another. Finally, we found our voices, and we talked nonstop for an hour, mostly about what life had been like in the prison camp and in Russian-occupied East Germany.

I bathed and changed into some of my old civilian clothes that I had left at my mother's house so many years ago. It seemed unreal to see my old clothes, which now hung loosely on me. This whole experience had the quality of a dream rather than reality. My mother fixed a meal of cold cuts and cheese with bread and butter and real tea. Food had never tasted so good in my entire life!

There was no full telephone service yet in East Germany—many such things had not yet been fully restored—so I could not call Lilo. I took about a twenty-minute streetcar ride to her apartment. When she heard the doorbell, Lilo thought it was someone from Neighborhood Control because she had her lights on when it was forbidden (electricity was rationed). When she opened the door and saw me, her expression was as unbelieving as my mother's had been. I was so excited that I thought my heart would surely stop! I stepped inside the door and we fell into each other's arms. Having her in my embrace was breathtaking, and I felt almost light-headed. We just clung to each other, both of us racked with sobs.

Then I saw Klaus and Alexander standing behind her. I knelt before Klaus and said, "Hello, Klaus," and he caught on to who I was and shyly let me hug him. Lilo knelt by Alexander, who was four, and said, "It is Daddy." I said, "Hello, Alexander," and he looked at Lilo and said, "He still knows me!" Lilo and I looked at each other and began to laugh, but the laughter abruptly turned to tears and we clung to each other as if we could never part again. Then we sat down and put the children on our laps and became a family again.

I was able to stay with Lilo and the children for several days, and it was pure heaven. I learned that when Alexander was born, Lilo had gone to a small private hospital, where she knew a doctor, before dark each night and returned home the next morning. The Russians had imposed a curfew at dark, and if Alexander had decided to arrive after dark and Lilo had been at home, she would have been unable to go to the hospital. The war had been over only three months at that time, and being in the streets after curfew was dangerous, because patrolling Russian soldiers would shoot without warning.

Lilo had lived with her mother at first. They lived by selling their jewelry and crystal and clothing to the Russians. But then a Russian official took over her mother's apartment and forced Lilo to move out, although her mother was permitted to stay and keep house for the Russian. Later, the Russians attempted to revive the old Leipzig fashion fair (Leipzig had been a fashion center before the war), and Lilo got a job modeling clothing there. From then on, she was able to make a living by modeling. Before I arrived home, Lilo had received a visit from an official of the Communist Party who told her that I would return home soon and that when I arrived they had a very good job for me in my old profession. That frightened me, because it meant they expected me and would come looking for me.

Lilo and I made plans for getting her and the children to West Germany. She could get a pass to visit me, as long as she left the children in Leipzig, so we planned that once

I got out she would visit me and then we would make firm plans to get her and the children out.

I wanted to stay with Lilo and the children for several days before going to Bremen. Klaus and Alexander had both been instructed not to tell anyone I was home. On my third day home, however, a long line of people had queued up at a milk store to buy milk, and Klaus called out to the milkman, "My daddy is here, but nobody is supposed to know!" A neighbor who heard that came immediately to Lilo and told her.

I quickly changed back to my smelly old uniform to catch the next prisoner train. I took a small shabby-looking suitcase this time, and put in it all the film negatives that I had accumulated from childhood through 1944. (When I had been assigned to Schörner's staff in January 1945, I had not taken my camera, because I believed I would not survive the war.) I was taking a terrible chance, because I risked being sent back to the prison camps if the Russians or East Germans searched us and found my negatives. But somehow to leave them would have been to leave my whole life until now in the hands of the communists.

I got on the prisoner-of-war train at the Leipzig railroad station. We pulled out of Leipzig and went to Marienborn/Helmstedt, at the border between East and West Germany. A small river separated East and West Germany, and there was a railroad station on each side of the river. The train stopped at the East German station, at the small town of Marienborn, and we disembarked. We all had our packages or shabby suitcases, and we were all wearing a mixture of our worn-out German uniforms and articles of worn-out Russian uniforms. They called us into formation, brought us to attention, and marched us across the bridge to West Germany, to the city of Helmstedt.

The tension mounted in each of us individually and in all of us as a group as we crossed the bridge, because once across that bridge we knew we were beyond the control of the Russians, and they could no longer pull us out of the column and send us back to a prison camp. When the front of the column cleared the far end of the bridge, the liberated prisoners broke ranks and began to cheer. As the end of the column melted into the cheering throng on the other side, we all spontaneously—almost as if on command—jerked off our Russian caps and, with a deafening cheer, heaved them into the river.

EPILOGUE

FROM HELMSTEDT, WEST Germany, we went by train to a hospital near Bremen for a medical checkup. I was thirty pounds underweight and suffering from severe protein deficiency. Von Burkersroda was also at the hospital, having arrived several days earlier with our original train. We stayed in the hospital three weeks while the staff fattened us up.

Lilo obtained a passport to visit me at the hospital, and we made plans to get her and the children out of East Germany. Children did not need a passport to travel between East and West Germany, but adults did. Our plan was for her to send Klaus to me, and then I would send her a telegram that Klaus was deathly ill and she should come immediately. The plan, of course, was that she would bring Alexander with her.

When I was released from the hospital, I looked up Count Schwerin, who had been released two years earlier and had established a business in Bremen. He gave me a job in his business, and when I was established with a job and a place to live, Lilo sent Klaus to me. Since I had only a sleeping room and Klaus had to go to school, I found a family who was willing to board him for me until Lilo and Alexander could join us. Then, as planned, I sent Lilo the telegram that Klaus was deathly ill and she should come immediately. The East German government refused to give her a passport, however, until she produced an affidavit from the physician attending Klaus. I found a physician who was willing to give me such an affidavit, and Lilo got her passport. By now the East German government was requiring passports for children, however, and they refused to grant one to Alexander. So Lilo had to leave Alexander with my mother when she joined Klaus and me in Bremen.

It took us one full year to free Alexander from the clutches of the East German government. My mother badgered the passport officials every day their office was open for the entire year until she wore them down. They finally found a loophole that enabled them to get rid of this pesky woman—the fact that I had been born in Brunsbüttelkoog, which was now in West Germany. Finally, we were all permanently together!

In April 1951, with financial assistance from the West German government, I entered the University of Rüstersiel, near Bremen. One year later, in April 1952, Sylvia, our first daughter, was born.

In September 1952, I went as an exchange student to Antioch College in Yellow Springs, Ohio. During the year I was at Antioch College, I recruited sponsors for my eventual return to the United States. I was determined to get myself and my family as far from communist rule as possible, both geographically and ideologically. I returned to Bremen in 1953 and received my diploma in April 1954.

I returned to the United States late in June 1954, with my family, on an immigration visa. After working briefly on a construction crew in Yellow Springs, Ohio, I joined the international division of a large corporation in early 1955. I retired in 1983 at the age of sixty-six.

The fates of some of the major people in this book are as follows:

General Weidling died in 1955 in Butyrka Prison in Moscow, according to von Dufving.

Oberst von Dufving spent ten years in Russian captivity and was released in 1955. His first two years in Russia were spent at Butyrka Prison. Then he spent two more years in a prison in Orel, from which he was sent to a labor camp at Workuta, north of the Arctic Circle, in 1949. On the way to Workuta, he met Raoul von Wallenberg, the Swedish diplomat imprisoned by the Russians at the end of the war (the Russians had claimed he died in 1947). At Workuta, the Russians apparently intended people to die, considering the prisoners' exposure to the weather, the hours of hard work, the quarters, and the inadequate food. It was also dark several months of the year and extremely depressing. Miraculously, von Dufving survived almost two years at Workuta and then was moved to a camp near Stalingrad, where he received his first mail from home in 1951. He spent the rest of his imprisonment in a camp at Asbest, in the Ural Mountains, and was released at the end of 1955 after German Chancellor Konrad Adenauer negotiated the release of the remaining German prisoners in exchange for improved West German-Soviet relations. Today, von Dufving lives in a small town near Cologne.

Major von Burkersroda lives today in Baden-Baden, West Germany.

Major Wolff became godfather to our daughter, Sylvia, but he dropped out of sight and I have not heard of him in many years.

Count Schwerin, now in his nineties, emigrated to Canada and lives today in Montreal.

ACKNOWLEDGMENTS

WE WOULD LIKE to express our appreciation to the following people for their contribution to the quality of this book.

Photographer
Negatives and photographs restored and printed by H. Clay White.

Manuscript preparation
Barbara Brusaw

Manuscript reviewers

Donda Thomasson	Carl Lewis
Barbara Brusaw	Mary Lewis
Pamela Fuchs	Edie Neyman
Ann Greiner	Marilyn Rueth
Paula Hawthorne	Delores Schlaack
Rita Joyce	John Thomasson

INDEX